The Stuff of Dreams

Books by Leah Hager Cohen

Train Go Sorry
Glass, Paper, Beans
Heat Lightning

The Stuff of Dreams

Behind the Scenes
of an American
Community Theater

Leah Hager Cohen

VIKING

VIKING
Published by the Penguin Group
Penguin Putnam Inc., 375 Hudson Street, New York, New York 10014, U.S.A.
Penguin Books Ltd, 27 Wrights Lane, London W8 5TZ, England
Penguin Books Australia Ltd, Ringwood, Victoria, Australia
Penguin Books Canada Ltd, 10 Alcorn Avenue, Toronto, Ontario, Canada M4V 3B2
Penguin Books (N.Z.) Ltd, 182-190 Wairau Road, Auckland 10, New Zealand

Penguin Books Ltd, Registered Offices:
Harmondsworth, Middlesex, England

First published in 2001 by Viking Penguin,
a member of Penguin Putnam Inc.

1 3 5 7 9 10 8 6 4 2

ILLUSTRATION CREDITS: Title page: Arlington Friends of the Drama; page 39: Creighton
Vallee; page 127: Doug Desilets; page 207: Molly Trainor

LIBRARY OF CONGRESS CATALOGING IN PUBLICATION DATA
Cohen, Leah Hager.
The stuff of dreams: behind the scenes of an American community theater /
Leah Hager Cohen
p. cm.
ISBN 0-670-89981-X
1. Arlington Friends of the Drama (Arlington, Mass.)
2. Theater–Massachusetts–Arlington–History–20th century. I. Title.
PN2297.A77 C64 2001
792'.09744'4—dc21   00-068578

This book is printed on acid-free paper. ∞

Printed in the United States of America
Set in Adobe Garamond
Designed by Nancy Resnick

To Joe, Rosy & George

Acknowledgments

I am very grateful to all the people at Arlington Friends of the Drama who generously entrusted me with their stories and gave me access to a place and a community they so cherish.

My great and continually growing thanks to Betsy Lerner and Barney Karpfinger, who amaze me.

And my deep appreciation to Lori Taylor, Jodi Silverman, and Tina Rathbone; Sam Freedman, as ever; Jane von Mehren and Jessica Kipp; Steve Roylance, who resurrected almost the entire book after the computer crashed; Sue Callanan and Jilan Yin, for watching the children while I worked; and Rose Redding, Barbara Coleman, Bob Olson, Peter Daly, Sandy Aune, Kitty Levin, Cheryl Pomerantz Bass, Mercedes Ellington, my parents, and others who gave me entry to theater when I was little.

Contents

Gutter and Stars

J ust before I turned eleven, my mother took me out of school for a month to work with a traveling theater company. The company was the Bread and Puppet Theater, and they would be performing, with a slew of local volunteers, at the Cathedral of St. John the Divine in New York. In the mornings we'd drive down along the Hudson from our small river town, take the West Side Highway to 125th Street, and pass under a great and lofty confusion of black girders that was like a portal to the neighborhood, or really a portal to the life of theater we were about to enter for another day, for it signaled those last few blocks of the drive, during which a happy, bracing kind of tension would mount. It was early autumn; just the mornings were cold.

Bread and Puppet was founded in 1963. It's based in Vermont, and has performed all over the world. It tells stories with music and giant puppets and things, and after every performance the audience can eat some homemade bread. Sometimes there is a big bowl of mashed garlic to dip it into.

This is from a piece, written as a sort of prose-poem, that Grace Paley contributed to a book about Bread and Puppet:

> ... *the beauty and usefulness of the huge puppet figures like legends out of history, the grey women of Vietnam the ridiculous evil Uncle Fatso the lovely oxen turning round and round in the dance of silent beasts the dance of the enormous washerwomen and their consorts   the great martyred figure of the Archbishop Romero bending again and again to the people of his country El Salvador   the white deer on the hill under the red ball of the sun   the white birds bravely carried that have flown before and after us on our demonstrations and have waited fluttering in the wind outside the jails of New York Vermont Washington ...*

The autumn that my mother and I came to the Bread and Puppet, they were performing a play called *Wolkenstein*. I don't know what it was about; I was ten; it was abstract; it seemed to be about sadness and responsibility and struggle and human nature. I was not uncomfortable with not understanding it; a lot of the grown-up world was like that anyway: accessible in threads of feeling, image, impression. The pageant had medieval music, and hand bells, and a great brass band that played "When the Saints Go Marching In." Before the performance, the audience could visit the bays around the nave and see the "sideshows," which were like living tableaux, depicting what seemed to be fragments of life: A gray-masked, gray-cloaked figure spun thread for a long, long time, then snipped it. A train pulled slowly away from a station and a puppet figure waving a handkerchief got ever smaller and smaller.

The first day my mother and I showed up as volunteers, we were taught to walk on stilts. It was lovely, out in a blacktopped courtyard area; we and others who had shown up to participate took turns wedging our feet into place under straps of old inner tube stapled to a footpiece, and members of the troupe bound our ankles and calves to the wooden stilts with pieces of cloth, and then pulled us to standing and walked backward before us, holding our hands, until we learned our balance. We were tall and surprised.

My mother was asked to be a mounted cavalryman, or really a

horse and rider all in one: she wore stilts and a knight's costume on top, and a giant horse puppet suspended from her shoulders around her waist. I was one of only a sprinkling of children, and too short to be a stiltwalker in the actual performance. I played a ragtag devil in the opening procession, and one of the dancers in the nave who led the audience out onto the street at the end, and I helped work an enormous bird puppet that fluttered whitely in the dark sky above Amsterdam Avenue every night when the play and the audience all spilled out there into the real world.

During the whole rehearsal process, we inhabited the great dim peace of the church, and the brilliantly, briskly golden tangle of leaves and grass and wildflowers and weeds that abutted it. We'd have our lunch out there, in the church garden, yogurts and bottles of juice from the deli, apples and chunks of cheese and granola bars from home, cupcakes and hamantashen from the Hungarian pastry shop across the street. We'd eat alongside other volunteers and the core puppeteers, noses beginning to run a little, fingers to redden, as the weeks wore on and it got colder. Peacocks that lived on the cathedral grounds would strut saucily across the grass, dragging their incredible tails carelessly behind them. A volunteer would roll a cigarette, another would play a recorder or guitar, and the taxis and ambulances and public buses would stream down the avenue.

Of course I longed to run away with the theater. There was another girl in the production, only a couple of years older than I, and she had grown up with the Bread and Puppet; had been performing with them since she was little. (Later I would get postcards from her from Amsterdam or Georgia: "I am playing a pig, a washerwoman, and a star.") In this production she was actually playing Wolkenstein, in a giant mask. They needed a little person to play the title role, because the character had to be lifted and carried on someone's shoulders. After a few weeks, she had to go home to Maine, and I was asked to fill the part. I didn't have very much to do, no lines or dancing, but at one point I had to scramble up a ladder to sit at a huge table, and drink purple "wine" from a giant cardboard wineglass with some stiltdancers; when we'd drained our glasses we flipped the painted cardboard around to the "empty" side. Then a hand bell would ring three times, and I would take off the huge, sweaty

Wolkenstein mask in a stylized way, and someone would lift me down, and I'd run back to the nave to be one of the dancers again for the end of the play.

I loved getting to play Wolkenstein, but not because it was a lead. There were no leads, no star performers, no curtain calls, no bows, no hierarchy of egos. Mostly you were masked, or you were playing *part* of a horse, or a dragon, or a group of mourners, or you weren't so much playing a part as moving a piece of cloth or working the arm of a puppet. You were all wearing the same thing—white on the top and white on the bottom—and you were subsumed into the production, into the group event of the play, the story, which was being told by action and sound and movement and stillness. I loved getting to play Wolkenstein because it let me pretend I was that much closer to joining the Bread and Puppet, to becoming one of the group of workers who all knew each other and made this experience happen over and over, made these stories play out again in country after country, city after city, town after town.

It wasn't that working with the theater felt truer to life than everything else: school, and chores, and riding bikes around the neighborhood, and going to the library, and taking a bath, and finding my barrettes, and scooping kibble for the dog, and playing jacks, and drawing paper dolls, and getting into squabbles, and setting the table. These were all equally true to life. But before that month with the Bread and Puppet, I'd never seen the stuff of dreams come seriously to life. I'd never seen grown-ups living out the boundless possibility of the dreamworld like that, without fear or shyness or apology. The members of the Bread and Puppet lived impractically, and imparted great joy and wonder. They took the bald matters of life on earth and restored to them their links to beauty and souls and suffering and passion.

The other thing that struck me that month, working alongside all those bodies—puppeteers, volunteers, strangers come together in the church, painting, stitching, hammering, assembling—was not just the camaraderie of the players—the way people would gather on the hard, cool floors of the church to play cards or stretch or share a bag of sesame seeds—but the camaraderie implicit in the act of storytelling in the first place, in the act of staging this whole elaborate saga, of striving to communicate, understand, see. Putting on a play is like holding out your hand to a stranger and saying, Come with me, let's visit this third person's history, let's visit this third person's heart.

A lot of people, I mean grown-ups, hear the word "theater" and they smile, a not entirely nice smile. Sometimes it's a smile glazed with condescension, and sometimes it's an unmistakable smirk. "Theater" is a bit of a silly thing, the smile says. "Theater" is not so far removed from the dress-ups and play-acting of nursery school. "Theater" is, well, a funny thing for grown-ups to engage in. Unless you make *money* from theater, of course. If you make money from theater, it really isn't a funny thing, it's more like a serious thing, more like a pursuit.

A lot of people hear the word "amateur" and they smile, too. "Amateur" is a soft, frail, rabbity word. It's a little bit cute but also a little bit embarrassing. We are embarrassed for amateurs, for those earnest souls who strive and receive no material recompense. The idea of the amateur is the idea of something tender and slightly disappointing, with no real standing in this society.

A couple of years after my experience with the Bread and Puppet, I fell in with our town's resident amateur theater. "Fell in" sounds sort of dark and seamy (and although there were among my friends' parents those who, I'm sure, felt the phrase apt, it does not, in fact, apply)—more accurately, I flung myself into, and was in turn scooped up by, the local community-theater group.

Elmwood Playhouse was housed in an ex-church a block off Main Street, just down from the Indian diner and across the street from a snug white fire station that looked sweet until an alarm went off, when it became the epicenter of a gigantic, blaring pulse of sound. (This frequently provided an unscripted and not necessarily effective layer of subtext to the drama unfolding across the street.) The theater building was not pretty from the curb. It had a big, broad, serviceable porch and a dumb metal door, painted brown, that was heavy to open, and no windows. The façade was white cement, peeling.

The charms of the interior matched those of the exterior: the theater was plain, cramped, and in a state of perpetual, if not extravagant, disrepair. The exception to this was the stage itself, or, rather, its multiple incarnations, for it was a versatile little space that was reinvented time and again, with ramps and lifts and trapdoors, balconies, staircases, and lofts. The stage, when set and lit and kindled alive by all of the amateur artists involved, was the one place within Elmwood that was not shabby, not homely, not sorrily crumbling apart, and it was probably all the more astonishing because everything else about the place seemed to belie the possibilities that flourished there.

I acted in one play, in one scene, and fell in love. I loved everything about it, loved the high-buttoned boots I wore and the way they clacked along the bumpy cement floor of the dressing room; loved the hush of the audience as the play opened, and the dark lumpiness of them breathing out there, beyond the dust motes in the stage lights. I loved the motley mélange of props crowding the back room where we waited to go on (this theater had no proper greenroom; we used the shop, and perched on sawhorses or prop suitcases); loved the watered-down Coke we used for claret, and the shaving cream we used for vanilla ice cream. I loved climbing up to the catwalk after my scene to watch the rest of the play; loved the stories of the theater ghost, and the occasional tantrum thrown by one of the production team, and all the sexual innuendo that whizzed delicately and cryptically among the grown-ups, just over my head. Above all I loved the building, both the plaintively shabby physical structure and the intangible fact of the place: a whole building existing only for pretend, for the elaborate, devotional practice of *play*, of playing, of exploring imagined lives.

I was on the cusp of adolescence, the exact period in which you are supposed to shed play, when you're supposed to get wise to what's real. But make-believe seemed so right to me, entering that hungry age, not as a way of breaking contact with the real world but as a way of imagining myself more deeply into its prospective possibilities. Focusing inward on one story was simultaneously an adventure outside of my own realm; the make-believe of theater seemed as instructive and daring a vehicle as the real-life explorations conducted by my peers at so many football parties and dances.

Throughout high school I worked at Elmwood, operating follow spots, running crew, assisting with props—sampling all of the more menial tasks the theater offered. I'd come home from school, do my homework, eat an early supper, and walk up the hill to be at the theater for a six-thirty call. We were an unlikely family, those of us who came together and apart with each show, in ever-changing configurations. There were dancers and lawyers, professors and librarians, cooks and salespeople, doctors and carpenters, and mothers and fathers and grandparents. There were gay people and straight people, healthy people and damaged people, people you couldn't wait to be around and people who were plain scary. A man who worked lights was convinced he'd once been abducted by aliens, and sometimes he made a high-pitched keening sound for no apparent reason. Community theaters tend to be sort of bastions for misfits, which isn't to say that they aren't also populated by the conventionally successful and adept, but that they are relatively welcoming and unexclusive places, and there is perhaps something about the work they do that may speak to those who are not most comfortable in the mainstream.

Certainly much of what might be called "theater behavior" would be unacceptable in other social institutions or workplaces. I don't just mean the ordinary titillating stuff: the traipsing about between dressing rooms half naked, the fact of actors' engaging in what would otherwise be adulterous kissing and fondling onstage, the unchecked use of curses and graphic language, scripted or not, that tends to flourish more easily in a theater than at, say, a meeting of the Jaycees, or choir practice, or the office. Not to characterize nontheater organizations as prudish, but it isn't for nothing that the theater world has often been associated with looser morals and a kind of dazzling but dangerous squalor. I suspect, however, that the "theater behavior" people really find most dismaying hasn't anything to do with a lack of moral boundaries, but with a lack of emotional ones. This is where theater's real power and threat lie.

In most environments, for most of our lives, social code restricts our emotional honesty, our vulnerability, and our expectations about the honesty and vulnerability of others. As we grow up, our interactions become circumscribed by these codes, like close-slatted fences, and we come to depend on them, could hardly get through a day without them. In the theater such fences are antithetical to the process, and must be knocked down. Even in the safest, tamest production of the most banal old chestnut, relationships and conflict unfold in public; people must make themselves more vulnerable than the daily code prescribes. The nature of theater is to expose, and in partaking of theater, whether as actors, crew, or audience members, we are ourselves made vulnerable, laid bare to feelings and reactions; to some degree we become participants in a story that asks something of us.

Not that we at Elmwood sat around the shop and discussed this stuff. In the day-to-day, night-to-night work of the theater, we were as shortsighted, narrow-minded, and ego-bound as human beings are wont to be most anywhere, most of the time. Our concerns were these: Can we get that set change down under fifty seconds? Is the house sold out for opening night? Does our third-act costume make us look fat? Could you tell our motivation in that monologue? Is the strobe light working? Did the ushers remember to come early and make the coffee for intermission? Will the fire alarm go off during our scene?

After rehearsals and performances, we'd often troop over from the theater to the bar right next door (which *was* dark and seamy; it was sometimes referred to as "The Star Wars Bar," after the famous bar fight scene from that movie), and someone would get me a ginger ale and we'd sit around a beer-sticky tabletop, this motley pack of us, old and young and conservative and progressive and black and white and flush and broke and happy and miserable.

In the first play I ever did with Elmwood, *Summer and Smoke* by Tennessee Williams, there is a scene in which the main character quotes Oscar Wilde: "All of us are in the gutter, but some of us are looking at the stars." It's at the end of the first act, and I'd generally be up above the audience by then, lying on the catwalk that jutted from the lighting loft, in among the people working sound and lights, and sometimes the director, who would climb there, too, with her pen and pad, to take notes, all of us quiet and watching up in the dusty heat right under the ceiling. I'd be in my costume skirt and middy blouse and stocking feet, because the high-buttoned boots clacked too much offstage. I loved watching the play night after night during the month-long run. I liked whiling away the time in the dressing room, too, chatting with the grown-up actors amid the bright jumble of flowers and hairspray and pots of rouge and pancake and cold cream, but that got dull. Watching the play never did.

The woman who played the lead was like a glass of water on a sensitive surface: the least of the earth's vibrations were made visible within her. She uttered the line beautifully, layeredly, charged with the flowery and pompous affectation that was trademark to the character, yet simultaneously conveying the character's equally true earnestness and hope; her very delivery conveyed both gutter and stars aspects of human nature.

For me, so many years later, I think the phrase captures remarkably well the peculiar nature of community theater. Here is a place where people's most base elements thrive: egos may be exalted, fed, stroked, and patted; jealousies may run rampant; tantrums may be tolerated and considered part of the culture. At the same time, here are all these strangers coming together—for nothing profitable, nothing useful, nothing tangible or lasting, for nothing more than such stuff as dreams are made of—all because of some unnamable, unstanchable desire to imagine themselves into other people's stories and relate those stories to others.

Nearly two decades later, I found my way to a small community theater in Arlington, Massachusetts—one of many thousands like it in America—and set about seeing what of the culture I remembered from Elmwood was equally manifest here. When I came to it, Arlington Friends of the Drama was embarking on an auspicious year: it had just celebrated its seventy-fifth anniversary, was embroiled in disputes over organizational changes proposed to help it adapt to the times, and was about to hold auditions for its most controversial play to date. I arrived eager to chronicle these events, but driven by an underlying desire that existed apart from them. This time around, I had come to community theater not in order to insinuate myself into its culture but to try to understand what that culture comprised, and to answer what it is about amateur theater that makes people not just desire but need it. This had for me become a small burning question, white-hot and fluttery, like hope.

The Stuff of
Dreams

One

Auditions

I n the September twilight a girl in a sweater and ponytail sits on the sidewalk and plays with a stick with a cat. The air is dense with normalcy and cricket song. Down on the avenue rush hour plods. Recycling bins dot the curb all up and down Maple Street like proclamations of sameness, most of them filled with empty plastic milk-jugs and seltzer bottles and the fortnight's bundled news, the familiar debris of respectable, predictable consumption. The last bin on the block, just beyond the girl and cat, is, as usual, somewhat nonconforming, overflowing tonight with stacks and stacks of unused cherry-colored ticket-order forms, and an improbable number of Coke cans. Beside the bin is heaped a peculiar assortment of scrap lumber: planks painted gold, plywood with elaborate shapes jigsawed out of it, a few broken spindles spattered lots of different colors. The girl dangles her stick and the cat bats at it once, with vague disdain. No one else is about.

It's the Thursday after Labor Day, with all the children of America back to school and the work force of America back in action, and you can feel it, the sigh of it: business as usual resuming its stride, life's gray minutiae lining themselves up once again in orderly fashion. Twilight drops deftly into dusk, and the girl and the cat rise from the sidewalk; the former slips inside a yellow house on Maple Street, but the latter prowls delicately in the direction of the building that generated the interesting trash, sensing some action there. The building, a Gothic stick-style former mission church, is home to Arlington Friends of the Drama.

Now at the corner a white car pulls up, a Ford Taurus, that most ubiquitous of American cars, only this one has a license plate that reads ACTOR 1. Moments later, walking from the bus stop down on Mass. Ave., past stately old houses with drawn curtains and smells of supper, comes a young woman with a jittery look and a script in hand. And then, from two doors up on Academy Street, a boy in cargo pants and an Adidas shirt lopes winsomely across his family's graveled drive and ducks into the theater's main entrance. The reason they, and others like them already inside the building, are here tonight is on the face of it simple—they have answered a call: *AUDITION NOTICE.*

The boy in cargo pants is not here to audition himself, but to help out. He is Matt Rehrig, aged thirteen, another neighbor of AFD and something of a devotee. His whole family is. Matt's father is the sound person on the stage committee and a trustee of special funds for the fund-raising committee; his mother edits the newsletter and is a member of the publicity committee. Everyone in the family took part in this summer's musical fund-raiser, *Stage Door Canteen*, with Matt, his mother, and his younger sister singing onstage, and his father acting as musical director. Matt is running a follow spot for *Funny Girl*, which opens in two weeks, and is here tonight to be the audition "runner" for the next show: he'll run people's audition forms up from the lobby, where their pictures are taken, to the casting committee, clustered front and center before the stage.

In the lobby, which is below street level and cool, he'll meet his colleagues for the evening, the two other audition aides. Dot Lansil and Lorraine Stevens are each more than a half-century older than Matt, and their collective years of membership at the Friends total more than seventy. Dot, a retired bookkeeper for a snowplow manufacturer, has a lively shock of white hair, which, along with the breadth and symmetry of her roundish features, gives her a leonine aspect. She carries a magnificent bunch of keys, mostly to various locks within the theater, from the tiny ones on the paper-towel dispensers in the bathrooms to the one on the back gate that's no longer even there. She comes to the theater every Wednesday morning, when no one else is about, and cleans the bathrooms. Lorraine, retired from managing the kitchen at a school for disturbed children, has an imposing, smoke-raspy voice and eyes that light mischievously with opinion. Her involvement with the Friends has been a family affair ever since she first went down and painted flats, toddlers in tow, thirty-plus years ago. Her three grown children were practically raised at the theater, playing with the prop swords in the aisles, later learning how to hang lights and dress sets; just last spring, two of them came back to work on a play her husband directed. Lorraine has baked and decorated opening-night cakes for the theater since 1975. Neither woman has the slightest desire to set foot onstage, and both have done more for AFD than they would ever tell you themselves.

When Matt arrives, Dot, who gets there an hour early, has already set up the card tables and the pair of ancient black-and-white Polaroid cameras in the lobby, and pulled the audition books—five fat looseleafs crammed with the alphabetized audition forms of the past decade or so—from the shelf in the greenroom. Should anyone show up tonight who has auditioned here previously, his or her old form and photo will be pulled for reference. Brand-new auditioners will stand against the large square of yellow jersey Dot has tacked to the wall and have their pictures snapped unceremoniously by Dot, two to a frame, to save film. Lorraine then snips the developed picture in two, staples the appropriate image to the appropriate form, and hands it to Matt, who runs it upstairs to the director. All somehow very professional and lemonade-stand at once.

Lorraine, when she comes in, takes up immediate residence in the blue easy chair by the fake potted tree, and organizes her equipment: stapler, scissors, staple remover. Dot keeps busy checking over everything. She doesn't like to sit, because it's hard to get up again; besides, as she says with a wink toward her backside, she does it all day. Only Matt, bright-eyed and affable, has nothing to do, and eventually inquires after change for a dollar so he can get some soda. When he started out as runner four years ago, Dot used to feel obliged to walk him the twenty yards home in the evening; now, at thirteen, he's perhaps outgrowing the job. Next year he'll be eligible for the first time to join the Friends as a student member, one of the very few young people in the theater community. Lorraine drums up the coins and orders herself a Diet Coke, no caffeine, while he's at it.

She and Dot are symbiotic, salty and retiring respectively, and chat with the easy familiarity of those who've been fellow clubbers for decades. They catch each other up on other members, no longer active but residing now in nursing homes. They disapprove aloud, but without any real vehemence, of the "strong language" in most of this year's plays. When Lorraine discovers she's out of staples and calls "Dot!" Dot answers reflexively "Sir!" and neither laughs; it's that old. Matt comes back with the sodas, plunking down the one before Lorraine, who delivers her standard thank you: "You're not *all* bad, Matthew. I don't care what people say."

Down the hall, the show's production team is waiting in the green-room. Not every backstage lounge area is actually green, but this one is painted a very deliberate, not to say strident, green, a sort of mossy-sagey-avocado hue, and is just one aspect of the generally swanky new digs the theater acquired in a major renovation completed last winter. New, too (to Dot's mild chagrin: more for her to clean), are four of the six bathrooms, as well as the new lobby and entrance, dressing rooms and makeup area, boiler room and box office: virtually everything on the bottom floor has been newly built or rebuilt, and though it doesn't literally smell of fresh paint, there is a new-shoes squeaky sharpness to the atmosphere that has caused a measure of homesickness among a certain set.

Tonight, however, a different sort of sharpness imbues the greenroom: the needling pressure of a flock of invisible question marks, pricking the air over everybody's heads. If the little chapter in the story of this community theater whose beginning is tonight is not monumental, not drastically different from the hundreds of other little chapters that have made up the story so far, it is nevertheless different enough to cause some special excitement and consternation. In a network of branching roots it might show up as a sharp turn, even a

tiny brand-new tendril. Certainly there is that wish among the production's creative team: to break new ground with this play, to accomplish something that pushes the limits of this community, that
makes possible new risks, new explorations in the future.

The play is *M. Butterfly*, by David Henry Hwang. Here is how the
play-reading committee described it in notes to the board last fall:
"Drawn from real life events, involving the strange tale of a French
diplomat who carried on a twenty year relationship with a Chinese
Opera star without (he contended) being aware that his 'perfect
woman' was really a man, the play becomes a powerful metaphor for
the exploration of deeper themes: the perception of Eastern culture
by the West, and the persistent romanticism which clouds and in-
hibits that perception." It premiered a decade ago, won the Tony, the
Drama Desk, and the Outer Critics Circle Awards for best Broadway
play, was made into a Hollywood movie, and has been produced by
at least a hundred nonprofessional groups, nationwide.

In spite of all that, the play was an iffy choice for Arlington Friends
of the Drama to include on its annual slate of five shows, and represents an unusual challenge for this group in two ways. The first relates
to content: central to the plot is an enigmatic love affair between
what the audience eventually learns are two men; also, the script calls
for one of the actors to undress completely onstage. The second relates to context: the mounting of this particular play, which is rich
with Asian themes, culture, politics, and characters, within the particular communities of this theater and this town, which are both pre-
dominantly white, European-American. In choosing to put on this
show, the theater has offended some of its own members and set itself
a task that it is frankly not at all sure it can meet.

Celia Couture, whom the play-reading committee selected last
winter to direct, is sitting, but barely, on the edge of one of the or-
nate, mismatched greenroom sofas, eating a Subway sandwich leaking
shredded iceberg lettuce, and listening intently while the set designer
and the costume designer discuss color schemes. She has come
straight from her job as a Hewlett-Packard business branch manager,
and is wearing a navy-and-white checked jacket and navy slacks with
simple, bold gold jewelry. She has short brown hair, the do of someone with more important things to think about, and incongruously

manicured plum-colored fingernails. Celia is forty-eight, and crackles with a kind of compressed energy that seems always to be seeking outlet. There is a physical density to her, a compact kineticism, as there is to a baseball bat, or a golf club, or a well-strung racquet. In fact, despite her movie-star name, she pretty much embodies the spirit of everybody's fifth-grade gym teacher. She makes people snap to, anticipatory, expectant, eager to be led.

Celia has been actively preparing to direct this play for ten months—literally ever since the play-reading committee submitted its proposed slate to the board of directors last November, for she is president of the board, and learned earlier than most what next year's prospective plays were. From her first reading of the script, she knew she wanted to direct this one, and her preparations for doing so have been extensive, including a trip to the New York Public Library for the Performing Arts to research the original production. Yet she is also the first person to say she doesn't know whether this play can be done in Arlington, Massachusetts. Even now, even tonight, ten minutes before auditions are due to begin, she still hasn't committed herself unequivocally to directing the play. The catch lies not in her faith in herself as a director, or in her faith in the theater's audience, but in that flurry of felt question marks: who will show up to audition?

Celia has made clear that she will not direct the play without a qualified actor of Asian descent in the role of the ambiguously gendered male lead. This is not an idle threat; once before, at another community theater, she stepped down as director when auditions failed to yield suitable actors; in that event, the play simply did not go on. *M. Butterfly* has been done with alternative casting, but this is an option she will not consider—partly in deference to the playwright, who makes clear in his notes that the part should "unquestionably be played by an Asian actor, and preferably a man," and partly in deference to her own artistic vision. Yet, in the theater's entire membership of over five hundred people, and even in the broader pool of "gypsies" who move about from one community theater to the next, no one can think of a single Asian man, let alone one physically able to pass for a woman, talented enough to make the complex part of Song Liling believable, and, not incidentally, willing to get naked onstage.

The scanty pool of available Asian actors within the theater's established circles is in a way the whole point—when the play-reading committee chose to include *M. Butterfly* on the 1998–99 slate, it was in response to a self-imposed imperative to select a play that would encourage multiethnic casting, as a way of broadening and diversifying its membership. But no one knows if this plan will work, if simply electing to do a show with Asian characters will lead to lasting future changes. No one knows if it will lead to Asian actors' coming out to audition, for that matter. In the months and weeks leading up to tonight, prospects have seemed discouraging. One rumor going around is that even the Chinese Culture Institute in Boston couldn't find an Asian actor for the part of Song when it did the play a few years back, and wound up casting an Italian-American in the role. This turned out to be false (the Chinese Culture Institute never even did *M. Butterfly*; the theater in question was actually down on the South Shore), but the story added urgency to the outreach campaign conducted by AFD members.

The kinds of outreach themselves speak volumes about the degree of preparedness the group has in taking on this goal—revealing its energy, its earnestness, and its lack of existing contact with an Asian community. AFD usually advertises auditions through several sources, from newspapers to Web sites. In the case of *M. Butterfly*, extra steps were taken. A couple of people on the publicity committee posted fliers in dozens of Chinese restaurants in all the surrounding towns. One member's co-worker's husband knew someone at the Chinese Culture Institute, and agreed to pass the message along. Slice of Rice, an organization for gay, lesbian, bisexual, and transgender Asian youth, was sent a mailing. The Asian student organizations and the drama organizations at all the area colleges were notified. Some members, in a display of either boundless enthusiasm or embarrassing desperation, depending upon your point of view, have actually been approaching Asian strangers in restaurants and shops and asking them to spread the news word-of-mouth.

Now, in the greenroom at seven-twenty-five, Celia gnaws one flawlessly lacquered nail and squints a little at those assembled, as she is wont to do when collecting her thoughts. She often manages to seem simultaneously alert and preoccupied, as though staying on top of the current situation while planning for the next. Beside her on the worn velvet sofa is Jeneane Desilets, aged three, eating a Happy Meal and feeding bits of it to a toy bunny. Wistful at Jeneane's feet is Baron Giagrando, a small gray terrier, all clicking toenail and jutting eyebrow. On various sofas and chairs are Nancy Tutunjian and Suzanne Spezzano, whom Celia has asked to sit on the casting committee; Molly Trainor, the costume designer; Doug Desilets, the set designer; Kelley O'Leary, the stage manager; and David Giagrando, the production manager, who has been addressing everyone who walks through the room with a rapid-fire "Are you auditioning? Why not? Then do you want to do props?"

It's time to head up. The group of them file up the back stairs, through the tiny shop that runs the depth of the stage, and out into the front of the house, taking residence in the front row of bolted seats. Dot Lansil has set up a folding table here for the casting committee, and Celia unloads her things: working copies of the script enlarged to leave room for notes, a hardbound blank book with pansies all across the cover, extra pencils, a wristwatch, her mug of omnipresent green tea. Behind the committee sit a smattering of auditioners; at first glance the numbers look disappointing.

Auditions are a weird thing, contrived and awkward, arguably never more so than at the community-theater level. In the professional theater, make-believe is people's stock in trade, a world people inhabit, with intention and craft, as part of their jobs. At the other end of the spectrum, the school show, children and even teenagers are not unintimate with make-believe and play on a daily basis. But for most of the rest of us, the activity of make-believe is at odds with the selves we are called upon to be, by jobs and family and society, for most of the minutes of our lives. Similarly, the act of exposing oneself emotionally, of being private in public, is at odds with everything society has taught us by the time we reach adulthood. Yet in the implausible environment of community theater this is exactly what people are asked to do, and never as nakedly as at the audition. By the time a show reaches opening night, actors have been partially protected from this nakedness: by the direction they have received, by the trust and familiarity that have grown up among the cast, and by the physical armor of costume, makeup, lighting, and props. At the audition they have nothing. They are arriving from days spent as office workers and welders, bookkeepers and bakers, tutors and homemakers, and being asked to step up and bare themselves, to play make-believe with strangers, in front of other strangers, out of context.

It's very difficult, and few people, on either side of the casting table, relish auditions. Celia and the casting committee share a sense of respect and admiration for anyone who has come to try out tonight, and a desire to put people at least somewhat at ease. So, while they wait for Matt Rehrig to come upstairs with the first batch of audition forms, and for (they hope) more auditioners to straggle in at the last minute (there are only eleven bodies scattered widely through the house, and some may not even be here to try out), the committee engages casually in what a script would call "business," meaning, in this case, sort of secondary physical actions: arranging pencils, putting on eyeglasses, stretching, turning around to acknowledge any familiar faces. The tension in the room is packed and moist as pound cake, but it's layered over with frivolity, like a dusting of confectioner's sugar.

The house is not overly large—it seats 194, on a gentle rake—but the vaulted church ceiling gives it a gravely splendid air, and tends to dwarf its inhabitants. It also renders the space perpetually dim, as do the heavy velvet drapes on either side wall, so that, even with all the house lights on, the room has a murky, cavelike feel. In the absence of natural light, with only the pooling shadows cast by a handful of incandescents, this chamber seems perfectly severed from real life.

Amid the light, nervous, pre-audition banter, Doug Desilets arranges his model of the set, which he completed late last night, on the thrust, a part of the stage that juts past the proscenium. A work of miniature beauty, made of balsa and plywood and rice paper and foam core, the model has real sliding doors and movable set pieces. Doug learned stage design twenty years ago—in the military, of all places, while working at the community theater on an army base in Germany. He's a trim man, with precise features and movements, and strong traces of native Michigan in his speech.

Marion, his wife, arrives now, late, straight from work, and clops down the aisle in pumps and business suit. Jeneane goes to her and up into her arms, holding a pink sippy cup. Doug and Marion ex-change slightly harried hellos. They have to take turns doing shows now that they are parents, whereas for a long time they worked to-gether on plays and musicals, doing as many as they liked, often four out of the five each year. In fact, Doug had been keen to audition for this play ever since the slate was announced last winter, but in the last few weeks has decided, reluctantly, that being in the cast as well as helping execute his set design would take him too much away from his family. Still, he and Marion are determined to support each other's continuing involvement at the theater, which after all is sort of the reason their family even exists: the two met here at the Friends, in the cast of *Barnum* eleven years ago; Celia, who directed that show, too, helped hook them up. Besides her directorial skills, she has a quiet but considerable reputation as a matchmaker.

In strides another late arrival: Maryann Swift, wearing a North-eastern University soccer T-shirt, and sunglasses shoved up on top of her curls. The cast will include three kurogo, a Kabuki term for "in-visible" stagehands; these three actors will be responsible for effecting simple set changes with stylized movements, and Celia has asked Mayre, as she is most often called, to do the choreography. She hugs Celia and delivers a loaded glance—Mayre is a great one for loaded glances—and changes into her soft black jazz shoes. She, too, is half of a theater couple recently turned parent, and is finding it harder to stay involved with AFD. She wordlessly hands over a stack of photos of her little daughter and, while the casting committee pores dot-ingly over them, retreats to the vestibule by the handicapped-access bathroom to mark the simple combination she will teach the audi-tioners.

Baron appears onstage and looks around open-mouthed, obviously delighted with himself.

"I just locked you up," says David, in the front row.

"Guess what," says Celia.

"Handicapped bathroom?"

"He'll whine."

"I'll hold him on my lap in the back." David collects the terrier under his arm and they disappear to the back of the house.

Marion heads home with Jeneane. Mayre comes out of the

vestibule and gives Celia a nod. Celia scans the house. A paltry eleven people. The play has a cast of ten. She gives no sign of dismay. Three of the faces are Asian; two of these, male. Already that's better than she'd dared hope. Anyway, there's still Saturday. She checks her watch. It's past time. She gives a sign.

David reappears hastily, dogless, in front of the stage. At thirty-two, he's the youngest member of the production team. He's in jeans and a Martha's Vineyard sweatshirt, cuffs extending right to his knuckles, like a college kid. He has bright, close-set agate eyes and a sharp sense of humor. "Good evening," he says, with warmth, and the auditions begin. Everything about his welcoming speech is de-signed to be just that. He thanks people for coming out on a week-night, jokes it'll win them extra points. He introduces the casting committee and the production team, tells the auditioners where to find coffee, and invites them to make a cup. He asks them to "feed the elephant" if they do—a little silver bank in the shape of that ani-mal, which perches always on the kitchen counter in the greenroom. "What else? . . . Oh yeah. This is now Arlington Friends of the Bath-rooms. We used to have two, and we remodeled, and now you go downstairs and every door you open's a bathroom, so if you have to go just open a door and it'll probably be one."

"Knock first!" interject Celia and Mayre in laughing unison. The locks are shaky.

Now Celia stands and moves back two rows to address the group. She knows five of the eleven. A few she has directed before. One sits on the AFD board with her. One works at Hewlett-Packard, directly under her. She addresses them all equally, in professional, cordial tones. She ticks off the commitments the show requires. They will re-hearse for six weeks, four nights a week, from seven to ten up until the last week or two, when they'll rehearse from seven to whenever. The part of the pin-up girl will require some nudity. The part of Song will require full nudity. Both Gallimard and Song will have to be very, very comfortable with the sexual situations. The two actors playing the leads will have extra rehearsals to learn how to work with their special wigs, costumes, and makeup changes. Three of the male characters will be required to smoke. Any questions? None? Good luck to everyone.

Auditions, Celia sometimes says, are the most important job she has as director. She sits down again, cups an elbow in the opposite palm, lays a finger against the side of her mouth. Dimples flash in and out of her cheeks. Her perpetual focus gathers itself, sharpens a notch further.

The stage at this moment bears traces of scenery from the upcoming musical, *Funny Girl,* so the actors will be trying out, incongruously, under brightly painted signs reading "Saloon" and "Track 2 New York" and "Keeney's Music Hall." They begin, all eleven, with movement, and they begin with their backs to Celia and the committee, turned protectively upstage by Mayre, who teaches them the simple combination. It's like that moment when the doctor leaves the room so you may undress in privacy: that queer politeness, illogical but somehow necessary to preserving an illusion of dignity. So the auditioners, clustered close to the lumber-cluttered back wall, fumble and grope for the steps, and learn them, and laugh very quietly with each other as Mayre runs them through it calmly again, and a fifth time, and then they face front, with johnnies on, as it were, and present themselves to the examiners.

Not all auditions have such a meager turnout. The previous ones, for *Funny Girl,* drew fifty. But that was a musical, a big, familiar musical, a funny, fluffy, old-fashioned musical. *M. Butterfly* is a serious play, with complicated, adult, and frankly darkish themes; no one ever expected it would draw fifty. Nevertheless, the numbers are discouraging. Eleven people for ten parts. Celia will have to get on the phone.

Here is the other fear: that the turnout tonight is prophetic and the show will fail at the box office in November. Half the old guard at the Friends have been saying as much all along: *People come to the theater to be entertained, not challenged or depressed. It's our job to make people happy, not to make them think.* Just as this play is only a single entry in a voluminous history, these sentiments are single notes in a cacophonous debate that has been going on for millennia: What is the purpose of theater? What is the point of art? That this debate continues, not only among artists and scholars in museums and ivory towers, but among sales clerks and chiropractors in church basements and barns, is testimony to its inherent, if surprising, relevance to human beings.

Right downstairs at this moment are two of the people not exactly wild about the choice of play. Dot's just going on what she's heard—nudity, a same-sex love affair, "adult situations" and "adult language"—and it just doesn't sound like something the Friends' regular audience would like. Lorraine has actually seen it performed, when the professional touring company came to Boston some years ago—or saw the first part of it, anyway; she fell asleep. She found it boring and wordy, and expects most of the core audience will as well, if they bother coming at all.

They're both here, though, as ever, doing their parts, and if you questioned them as to why they're volunteering to work on a show they don't entirely approve of, they'd look at you as if you had some mild brain damage. And that's the difference between the old guard and the kids, the fickle gypsies of today, who come and go from theater to theater, often without even joining as members, without paying their dues, literal and figurative, but only drifting toward the plays or the parts that appeal to them and then drifting on again. People like Dot and Lorraine are here not for the play but for the organization. Among the old guard, the Friends is referred to as "the club," the physical theater as "the clubhouse." And disagreement about a slate, or even dissent and political infighting among the members, are never reasons to quit, but evidence of an impassioned, committed constituency. Which is graying.

It's no secret that the board is worried about this trend. Sixty-six percent of members are over fifty, only 16 percent under forty. The planning committee, in reporting results of a membership survey conducted this past winter, put it in no uncertain terms: "We're not getting any younger. . . . We need to cultivate members, particularly in the 31–40 age group, if AFD is to have a future." The report warned that "there is no 'next group' at the moment to take over running AFD," and recommended diversifying the regular season to include offerings designed to appeal to younger members, as well as adapting to the schedules of people in this target age group, who may already have huge time commitments to work and families.

Everyone who works at Arlington Friends of the Drama is a volunteer. On each show, the director receives a five-hundred-dollar stipend, which generally just helps defray out-of-pocket expenses (most every director winds up adding some of her or his own money to the play's budget, and it isn't uncommon for a director to donate the entire stipend back to the theater). The only other exception to the all-volunteer status is when AFD produces a musical, in which event the musical director and musicians are paid; this relates largely to precedent and even more largely to the shortage of available people to assume these jobs. That's it. No one else is paid, not the people who show up virtually every Tuesday and Wednesday night and Saturday morning to construct sets, not the people who landscape the front of the theater, not the people who manage the budget, or design the costumes, or pay the bills, or run the box office. Certainly not the actors, or the stage managers or production managers. Certainly not Dot, for cleaning the toilets, or Lorraine, for icing the cakes. And at one time this presented no problem, and there was no shortage of bodies eager to assume these tasks.

In 1913, Arlington staged a civic pageant in which virtually the entire town participated. The program, given on the shores of the Upper Mystic Lake over the course of three performances, before audiences of fifteen thousand people, brought to life a staggeringly ambitious hodgepodge of history and myth, from Paul Revere's midnight ride to the landing of the Vikings; from English Morris dances to French harvest rites; from Robin Hood and medieval heralds to Greek maidens and Roman peasants, Pan and satyrs, dryads and naiads, the Winds, the Months, the very Hours.

The dreamer-up of this pageant, its author and initiator, was Vittoria Calonna Murray Dallin, one of the town's most prominent citizens. She had already penned two other pageants, "The Pageant of Education," presented in Boston in 1909, and "The Pageant of Progress," presented in Lawrence in 1911. She had just completed a term as president of the Arlington Woman's Club when, at a regular meeting of that group, the idea of starting a pageantry movement in Arlington was officially born.

Arlington's pageant was hardly unique, or even particularly unusual. A sort of pageant fever had burned across the country during the past five years, and would continue for another five. Scores of pageants were written and staged, from Marietta, Ohio, to San Francisco, from Pittsburgh to the Bronx to Cornish, New Hampshire, and in every one, magnitude played a principal role. The arenas were measured in acres, not feet. An audience of thousands was commonplace. The pageant in St. Louis boasted a *cast* of seven thousand, and attendance by half a million people. The one in Hadley, Massachusetts involved nine towns in a mile-long procession. The one in San Gabriel, California, was given daily for months on end.

Whence this craze? It seems redolent of a desire to reconnect with ancient pagan ceremonies, or at least with the theater tradition of the Greeks: masses of people gathering in the amphitheater for a communal experience of catharsis. In fact, it was more directly fueled by the recent swells of immigration and the commensurate anxiety, on the part of longer-established Americans, about protecting a certain hallowed and pristine version of America. The deputy commissioner of education for Massachusetts, addressing the topic of pageantry in 1912, wrote, "There is no better way to induct immigrants and their children into a knowledge of American history and institutions. . . . And an abiding sense of the stability of society is gained." And in his *Handbook of American Pageantry,* written two years later, Ralph Davol extolled the pageant as "a great civic rite, through which the non–English speaking immigrants to the Land of Promise may be taught their parts as 'flag-makers of the nation.'"

But induction works both ways. Control yields to access; one-way instruction yields to accidents of mutual understanding. Percy MacKaye, a prolific and voluble proponent of "civic theatre," and author of several pageants himself, wrote in his book *Community Drama,* "Neighborliness in a little town may beget the neighborliness of nations." He saw community-based theatrical events as a means of "resolving the estrangement and conflict of social elements into harmony," and he called the new art form the "theatre of democracy." Others took a more radical approach, harnessing the grassroots theater movement as a tool *against* the status quo, seeing ways to use it instead for empowerment of the disenfranchised and for social change. In big cities from New York to Chicago to San Francisco, settlement-house theaters were started; the suffragettes gave pageants rallying for the right of women to vote; the International Workers of the World staged a pageant in Madison Square Garden.

However multifarious or even confused the nature of the pageantry movement may have been, what emerges is this: the Arlington Pageant in no way constituted an isolated or chance event. A movement of community theatricals was causing literally millions of people, across the country, who did not think or act or speak alike, to get together and make art. And if one looks beyond the merely recent trend in America to the much older tradition of pageantry and masquery in Europe, and beyond that to the really ancient customs of staging history worldwide, of acting out the important stories within a culture, telling them again and again in vivid, ritualized group ceremonies of color and sound and movement—then it becomes clear that the pageant in Arlington in June 1913 is one minuscule iteration within an infinite pattern that is part of the weave of human existence.

And none of this makes it less noble or holy or magical or breathtaking.

On the contrary.

The fact that size figured so importantly in virtually all of the pageants was no coincidence. The scope and breadth of the production process may ultimately have been more significant to the community than the content and quality of the performance. In Arlington, more than a year's worth of preparation went into the pageant's making. More than two dozen subcommittees. More than six hundred performers (not counting livestock). The idea was hatched over teacups held in the tidy white hands of the most proper ladies in town, a great portion of the money ($9,882.23 in the end) was raised by the most privileged and well-known citizens, and the reins held by those best acquainted with power (a judge, the superintendent of schools, and the president of Arlington Co-operative Bank were among the members of the executive committee). But in a kind of inevitable twist, the majority of people working to bring it off were not the elite. They were celery farmers and ice cutters, streetcar operators and putty gun-ners, tailors and grocers, mail carriers and chimney sweeps, clerks and domestics and washerwomen—many of them too newly arrived from distant poverty, oppression, famine, and pogrom to exist yet in the pages of the town directory.

The assortment of people in the grandstand constituted a second spectacle, not really any less momentous than that on the stage: in the sea of spectators' fluttering hair-ribbons and stately top hats, of white mustaches and newsboy caps, of cheeks burnt rosy and those kept sheltered from the sun, was a picture of a town, a profile of a community not necessarily harmonious, not necessarily loving or united, but here anyway for an afternoon together.

Something had brought them all out together by the lake.

A play.

> *Arlington really surprised itself, or rather it has discovered itself in the pageant, in which all classes in the community were represented, for there was fine spirit and fine dignity and intelligence in every bit of the work and in the entire affair.*
> —Boston Globe, *Saturday, June 7*

> *The pageant which has been enacted the last two days in this town of 12,000 persons in the Boston metropolitan district probably never has been equaled in this country as a purely civic function, for all classes in the community participated in the affair and all classes in the community had been working for months to make it the success that it was.*
> —Boston Herald, *Sunday, June 8*

The tasks were quite literally innumerable, and eclectic, and meted out to so many different hands that no one could claim a comprehensive awareness of all the work that had been done or all the workers who had done it. Who could name the high-school pupils who typed out copies of Mrs. Dallin's script? The men and women who mopped the floors of the churches and clubhouses where individual episodes were rehearsed? Those who at the eleventh hour built additional rows onto the grandstand? Everyone who gave an evening to stitching banners or cutting out patterns? Everyone who ventured into an attic to search for old muskets, flags, farming equipment, military uniforms, shields, swords, lanterns—properties for the historical episodes?

In the end, no single person knew every inch of the pageant, and every person who worked on it could claim it as her or his own. And the work made it real, the fact of the work. There were those, at the outset, who scoffed at the whole project, or, worse, were actually offended by the idea of so much time and energy being wasted on a goal this frothy and insubstantial—a sort of pink and fluty thing, with grown women (pillars of society!) dressing up as fairies and nymphs (scantily clad!) and prancing and dancing about like children caught up in veils of make-believe. And even among those who were moved by the idea, by the notion of a grand-scale re-creation of historical events and ancient mythology, by the relative values of Culture and Art—even among those, some found it initially hard to justify such expense, such outpouring of the town's energies. To all such doubters, then, by the civic merits of the extravaganza, the ways in which it exemplified the true spirit of democracy, and the productive channeling of the wayward impulses and leisure hours of a newly heterogeneous society into a form of homage for the wholesome past— by these outcomes the pageant redeemed itself.

The truth is that it *was* froth, airy and insubstantial, inasmuch as the pageant was staged for no quantifiable or tangible gain, and inasmuch as it *was*, after all, a great effort of make-believe, of child's play, of let's-pretend en masse. But among plenty of others in the audience and in the cast and crew, there was no particular need for justification or redemption, or even for an accounting of the pageant's net merits. Among them resided no need to tally or classify the pageant's worth, or to locate the precise whereabouts of that worth, either in the brilliance of the actual spectacle, or in the spirit of the town's pulling together, or somewhere in the alchemical reaction between those two. Among them, the worth would not be named or chronicled, but felt.

When analyzed today, eighty-five years later, it yields nothing but a disparate heap of everyday acts: a clarinet player wetting his reed, a woman leading a cow by a rope across a field, a man cobbling together lengths of wood, children practicing dance steps up in their bedrooms at night. The pageant was like a fantastic cake whose workaday ingredients have been transformed in the baking into something wholly unlike the sum of its parts, into something sublime. All of the tasks that went into the pageant seem prosaic when considered by themselves, yet when taken together become something more like the grave and mysterious goodness of a town.

All of the reasonable aspects of the pageant could be parceled into scholarly-sounding boxes: Civic Motivation; Sociological Impact; Economic Effects; Reinforcement of Political Values. The event could be examined in terms of social hierarchy, preservation of classical ideals, group dynamics, and power plays. The pageant could even be recognized as having afforded some ladies a socially sanctioned opportunity to preen a little, to show their legs and wear feathers in an otherwise tight-laced society, and having afforded some men a chance to fire their weapons in peacetime, and sport uniforms and die safely in battle—as having provided, in other words, a great and lively feast for the individual ego.

But it remains, finally, mysterious. The people of Arlington put on a play. This is extraordinary and at the same time commonplace. It's something that, in some form, their ancestors did, something their descendants are nearly certain to do.

People put on plays.

Why? Why that outpouring of time and money, sweat and heart? Why the willing assumption of risk? There *is* risk involved, public and personal, financial and emotional, to the mores and self-image of the town, and to a person. All for something whose gains are abstract, unproven, ineffable. For something that lasted three days and vanished.

> *This tapestry hung on the walls of memory will ever be a priceless possession of all who were in any way connected with the Pageant. As the years go on they will more and more realize what a privilege it was to lend their aid in a movement, which above all things, did much towards fostering, for a time at least, the community spirit.*
> —*Mrs. Vittoria Dallin*

Ten years later, when pageant fever had abated and something called the little-theater or community-drama movement was taking hold across the land, the Woman's Club founded Arlington Friends of the Drama. Mrs. Dallin was elected president. And the members of the group began to put on plays.

Now, on the cusp of the twenty-first century, the group perseveres, but times have changed, and people's levels of commitment have waned. Everyone's simply busier—that's the accepted wisdom, only how can that be, wonder older members, some of whom remained committed through the Depression and wars, through years of raising children and working jobs, through divorces and deaths, through nursing dying parents and dying spouses. Through all of this, for many older members, the Friends was a respite, a source of happiness and connection, a way, even, of getting through difficult times.

But now, if people aren't literally busier, they're busier in different, less community-oriented ways. Women are working outside the home; men are spending more time with families; people in general are moving more often, commuting greater distances to work, and spending more time isolated in front of television and computer screens, all of which have affected community involvement and identity. The National Commission on Civic Renewal recently conducted a two-year study into the decline of civic involvement. Their final report, titled, "A Nation of Spectators: How Civic Disengagement Weakens America and What We Can Do About It," states that "our overall civic condition is weaker than it was" a generation ago, thanks in part to a decline in membership in "the associations of our civil society . . . from churches to soccer leagues to reading circles to social movements, from colleges to symphony orchestras to volunteer fire departments."

Not all the news is quite so discouraging. Another reason for divided loyalties among younger members is the increased number of community theaters. AFD is now one of about forty-five in the Greater Boston area; an exact count is difficult, because new groups crop up and dissolve every year, but everyone agrees that there are far more now than there were fifteen or twenty years ago. AFD claims to be one of the ten oldest continually operating community theaters in the country. The American Association of Community Theatres, founded in 1986, estimates about ten thousand community theaters nationwide, with over a million active members. Still, that the nature of both "community" and community theaters is in flux, in a way that spells trouble for an old, club-oriented amateur-theater organization, is evident, and AFD has begun addressing the matter overtly, with efforts to change its own structure and goals in order to keep up with the shifting community around it.

The figurehead and chief practitioner of those changes is at this moment sitting upstairs in the front row, squinting intently at the stage and searching for signs of chemistry between the two men reading lines together there. Celia, entering her third and final year as president of the board; Celia, the businesswoman in real life, managing three different Hewlett-Packard branch offices; Celia, who as president has moved the site of board meetings from the comfortable clutter of the greenroom or the den of someone's house to a sleek and polished conference room up at her Burlington office, is the most visible proponent of change and most obvious target for people's dismay and anger. Under Celia, the massive renovation was carried out, incurring a $150,000 mortgage when before there was none. Under Celia, a radical change in the membership structure has been proposed and is now under heated, even divisive, debate (according to its supporters, it would eliminate an archaic and elitist hierarchy; according to its detractors, it would degrade those who have worked hard to achieve "active" status, and leave the theater vulnerable to being taken over by outsiders). And under Celia, this play, this daring and some would say disgraceful play, *M. Butterfly*, is being produced, draining talent and energy from some of the group's best workers, and dollars from its coffers, at the possible expense of offending and driving away some of its most loyal supporters.

Not that Celia could care less at this moment. She is fixated on the action onstage, a scene between the two leads, Song Liling and René Gallimard, the opera star and the diplomat. In the past hour, the committee have viewed all manner of scenes and combinations of actors. They have seen a stocky young woman, deadpan and callous in her delivery, give a terribly funny reading as Comrade Chin, Song's contact within the Chinese world of espionage. They have seen a wiry young man, at his first audition ever, give a charmingly rough reading

in a Boston accent so broad it bordered on parody, as Marc, Gallimard's boyhood friend. They have seen five Gallimards, ranging from
beautifully clear and subtle to frankly all wrong, and two Songs, each
compelling, and each awfully tall to pass believably for a woman.

Five minutes ago, Celia whispered to the committee that she was
going to start doing a more intimate scene now between the male
leads. Then she raised her voice. "Gentlemen, be as physical with
each other as you are comfortable being, given that this is an audition." She said this with all the inflection of a DMV clerk asking the
next person in line to step forward, and in this way helped make the
instruction seem businesslike and routine. The level of respectful silence in the house grew, and the actors she called took the stage with
concentration.

The scene is two pages long. It begins with hostility and ends with
Song agreeing to become Gallimard's lover. The actors approach it
bravely; Gallimard strokes Song's cheek, Song kneels before him and
kisses his fingers; Gallimard embraces Song from behind, with confidence and tenderness and longing. Five times the scene is run, until
each of the Gallimard hopefuls has had a chance. Each of the pairings
is different, some strained, some more believable, some believable but
too clumsy, or too harsh, or just ill-matched. Once or twice, for a
moment, real characters are inhabited, a real relationship seems to be
unfolding. "Okay, thanks, guys," says Celia, sounding grim, after
each reading. She herself is unreadable, has addressed everyone in the
same tone. The rest of the committee is equally affectless, jotting a
note from time to time, otherwise treating the whole thing with an almost leaden sobriety.

That all changes when they announce a break and go hole up in
the rear dressing room downstairs, Celia and Kelley and Molly and
Nancy and Suzanne and Mayre and David and Baron, all crowded
against boxes of ribbons and elastics, piles of shoes and top hats, racks
of wedding dresses for one of the Ziegfeld Follies numbers in *Funny
Girl*. Baron runs circles in the middle of the tiny room, and Mayre
says, in a dry, factual tone, "He needs to stop that," and sips from a
cold cup of cocoa. Celia plays with a prop cane. "You can't be here—
get out," she says to David, because he's been on the fence about
whether to audition as well as produce. "No, no, I made up my

mind," he insists. "No, I did, I promise—I'm not auditioning." He perches next to the sewing machine on the folding table, swinging his legs. Kelley takes a folding chair, Nancy squats on her haunches, Suzanne leans against the full-length mirror, and Molly swipes at a pink boa, which had come creeping down from a shelf like an amorous snake onto her shoulder.

"Which one?" says Celia, with no preamble. That she's tackling the part of Song first is understood. Whether or not the play goes on is completely predicated on finding an actor who can convincingly portray a woman. She turns to Molly, the costumer. "Well, first, which one would be easier?"

"Neither one's easy," pronounces Molly, never one to promise what she doesn't know she can deliver.

"How tall are they, anyway?" asks David, because that question is on the audition forms, and Kelley looks it up.

"Five ten and six feet."

"Shit."

"I envision him constantly bent," says Celia.

Both Asian male actors had strong qualities, but the group keeps returning to the taller of the two, the one named Patrick Wang, who had a kind of stillness and guileless grace that read from the audience as more intriguingly vulnerable, and more feminine, than the rather conventionally, coquettishly female mannerisms the other actor had adopted. Patrick also had a prettier face, and a pretty vocal quality, opine Kelley and Suzanne.

"I think the depth is better in Patrick," says Celia. "I'm trying to watch his hands when there's not a script in them. The one place I noticed it was the mirror exercise. Which was brilliant," she adds to Mayre, who had ended the movement part of the auditions by putting the actors through this old chestnut of an activity, a staple of beginning acting classes, in which one actor tries to follow the movements of another so closely that he could pass for a mirror image. It was intended to let the casting committee see who moved well and could be cast as a kurogo, but the exercise has the side effect of shedding light on how people work together, how closely they observe, how well they communicate nonverbally, how focused and supportive they might be with fellow cast members.

"Okay. Any of the Gallimards strike you?"

The conversation here is completely different, because several people on the committee know four of the five men who auditioned for this role, and past experiences come into play: who has a problem learning lines, who does wonderfully in auditions but never improves beyond that, who is full of nervous mannerisms today but will take direction and grow into the part by opening night. They discuss who seemed comfortable with the physical intimacy. They discuss who seemed really to understand the part, who interpreted the character best. They discuss height. One of the favorites is a good deal shorter than either Song.

"There's only so much I can do with lifts," Molly reminds the group, direly.

And they discuss politics. Three of the five men are active members of AFD, and each of these does a tremendous amount of work for the theater. One helps build sets for virtually every show. Another manages the theater's Web site and takes almost all the publicity photos. A third sits on the board as head of the play-reading committee, and in that capacity played a huge part in actually getting this show on the slate; he has also made no secret that for the past year his heart has been set on playing Gallimard.

It is official policy at AFD, when casting a play, that if two candidates are of equal merit for a part, and one is an AFD member and the other is not, the part shall go to the AFD member. No one pretends otherwise, or apologizes when explaining this policy, and if there are those who believe it helps foster the aura of elitism or exclusivity that is sometimes mentioned when people speak of the Friends, there are as many others who say it's just and, what's more important, practical. The organization's utmost goal is not to produce great theater or make outsiders feel welcome (although these are certainly among the goals) but something more Darwinian: to survive.

Not official policy, but just as practical, is to weigh in what *sort* of member an auditioner is—how active, how loyal, how well connected and well respected among the other members—in other words, to take into account the politics of the theater and what role the auditioner plays in them. In this respect, paying the membership fee matters less than playing an active role as a member. As the organization's current leader as well as director of this play, Celia is in a doubly charged position. More than once during the casting discussion she says, "To put on my president's hat for a minute . . ." This is not cynical Machiavellian stuff. In community theater, you have to think at least as much about the *community* as you do about the *theater*. Concern about the former may compromise the latter; on occasion it undoubtedly does. But concern about the former is also what makes possible the latter.

On the other hand, Celia has a reputation for flouting casting expectations, often to the surprise and delight of actors and sometimes to the consternation of those who monitor the organization's political climate. She is known to cast against type, specifically against age and ethnic type, but also against the auditioner's own self-perception. Several actors who have worked with her talk of Celia's possessing an uncanny ability to see things in a person that the person has not yet discovered within herself or himself, and to help bring those qualities out in the rehearsal process. On the political front, her most famous departure from the expected occurred in *Grand Hotel* four years ago, when she cast an outsider as the lead, passing over the man many people had believed was destined for the part: a longtime and greatly admired member named James Grana.

Jimmy, as he is more often called, is currently sitting upstairs with the other auditioners; he is the head of the play-reading committee, the man whose heart has gleamed bright on his sleeve for the past year. He is the driver of ACTOR 1, having waited for that license plate to become available for four years. (Nobody was using ACTOR 2, the registry informed him when he first inquired, but he demurred; what message would *that* send?) This is his first audition for Celia since she chose not to cast him in *Grand Hotel.* And he is the one subject that arouses a bit of heat among the casting committee tonight, for, even within this small group—hand-picked by Celia, as is her directorial prerogative—there are staunch Jimmy-supporters and those who are just neutral.

Jimmy has thick silvery hair and a craggily handsome face. Tonight he is wearing a blue shirt and a tie with white trousers, about which he earlier took pains to explain, "I know you're not supposed to wear white after Labor Day, but in the script at one point it says he's in a cream-colored suit, and this is the closest thing I have." He has been a member of the Friends since 1977, and in addition to acting, directing, and serving on the board, he's had an original play produced here. He is broadly hospitable in the way of a great, shaggy golden retriever, greeting each scene partner tonight by name and with a large, solid handshake. He is also the only person to have won the best-actor award at the Eastern Massachusetts Association of Community Theatres festival five times. Gallimard is a dream role for an actor seeking challenge; he must transform himself onstage from an insecure adolescent to a hubris-impaired, overly confident lover and diplomat to a savaged, spent older man on the verge of madness and suicide. Clearly the sort of role to provide another shot at best actor, and AFD, which does not enter the competition every year, has already announced its intention to participate this spring—with a cutting from *Butterfly*.

Jim has not given a stunning audition. Nerves have affected his performance, which is coming across as somewhat overwrought, as if all the tension of the past ten months' yearning for this role has been funneled into these few scenes, which cannot bear the load. His interpretation of the character is more mannered and insecure than what Celia has in mind. He has rattled the change in his pocket so noisily that Celia had to interrupt him twice to ask him to quit it.

On the other hand, his audition doesn't suffer from lack of passion, commitment, or thought ("Problem is, he's *over*thought it," Celia says). And he's a known quantity, so that whether or not his sense of the character matches Celia's at this point doesn't necessarily matter ("We know Jimmy responds to direction," she observes). Perhaps most important, he's emphatically human onstage, never cardboard, never aloof; he gives himself away to the audience—if not always perfectly, then fearlessly.

Of the other contenders, the favorite is also the shortest, a fact the committee argues and sighs over again and again in this hasty meeting among the costume racks. Appearance ought not to matter—but how can it not, in this play *about* appearances? Already they are asking so much of the audience, straining the audience's credulity so far—can they really afford to push it further? But his reading was so beautiful!

At last they agree to table this discussion until Saturday, when they've seen who else might show up—potential Songs as well as Gallimards, for the proper pairing is almost as important as talent alone. The committee moves on to supporting characters. The one woman who seems to be a shoe-in—the acerbic Comrade Chin with the killer comic timing—has scheduling conflicts during production week, the all-important last week of rehearsals before opening night. No one else seemed just right for any of the supporting roles, although one woman, who, as Mayre points out, "moved really pretty," is a potential kurogo, and one man—the young tough with no experience and the heavy Boston accent who read for the part of Marc, Gallimard's cynical, lascivious boyhood friend—made them all grin. "He did great with the 'boob' line," observes Celia, resting her arms on the prop cane, which she now wears behind her neck like a yoke. "Well, you know he's had that conversation before."

In the end, they decide they don't need to see any more scene work tonight, but agree to invite eight of the eleven to callbacks on Saturday afternoon. The callbacks will let the casting committee see all the top candidates paired up with one another, as well as show who can follow direction, for Celia will interact more with them on Saturday. Some directors may use callbacks politically also—again, unofficially—as a kind of courtesy to members who are not being considered but who might be unnecessarily hurt or offended if not invited, at least, to callbacks. The committee now scatters briefly, to bathroom and soda machine. Kelley and Nancy go off to raid the secretariat—a storage closet built under the stairs in the lobby, so named because the theater stationery is stored here, along with any candy left over from the intermission concession—but come up empty-handed.

They reconvene upstairs, in the house, where nothing has changed: the auditioners all waiting in their bolted seats, the light and shadow, the dust motes and scenery, all just the same, suspended in the timeless, cloistered unreality of the theater. David apologizes for making them wait, explains they won't need to do any more scene work tonight, and says they'll notify people regarding callbacks by phone. (It's too small a group, and too few are *not* being invited, to announce the list in front of everyone.) And then that's it. They begin to drift out, the brave eleven, those who've been members forever and those who've never set foot in here before, and among whom a tenuous camaraderie based on shared vulnerability is already dissipating.

Back at the theater, the committee members are gathering car keys and jackets. Celia, Kelley, Suzanne, and Mayre all live in Tewksbury, a forty-five-minute drive north. Molly, in Malden, has a half-hour drive, as does David, in Braintree. Even Nancy, who lives the closest, in Watertown, is two towns away from the theater. All further evidence of a breakup of community at AFD, where once you had to be an Arlington resident to join. They begin locking up, turning off lights. Doug left long ago; he still hasn't gotten over not being able to audition for this play himself, and he couldn't stand to watch others do it. Matt and Dot and Lorraine are also long gone, not having exactly had a bevy of auditioners to process tonight. But: "We already did better than we thought we might," David reminds everyone as they file out the back door, and this is true—not one but two Asian men, and both worthy of consideration. And maybe more on Saturday. Good-nights are said, and car engines cut the quiet. For the first time in all the months of imagining this play, Celia drives home thinking it will really happen.

Behind them, Arlington Friends of the Drama stands empty, behind the grander civic buildings, in a neighborhood of family homes, its painted-lady flamboyance drained away by the night, just the shape of it etched steep and gray against the navy sky. At such times you remember it was in the last century a church, which fits, in a way: a church being that other place where neighbors congregate against the odds, for neither profit nor practical purpose, but for reasons ineffable and deeply felt and as old as humankind.

On Saturday two more possible Songs show up: a slight, delicate man from Thailand who puts on his audition form that he's worked as a female impersonator, and a sweet-faced man from Taiwan in an eggplant silk shirt with a dancer's posture. The committee members dig elbows into ribs, exchange meaningful, eyebrow-waggling smiles. The female impersonator moves wonderfully, but his acting is stiff, and his accented English difficult to understand. The one in the silk shirt, though not right on target, has some nice moments. But later, in the dressing room, Celia puts it bluntly. "I think the other two were frankly better actors."

"How tall was the other one again?" asks Nancy.

"Which, the one in the argyle sweater or the tall one?" asks Kelley.

"I don't give a shit if he's a giant, if he's a better actor," Celia cuts in. "We'll put Gallimard on stilts if we have to." And this is when the committee and production team really know, for certain, at last, that Celia is committed and there will be no turning back.

Saturday does yield a talented, confident, and funny Marc in the person of Tom Dinger, new to AFD but a theater veteran, and a game pin-up girl and mistress in the person of Carolyn Torrey, who has never before acted in a straight play but disarmed them all by uttering the penis monologue with good-natured ease and an endearing blush. Saturday also brings the two Michelles: Michelle Aguillon, a tall, strong Comrade Chin with an expressive face and no scheduling conflicts; and Michelle Estrada, a startlingly beautiful kurogo dancer, diminutive even in her mega-platform shoes. All four are offered these roles, and accept. Grace Butler, an active member who most recently appeared opposite Jim Grana in last spring's Noël Coward play, is tapped for the part of Helga, Gallimard's wife. And Jimmy emerges as the obvious best choice for Gallimard. Seven out of ten parts cast: they are short one kurogo, one Anglo male supporting actor, and, of course, one Song.

On Monday night the Songs are called back a final time to read with Jimmy. One of the four, the one in the argyle sweater from Thursday night, has dropped out, citing scheduling conflicts. The other three present themselves with quiet dignity, awaiting direction. Celia is all business. She dimples frequently and deeply, but hers are the kind of dimples that are as likely to indicate a frown as a smile— or, most often, simply intense concentration.

Jimmy, now cast, is broadly relaxed, and eager to make everyone else feel that way. "I took the change out of my pockets," he announces cheerily, bounding onstage. "But I've got Tic Tacs today." He displays them and offers one to his scene partner, whom he calls by name.

"Just don't rattle 'em," Celia retorts from below. "Okay, go."

She puts the auditioners through their scene work in rapid succession, sometimes giving terse directions ("Try to minimize yourself physically," "Avert the eyes," "Flirt"), and offering no indication of her reactions. After an hour of this, the committee breaks and, too impatient to travel all the way downstairs to the dressing rooms, gathers in the set shop tucked just behind the stage. No one can figure out how to turn on the regular lights, so they meet in the clandestine glow of a blue bulb.

Celia dimples without smiling. "Did any of that help anyone?"

"The voice of Patrick blew me away when he made the transition to being a man," says Nancy.

"But that same resonance doesn't work as a woman," says Kelley.

"Who do you think Jim connects with?" asks Celia.

"Bernard."

"Yeah."

Celia nods, but it's difficult to tell whether she's agreeing or just acknowledging their opinions.

"I'm having a hard time with the height of the two tall guys," says Mayre.

"First of all, we have to get Jim to stand up straight," says Molly. "I can probably find him some shoes with a little bit of an extra heel, but I can't do too much or he'll look like he has platforms on."

"I think we need to look at them," says Celia. That, of course, is what they've been doing for the past few days, but this time, when they tramp back into the house, she asks the Songs to please remove their shoes and shirts. The men comply and stand onstage in a row, Jimmy, clothed, among them. They face forward and, when directed, turn upstage. The committee regards them from the back of the house, silently assessing and comparing heights and builds and believability, and the men, passive, naked to the waist, offer themselves to the gaze of these women.

Then Celia says, "All right, gentlemen. Thank you very much," and shoelaces get tied and shirts buttoned and the Songs collect themselves to depart. "Thank you," repeats Celia. "You should hear from us no later than tomorrow morning."

When they and Jimmy have cleared the house she says, "Okay. Talk to me."

"Patrick seems to have thought it out."

"He has the demureness."

"There's an intensity and mystery to Patrick."

"Yes!"

"But Bernard carried over all the notes you gave him Saturday. He really worked on it."

"Patrick's height bothers me."

"It bothers all of us."

"I think he's going to make up as a prettier woman, though."

"He's very, very smooth-skinned, which has a lot to do with the believability."

Celia weighs in. "I think Patrick is the more intelligent actor. He could play the depth. And when we get past working the physicality to death, I need someone who can interpret the script."

No one has anything to say against that, and their faces go into reverie for a moment, mentally inserting Patrick's name on the nearly complete cast list, picturing the ramifications. There's enough in place to begin to fantasize. It's really going to happen, this play; it's really going to get staged here, in Arlington, Mass. It may occasion shock and disgust; it may occasion adulation and epiphany. If it works at all, a slice of something Other will illumine the stage of this little woodframe theater for a handful of nights. Which will itself be marvelous. As one longtime director at the Friends says, a production is never as fine as before the first rehearsal, when it shimmers exquisite in the mind of the director.

"Well," utters Molly, eminently reasonable, snapping them back to reality. Her hair is the double-take color of an orange poppy, very short and very straight. She looks over the tops of her little round glasses and delivers the final flat word: "Everyone's going to have to work on Jim not to slouch."

TWO

Lonelyhearts

I n a cupboard in the greenroom there are two mildew-speckled
cardboard boxes with FINCH PAPER printed across the tops. They
are the repository for a couple dozen logbooks of various shapes
and sizes and quality, which all together contain the minutes of the
board of the Arlington Friends of the Drama from 1923 to the present. The first book in the first box is a two-ring black binder filled
with ordinary yellowed looseleaf paper, and the first page is inscribed
in fountain pen, in a looping, womanly hand:

> *January 16, 1923*
> *A meeting was held at the house of Mrs. Dallin on Saturday,
> January 16, called together by the hostess.*
> *Questionnaires were handed around and filled out securing
> information in regard to the special fitness of each one present in
> regard to dramatic art. Mrs. Dallin was chosen chairman and
> Mrs. Tibbetts, Treasurer and Mrs. Waterman, Secretary.*

It was voted to call the new organization the "Friends of the Drama."

The pages that follow, in all of the books, continue in the generally dry tradition of minutes everywhere, although every once in a while the arrival of a new recording secretary is evident not only in a change in handwriting (or typewriter), but in a more arch or playful style of reportage. Some years are muffled by near-illegibility, others partially obscured by the extreme laconism of the recorder, but the existence of these documents at all is remarkable, and it is tempting to think that they must hold the secret of the group's long existence.

The logbooks are not the only contents of AFD's archives. Above the cupboard, occupying two rows of bookshelf, sit twenty-five fat scrapbooks containing seventy-five years' worth of programs, photographs, newsletters, and newspaper clippings. These, unlike the minutes, offer more immediately accessible amusement and are well pawed over; some of the spines on the older, clothbound books have been almost completely severed from their bindings, attached by only a few dry threads. During rehearsal breaks, people come down and flip through these for fun, exclaiming over ten- or twenty- or thirty-year-old pictures of current members, marveling over the seventies fashions, the fifties hairdos, the intrinsically glamorous thirties portraits. The sense of history and lineage the scrapbooks convey is powerful.

Overseeing and keeping up this collection for nearly the last third of the group's history is the woman people call the godmother of AFD, Nancie Richardson. Nancie is tall with short taffy-colored hair and big square-framed glasses and a softly pretty face. She is not an actor, not an artist—not really, as she is quick to say, a theater person. She came to AFD a quarter of a century ago, when she was in her twenties and new to the area, simply in order to meet people, which she did: she met her husband and those who would become the majority of their close friends at AFD. Before community theater she'd tried meeting people through adult-education classes; she took everything from the history of Cambridge to pottery to tap-dancing to palmistry, all to no avail—people never went out for coffee or anything afterward. And then a co-worker at the environmental firm where she was a secretary invited her down to a set-building night at AFD, and it finally happened: she walked in and was handed a paint-brush and treated like a welcome newcomer to a warmly quirky social club.

If two components of community theater are actors and techies, Nancie represents a third sector of the population, at least as impor-tant and dedicated as the other two: those who are here because it's a second home, in a quite literal sense. The number of people in official possession of keys to the building is at any given time rather large, in-cluding anyone with a position on the board or a committee of the board, as well as a handful of top staff for the current production (perhaps forty or even fifty in all). The number of people in *unofficial* possession of keys to the building far outstrips this. For one thing, no one actually follows people around asking them to turn in their keys when their board positions have ended or their productions have closed. For another, there are several members of such long standing and high esteem, who do so much invisible work for the theater on an ad-hoc basis, that for them to possess keys is not only fitting but prac-tical. Nobody actually knows how many AFD keys exist, or in whose hands they reside, but nobody is terribly concerned about this, either, since AFD is a clubhouse and members are encouraged to treat it as such, to come and go as they please, to poke their heads in whenever, whether for five minutes or five hours, whether on theater business or simply in order to fix a cup of instant coffee down in the greenroom and chat.

To Nancie Richardson, who has, almost in spite of herself, become a theater person over the past twenty-five years, wearing virtually every AFD hat (save actor's) from president's to floor sweeper's, the theater remains most importantly a front porch, a watering hole, a hearth. What she calls her favorite AFD anecdote (really more of a tableau) is disarmingly simple. One night, quite late, a week before some play was opening, she walked into the house and saw onstage three volunteers all completely intent on getting the set finished: a man in his mid-sixties, another in his early forties, and a boy of thir-teen, representatives of all three generations working together and speaking with one another as equals. That's the whole story. Her eyes water when she tells it.

Her love of the place stems so clearly not from a love of theater in itself but from a love of this community that happens to have as its focus the production of plays. She refers to the edifice as "the old girl," and to the organization as "a kind of lonelyhearts' club." So it seems just right that Nancie is, among ninety other things, the theater archivist, in charge of preserving a record not only of its business dealings and artistic accomplishments, but also of its essence. The scrapbooks she compiles today, the events she chronicles, will go beyond budgets and programs to relate the very character of the club to future generations.

As for the character of the club hitherto, it has not, despite the picture sometimes so stridently presented by long-time members in an effort to caution against change, been wholly static. Debates over the policies which collectively define the identity of the group pepper the logs and scrapbooks. And communities, like people, by their nature are perpetually in flux, constantly in the process of becoming. Still, the club's history is specific and unalterable, and in several key ways comparable to that of the other "little theaters" (as they were called in the teens and twenties) that had sprung up across the country around the same time. Through the logs and scrapbooks, a definite picture emerges, one aspect of which is a perpetual lack of consensus as to what its identity should be.

The club's very name was an issue of some indecision throughout the twenties. At one point, the group held a contest to select a new name, boasting a prize of ten dollars in gold; there is no record of whether anyone ever received that prize. The only name change that did take place occured in 1933, when the group moved into its permanent home on Academy Street and began incorporating the name of the town into its moniker. One would love to know the story behind the early proposed change: Who argued for "Guild," and why? Who argued against? Was there very much laughter during the debate, or did teacups rattle angrily? In the end, what did the decision symbolize for the women of the club?

The women and the teacups one can safely surmise. Besides Mrs.

Dallin, Tibbetts, and Waterman, there were also Mrs. Hoxie, Moody, Yale, and Perry, a female Dr. Ring, and two Misses Lenks. By the second meeting, held the following week at Town Hall, twenty-nine women had become charter members by paying dues of two dollars each. The surnames at these early meetings and for several decades hence would be familiar to anyone who knew the most influential and well-established families in town. As a direct offshoot of the Arlington Woman's Club, the Friends of the Drama inherited a certain social pedigree that influenced its conduct well into its fifth decade. As late as the 1960s, general business meetings ended with the serving of tea from a Shreve, Crump & Low silver service. Designated pourers—often newer members of the club—wore white gloves and were named in the minutes. Being asked to participate in this way was a high honor; it meant you'd arrived.

Archival materials from the early days of the Friends carry an air of carefully constructed grandeur. The membership held whist parties and bridge parties to help raise money, and occasionally organized their meetings around a theme. ("February, 1924. The February meeting of the 'Friends of the Drama' was held at 'Ye Lantern' on the evening of February 28th. The meeting was a Dickens' evening with many members in costume.") Their own members presented oral reviews of area productions. ("February 13, 1930. Mrs. Roscoe Perry gave a really splendid review of the play now at the Plymouth Theatre, 'Little Accident.' This play, being an extremely broad sex-play, was reviewed with great dignity and propriety, all the objectionable parts being skillfully dodged.") They sponsored talks on the little-theater movement by college drama professors, and sought the advice of experts and presidents of other community theaters. ("February 12, 1931. Mr. Belford Forrest, dramatic director at Emerson . . . said for us to be friendly, frank and truthful in our work to attain the best results.") Even the post–business-meeting social hours abided by a strict sense of decorum, as dutifully recorded in the minutes. ("January 15, 1931. Mrs. Hosmer Johnson sprang a surprise with refreshment. Orange cake and delicious punch strictly within the law were served.")

But for all the air of archaic refinement, the early days of the Friends were marked by many of the same dilemmas that face the group today. Chief among these were the very issues Celia Couture had just raised so controversially in 1998: disagreement over what the rules and categories of membership ought to be, compounded by concerns over how to encourage more active participation among members, how to recruit new and younger members, how to present the club with a friendlier image to attract would-be members, and how to strengthen overall the club's financial position. Contrary to the perception of many current members, these concerns are hardly new to AFD, as a glance through selections from minutes over the decades illustrates:

January 28, 1928
   General discussion as to ways and means by which more in-terest on the part of active members might be aroused.

December 13, 1928
   Cards were given to each Active member with the request of the President, that each member express just what he or she would like to do in the way of being active.

February 1946
General Recommendations:
   . . . more hospitality and warmth be shown new members. The most common criticism from new members is that nobody pays any attention to them. . . . Some person fitted for the duty should be selected to talk with new members personally, intro-duce them to other members, find out what activity they wish to do, and follow up.

March 9, 1946
Recommending:
   That a Friendly Committee be organized to work out a pro-gram of "friendliness" going beyond mere card writing.

October 6, 1951
   It was suggested and decided that we have a clubhouse clean-ing and repairing bee, to be held on Saturday, November 3rd, from Noon until Exhaustion, with supper served at the club-

house. This bee is to be held for the dual purpose of re-awakening enthusiasm among members, and to accomplish many small repairs about the building.

March 16, 1952
   We had a discussion on the different types of membership and it was voted that the President appoint a committee to look into the advisability of having one membership or different types of memberships and the fees for each if any change.

It's all there—the fretting over the apathy of members, the bickering over who should be granted membership and what categories of membership should exist—all issues that the theater faces today. Only, seen this way, in the mellowing light of a cyclical history, the problems seem less urgent, less threatening. If the same demons have been dogging the Friends all these years without doing real harm, why fear the group will succumb to them now? Through depression and war and the advent of television and computers and commuters and all manner of social and economic change, a few people have continued, against reason, to want to make theater.

That no one can explain or account for the group's survival makes it all like a giant round of Trust—one of those theater games acting students are always playing. In one variation, they cluster at the base of a platform, on which one individual must close her eyes and fall backward, rigid, only to be supported by unseen hands. In a way, that's what the Friends have always done, pitched themselves into the air and felt hands comes up to meet them, never emptiness, always hands. It's nice to picture them, those women of the club's earliest days, in all their primness and properness, in all their pearls and gloves, closing their eyes and stepping off cliffs and finding themselves held aloft, their long skirts belling somewhat in the open air.

One notable instance of their committing such an act, figuratively, coincides with the acquisition of the most obvious asset to their longevity. In 1933, when the Episcopal congregation which had occupied the little building on the corner of Maple and Academy Streets announced it would be moving into a new, more permanent home at the other end of the block, the women of AFD outbid the

Oddfellows and bought the old mission church for their theater group. Much mention is made in the Friends' lore of "an initial nest egg" contributed by Mrs. Gracia Bacon Moody to establish a building fund, but the books show this nest egg to have been a mere fifty dollars. That means that, around the height of the Great Depression, a little group of local art-lovers chose and proved themselves able to raise $8,150 for the purchase of a theater clubhouse.

The following summer members spent transforming the space into a functional theater. From a pamphlet written for the fiftieth anniversary:

> *The chancel was raised and converted to a stage, the pipe organ site became an electrician's loft, the rector's study became a kitchen and lavatory, the choir room became the Green Room, and the small cellar was turned into dressing rooms and work area. The pews remained, a reminder of the theatre's architectural heritage, until 1947, when the friends received a gift of used theatre seats. . . .*
>
> *In the mid-1930's, the heating system was changed from coal to oil and—because storage space was needed desperately and a lounge was strongly desired—the enlargement of the small cellar into a full basement was begun. "Digging Parties," equipped lit-*

erally with spoons and spades, picks and blowtorches, buckets and bare hands, attacked the dirt and boulders. Finally, by the mid-1960's, with some professional help, the job was completed. Additional storage rooms, restrooms, and a smoking lounge were in use, and the theatre was completely refurbished.

Now, with the renovation completed in 1998, the theater has again been totally refurbished. The old concrete floor in the basement had literally been crumbling away with every step; whenever anyone swept, a layer of concrete dust was launched into the air. The contractors hired to enlarge and finish the basement discovered that the old foundation had been assembled without any mortar—its stones held together with only loose earth—and professed amazement that the building had stood all these years. The old smoking lounge was done away with, and the new handicapped-access bathroom and elevator entrance were put in, and rather jazzy tiles were laid in the new lobby, and a hundred other things, but in many respects the building hasn't changed much. From the outside it looks almost exactly like photos taken when it was still a church. The renovation even made possible a kind of pentimento effect, turning up some buried artifacts from early days—an old gas jet that had lit the original church, a kneeling bench that had been tucked into a hole under the ladies' dressing room, a stained-glass window behind the wall and layers of insulation in the old library—and these items will now be cleaned up and incorporated in the structure's newest physical incarnation.

The logs, in their own funny way, are gorgeous little treasures, filled with flotsam and jetsam, quirks and vanities. They are the ultimate artifacts, and through them the early days of the group become animated and more closely appreciated. But their importance extends well beyond understanding the history of Arlington Friends of the Drama. If, as the Friends claim, based on dates compiled by the American Association of Community Theatres, AFD is among the ten oldest continuously operating community theaters in the country, their history is particularly valuable in illustrating the story of American community theater, and to have it so comprehensively preserved, whether a testament to the forward-thinking good sense of its foremothers, or to their skewed sense of self-importance, or simply to their packrat sensibilities, is fortunate.

American community theater, or "little theaters," grew out of a particular set of circumstances. In 1870, the country had about fifty permanent resident theatrical troupes, as well as a touring system which brought road shows to towns and cities across the land. With the completion of the transcontinental railroad, the popularity and number of touring companies soared. By 1886, more than 280 of these transient bands of performers, mostly originating in and booking out of New York City, were traversing the country, with vaudeville and burlesque as well as more classical programs; at the same time, the number of resident companies had decreased to four. Then, in the early twentieth century, the popularity and consequent number of bookings of these touring shows began to dwindle, due largely to competetion from two new phenomena: spectator sports and motion pictures. The "road system," as it was called, collapsed. No more theater came to cities and towns and villages; the old opera houses sat dark and empty; and there were no local resident theaters to fill the void.

Into this theatrical vacuum the American community-drama movement was born. Not everyone who aided it saw it as a movement; even at its birth it didn't have a monolithic identity. But in any case, it proliferated. Between 1911 and 1917, over fifty of these "little theaters" had been established; by 1925, nearly two thousand of them were registered with the Drama League of America. The movement was hailed and heralded with terrific importance by a number of august proponents in the theater world, who, whether indiscriminately projecting their own views and desires or recognizing core elements that really did exist throughout, linked it with rather feverish enthusiasm to everything from spirituality and godliness to democracy and social service.

It is precisely because our peace is so devoid of organized, constructive imagination, that the organized destruction of war appeals so potently to the imaginations of men, by giving scope for their qualities of spiritual heroism . . .

What the world is waiting for is to be found, I believe, in the basic method of social service involved in Community Drama.
                                                        —Percy MacKaye, 1917

Back of all little theaters of America lies one dominant motive. It you want to define it at its highest, you call it the creative impulse. It you want to estimate it a little more realistically, if you want to risk looking at it in its lowest form, then you talk about a kind of exhibitionism. This desire to show off is an odd angle of a general human impulse to be doing something and doing something important. . . . It cannot destroy the reality or the importance of the dramatic impulse. It cannot annihilate the pleasure and the value that almost all humans get from the vicarious experience of the theater. The actor and the spectator win to a greater human sympathy with human nature; even the stage-hand and ticket-seller get a special thrill from the making of a theater. There is a little of godhead here.
                                                        —Kenneth MacGowan, 1929

This is American Theatre!
It is the non-commercial and community producing groups, existing all across the country, that are responding to the desire of the American people for a non-merchandized, personal theatre. It is very largely through them that a national theatre is coming into being. They are closer to the people than any professional theatre can be and, therefore, at their best they present a truer and more fundamental reflection of American life and thought.
                                                        —Gilmor Brown, 1939

While the scholars and interpreters of the field were busy attributing lofty ideals and meanings to the movement, the actual little theaters themselves were formed under a more motley variety of auspices. Some of these were motivated by a desire to play out an artistically adventurous experiment in amateur theater, similar to Konstantin Stanislavsky's beginnings in Russia, or Max Reinhardt's in Germany, or André Antoine's in France, or the Irish Players of Dublin. In this regard, the American community-theater movement was not entirely detached from similar work going on around the same time in Europe. Others approached the project as a social mission, with self-appointed missionaries spreading the democratizing, enriching benefits of theater to settlement houses in the cities, and prairies and farms across rural America. But the typical community theater was not created in the service of a social movement so much as in the service of its own rather more circumscribed social circle, as in this wicked send-up Albert McCleery relates in his 1939 book, *Curtains Going Up*:

> *The dowager took command. She surrounded herself with faithful henchmen, and the amateur theatre in this country was born. . . . There were a dozen or so ladies of indefinite age who always hovered around the edge of any movement whether they knew what it was all about or not.*
>
> *These the dowager assembled in her drawing-room and over tea cups founded the Little Theatre. The American matrons of that period, said Edith Wharton, 'Met culture in bands, since they were afraid to face it alone.'*
>
> *That they ultimately put on a play is a miracle. But the play went on, tickets were sold, and the husbands slept soundly through it all. Nobody got the chance to act on the tiny stage unless they first produced their birth certificates and proved they were socially house-broken.*

It would be a disservice to apply this description too finely to Mrs. Dallin, Moody, Tibbetts, Waterman et al., although the temptation is great; it would seem to fit so neatly with the details we do have about them. But the patness of the stereotype is its own undoing. In mocking the "dowagers," McCleery underestimates them and misconstrues their efforts. Extrapolating from his caricature, who would predict these groups would last and flourish into the next millennium? His description cannot be counted as useful for adding to what we know about the founding mothers of AFD, but it does help locate them, and the process by which the Friends came to life, as being typical of other little theaters of the day.

All of this helps to establish the Friends' documented history as being squarely typical of the little-theater movement. But the logs and scrapbooks, for all their value as a link to an episode in national history, and as a particular record of one group's process of evolving and sustaining its existence throughout three-quarters of a century of change, do little to shed light on the deeper mystery of community theater: why we have it at all. Despite their decades' worth of carefully preserved minutes and fountain-penned minutiae, in the end they disappoint.

Really there is nothing in the books that addresses that core secret any more lucidly than the simple presence of the guardian of those books—Nancie Richardson, and the way she tears up when she relates her favorite "anecdote," or the way she stops by the theater on her day off to clean out the fridge. Her passion for the Friends—coming, as it were, from a self-professed nontheater person, and expressed through the most menial and humble of actions—has a kind of uniquely illuminating purity; through her it is possible to glean some of what has made this place so necessary to so many for so long. Her feeling for the place is as valuable a tool for understanding its riddle as are any number of years' worth of news clips or budgets or box-office reports.

To call it a "lonelyhearts' club" might be seen as narrow, or even demeaning to those who flock here. But we are all of us lonelyhearts on this earth. What better place to flock to than a front porch where stories are told—not only told, but played—and in which we are each needed to take part.

Three

Preproduction

Before the first audition even takes place, they are behind. *Funny Girl*, the first show of the season and *Butterfly*'s immediate predecessor, is indirectly the cause of their late, shaky start. What happened was this.

Barbara Tyler, the director of *Funny Girl*, has a passion for doors. Apparently. At least she takes endless ribbing for such supposed passion. It seems that, in shows past, during blocking, she's had a relaxed attitude toward entrances and exits, instructing the actors to go off and come on from as many different locations as strike her fancy at the time. Then, to hear her closest friends embellish it, once the actual set is erected, it becomes necessary to reblock the show or else take sledgehammer to flat, in order to poke in a few more holes.

This sort of thing is recounted with much obvious pleasure by Barbara's theater cronies, to whom she'll reply, as likely as not, with some sly and side-splitting crack. Two of these cronies, Betty Finnigan and

Ellen Kazin, are involved in *Funny Girl* with Barbara—Betty as the production manager, Ellen playing Fanny Brice's mother. These are women of some threescore years who greet each other with, "What do you call that getup you're wearing?" and call each other by their last names. They have so perfected the art of rapid deadpan repartee that chancing upon them in the greenroom is like stumbling upon the Tyler-Finnigan-Kazin show, and the younger people gathered around watch the three women like fans at a tennis match.

At any rate, it happened again, the thing with the doors, or something like it. This time it was a case of overabundance: too much set for AFD's narrow little stage. Two weekends before the show, the set crew finished constructing a couple more interiors, only to be informed that these pieces were being nixed: not enough time, space, or workers to maneuver them on- and offstage. As it was, *Funny Girl*'s *cast* would be hard to cram onto this stage, let alone the elaborate sets. So the construction crew hacked them apart again, amid much grumbling, and the production team eyed what remained (some four reversible walls on castors, a bar, a ticket booth, two movable flats representing different interiors, and the entire Follies set, complete with stairs, platform, backdrop, and Mylar curtain, not to mention all the pieces of furniture that had to be lugged on and off and stored in the claustrophobic alleys that passed for wings) and called Celia.

The problem was this: no stage crew. Not a person. Betty Finnigan, as the show's production manager, had called everyone in the membership who ever claimed an interest, and then she and Barbara turned to family and friends and acquaintances, and except for successfully roping in one of Betty's brothers, they came up empty-handed. The worst of it was that, by their reckoning, *Funny Girl* was going to require a stage crew of a whopping ten to get everything done in the brief intervals between scenes, even with the reduction in scenery. So the big guns were called in, Celia and a few other board members, the designated few in this current era of the theater's history who will put themselves between a show and disaster. In the life of the theater there have always been disasters, just as there has always been a core group to handle them, those who have kept the organization going no matter what. The thing is, one can't help noticing, this sort of disaster has been threatening more and more frequently these days, as a sort of generalized apathy spreads like an epidemic through the community.

Celia's solution: she stepped in herself as crew chief, and helped cobble together a running crew that borrowed heavily from her *Butterfly* team. And then she forfeited two of a possible eight weeks of *Butterfly* rehearsals in order to work *Funny Girl*. It wasn't really a matter of heroics or noble gestures, and it wasn't a decision she particularly labored over. It wasn't exactly a *decision* at all; it was a response, it was *the* response, to the situation at hand. You see a carton of eggs teetering off a shelf; your hand goes out.

It was also the first time many people at the Friends had the chance to see Celia out of her board member's hat, out of her director's hat, and in the humble blacks that stagehands wear for camouflage. There was Celia sweeping, Celia sweating, Celia crouching to apply glow tape, Celia lugging the chaise and the armchair, holding back the curtain for the actors' exit, extending her hand to help them up the stairs in their high heels, guiding them with her flashlight through the choked dark alleys of backstage. Of course, she was still crew *chief*, still in charge, organizing everyone, hissing instructions to the haphazard, hastily assembled crew between set changes, signaling furiously to lower the flag, or open the curtain, or just shut up the backstage chatter. When the fake mantelpiece broke loose from the set of the mansion during a set change one matinee, it was Celia who took over, urgent and grim, barking out orders for *Drill! Screw! Extension cord!* with the same bluff authority with which doctors in the movies bark, *Scalpel! Suction! Sponge!*

But those working the show were also surprised to witness her playing against type, for often she seemed to be having almost childlike fun with the show. She'd maneuver herself into the tiny gap between the set and the piano, to sway and rock amid the seven-person orchestra wedged into the stage-left wing. She'd whisper-sing the musical numbers behind the curtain, punching her fist in the air to the beat. She doubled over with silent laughter when one of the stage crew, lagging during a set change, got stranded onstage and had to spend an entire scene crouching in consternation behind a prop clothes rack. When the fire alarm went off just before one evening's performance, and all the audience and cast and crew had to bundle out onto the street, the showgirls goosepimpled and shivering in the chilly lavender evening, Celia, grave-faced, dealt with the firefighters and later helped usher the audience back in, but she also laughed as hard as anyone when the cause of the false alarm turned out to be too many candles on Ellen Kazin's sixtieth-birthday cake.

For Celia, regarded by much of the membership as a tough, pragmatic leader, all business suit and command, the *Funny Girl* experience may prove unexpectedly useful. As a president who has been resented for approaching the club too much like a business, Celia has spoken of the need to win people over, to convince them she's not the enemy. An unintended side effect of the *Funny Girl* experience may be just that. She's now done a favor which may be returned sometime when *she* is desperate.

But the immediate result is that they are two weeks behind before they've even begun. Two weeks behind on a production so complex, so difficult, both artistically and technically, that it was going to be a challenge to pull off in the best of circumstances. And, somehow, following in *Funny Girl*'s wake makes the task at hand even more daunting.

Funny Girl was everything that *Butterfly* is not: hummable, old-fashioned, with a large cast and spangly costumes, a crowd-pleaser and, above all, an entertainment. In the end, in spite of all the technical worries, *Funny Girl* shone, and not only at the box office. The woman playing the lead, as various departing audience members were heard knowledgeably to remark, was every bit as good as Barbra Streisand, and the dancing was wonderful, and the costumes were divine, and the character actors funny, and the whole spectacle was thoroughly enjoyable. It got the loyal audience out, gave them what they wanted, and set the standard for this year's plays to come. One thing about *M. Butterfly* is certain from the outset: no matter the artistic heights it achieves, there's no way it's going to elicit the kind of response *Funny Girl* got.

It isn't that Celia wished she'd directed *Funny Girl* instead—*Butterfly* was her prize all along—but to be late, to be scrambling before the first rehearsal has even taken place, on a play that so many seem already poised to shoot down, is not how she wished to begin. Reports have trickled through of at least one member who didn't renew this year, troubled by the presence of this show on the slate. A handful of other members have voiced—outright, or through proxies—their extreme disapproval. What Celia hasn't broadcast widely is that one of the most emphatic of these shares her bed. Since Celia introduced her husband of four years to the world of community theater, Gerry Couture has on occasion ventured affably if skeptically down to the ex-church at Maple and Academy Streets, to help build sets or sell refreshments. But it's still deeply weird to him, and by his own cheerful admission he cannot really grasp that adults actually do theater as a hobby. The thought is enough to twist his lips in a grin of embarrassed indulgence.

The couple met on a blind date, and clicked as opposites more than soul mates; they seem to both marvel at and revel in the qualities that set them apart. Gerry grew up in rural New Hampshire, pretty well oblivious of theater, and after a stint in the service has worked as an environmental health-and-safety inspector for the same company for twenty-five years. In contrast to many of the people encountered within theater circles, he comes across as being artlessly at ease with himself and the world, refreshingly unburdened by complex interior or existential dilemmas. He says he respects Celia's theater work without understanding or being moved by it. "Some people get emotionally into a story," he explains, in his immensely and enigmatically appealing way. "I never do." No play or movie, he says bluntly, has ever made him *feel* anything. His taste is for nonfiction: documentaries about war, volcanoes, that sort of thing.

The chasm bothers neither spouse in the least. In a sense it's been useful to Celia, who usually asks Gerry to sit in on a rehearsal late in the process: his reactions come from such a different perspective that they afford her a more rounded sense of the play and how it's coming across. Gerry never shrinks from saying that something bored him or bugged him, or that he just didn't get it. But until now he's never been quite so unequivocal about his negative opinion of a play.

"A pig show," Gerry calls *M. Butterfly,* with a beguiling mixture of good nature and conviction. "Sick." Not that he would dream of standing in Celia's way or arguing her right to direct it, but neither is he shy about his position: it belongs in the wacky streets of New York and not in Arlington, Massachusetts. "Artistic," he snorts. "So's a stripper's act." And that's that. He'll probably still help build the set, if requested, but don't ask him to see a performance.

Celia can take it in stride from Gerry; what's more worrisome is that his may be the general reaction as well. Last year, when the board voted to accept the play-reading committee's entire proposed slate, the decision had not been particularly fraught or contentious. That *Butterfly* pushed AFD's envelope was obvious, but for the most part board members felt it would be a kind of feather in the theater's cap—to pull off such a challenging piece would be a triumph for a community theater, and help establish AFD's reputation as an artistically committed organization, not just a social club.

A lot of community theaters try to offer blended seasons, a balanced diet of safe and risky offerings, designed to keep the group both fiscally viable and artistically exciting. Whether or not audiences have heard of a play or its author has a great deal to do with whether or not they'll turn out. From a box-office perspective, the old chestnuts can be gold, especially when the audience is disproportionately older, as is AFD's. If a play has been made into a movie, even a lousy one, it can make a positive difference in terms of ticket sales. If it's won a Tony, noting that on the advertising flier may help. Any sort of name recognition at all will help to sell a play. But the greatest determinants of a play's ticket sales boil down to these: cast size (because a large proportion of audience members often wind up being friends and family of the cast), whether it's got music, and whether it's got laughs. Musicals and comedies are the big draws of most community theaters.

The whole reason other plays get produced at all—"other" meaning artier, or more experimental, or intellectual, or provocative, or political, or emotionally intense—is that some people, a passionate minority, want badly to do so. Some of these people think it's important for the community, that it's part of community theater's mission to provoke, and that audiences should leave a theater stirred and questioning. Some of them think in smaller, more individual terms. The motive may be selfish, a desire to see what one is capable of as an actor, a desire to push one's own personal craft to a deeper level; or it may stem from an intellectual or spiritual curiosity, a desire to cross frontiers of experience and understanding. Whatever the motive for producing them, these "other" plays rarely bring in the crowds that musicals and comedies do, and are generally the subject of some grumbling and eye-rolling among the majority of the membership. On the other hand, that they are frequently the most dense with talent does not go unrecognized.

The latter is overwhelmingly true of *Butterfly*. The team Celia has assembled is premium—and hard-won; nearly everyone had to be coaxed and cajoled a little. But she began recruiting as early as last winter, and won commitments from several top people as a result. In fact, that they are already behind seems doubly unfair, considering the amount of work several of them have been putting into the show for months already.

At a production meeting three weeks before auditions, everything had seemed to be coming together promisingly. At seven o'clock in the greenroom on that sultry evening, beneath the muffled din of hammers and power tools being used to build the *Funny Girl* set over their heads, Doug had shown Celia a rough model of the set he'd designed. "You're a genius. That's exactly what I had in mind," she said, shaking her head in wonder, but also in confirmation of her expectations: it was just like Doug to come through this perfectly, this precisely.

The set was sparse and elegant. It comprised a platform fronted by sliding doors, which opened onto a long, curvy ramp; a couple of huge standing fans, which would be made of sized muslin; and a folding screen covered in rice paper so it could be backlit for different effects. Everything was black except the rice paper and muslin and one other thing: a six-foot circle jigsawed into an intricate, Chinese-looking element, which would be painted red and affixed to the sliding doors so that, when open, the circle would split in half. The element, Doug was explaining, had come from one of his daughter's picture books; the Desiletses had adopted her in China a little more than two years earlier. Doug had copied and then altered the element slightly; he wanted to avoid accidentally using a symbol that might have a specific, unintended meaning.

That partial scrupulousness with regard to cultural authenticity is typical of the production as a whole. At every stage, in every aspect, from choreography to makeup to props to design, acknowledgment is made of the importance of particular meanings and techniques within Chinese and Japanese culture, but these meanings are not fully explored or explained. The research Celia and the others have done is substantial and impressive by community-theater standards—Celia has compiled an entire looseleaf-full of notes on Asian culture, Asian-American culture, identity politics, transcripts of a talk given by the playwright, notes on the opera *Madame Butterfly*, etc.—yet the lack of any adviser with an actual knowledge base in the subject is evident. The production team consults books on the stylized movements of the Chinese opera, for example, but the choreography the dancers will learn is a vague approximation thereof, no one on the production team having been schooled in the art. At the end of the play, when Gallimard commits seppuku, the specifics of the ritual are a bit altered and fudged. This whole approach, a mixture of earnest scholarship and naïve guesswork, this reproducing of the play's specific cultural aspects with a sort of best-effort fallibility, begs the question: what business does a provincial white theater group have attempting a work based in a culture about which it knows little?

The questions that logically erupt from this one are Hydra-like: What business does anyone have producing theater of another culture? of another era? of another religion? What business does anyone have attempting to understand and relate the story of another? What business do healthy people have portraying the sick? Happy people portraying sufferers? Privileged portraying the oppressed? What business does anyone have acting a part, passing herself or himself off as another? Is it all, in a way, insults and lies, appropriations and bastardizations, disingenuity and damage?

Doris Chu, director of the Chinese Culture Institute in Boston, the one Chinese theater professional consulted by AFD, was never asked whether she felt AFD was acting inappropriately by attempting *M. Butterfly*. Nor was she asked whether she felt the part of Song must be played by a person of Asian descent. She was asked only to help spread word of auditions among the Asian male actors she worked with. Her response was that there were nearly none; at her last auditions for a CCI production, the turnout was fifty Caucasians and three Asians. And that is part of the whole story of East-West relations that *M. Butterfly* seeks to illuminate, a story of cultural stereotypes and cultural barriers, of expectations that limit and define and eventually create their own reality. A long dearth of acting opportunities for Asian people has helped create a dearth of Asian actors. Had Doris Chu, however, been asked either of the former questions, her answer would have been no. She does not believe that people must portray only that which they have personally experienced; she does not believe that only Asian people should be cast in Asian roles. "Any actor can play any role," she says. "Art should have no barrier."

Certainly the politics surrounding this issue—a whole history of denied access and forbidden expression—complicates the question. But if Doris Chu's answer is problematic in light of the politics, it is also deeply hopeful, positioning art as a tool to be used for illuminating and overcoming the very same ills. And lifting regulations as to which actor can play which part seems, theoretically at least, integral to accomplishing such a goal.

If theater is a way of exploring the lives and stories of others, perhaps acting is a heightened form of this endeavor. Instead of bearing witness to another's experience, the actor attempts to come even closer, to experience it herself or himself. In this regard, she is more than anthropologist, more than psychologist, more even than storyteller: she is an empathic journeyer among fellow humans, trying on different lives, connecting to others through her own wondering core. And as a surrogate for the audience, the actor may help an entire houseful of people to be willingly transported in thought and feeling to new kinds of experience and understanding. In this context, the fact that a basically white, middle-class, suburban New England organization, in spite of a certain cultural and political naïveté, should want to mount this play—about a culture that we have kept foreign, that we have mystified, stereotyped, and misunderstood—*and* about the disastrous effects of doing just that—speaks of bravery and hope.

A song from the musical *Promenade,* by Maria Irene Fornes and Al Carmines, goes, "I know what madness is; it's not knowing how another man feels / A madman's never walked in another man's shoes."

By this definition, theater is a form of edging toward sanity.

At that August production meeting in the greenroom, after Doug finished "walking" the others through his dollhouse version of the set

("It's all to scale . . . and these pieces can move around . . . these are hinged, these stationary . . . and we'll put little curves here, to give it an Oriental feel. . . . You'll be able to project patterns on the fans with gobos . . ."), attention turned to Don Richardson, who, as set tech, would be responsible for the actual construction. Don and his wife, Nancie, are sometimes referred to as the godparents of the theater. He joined some thirty years ago, and has always been active, but since he retired last year as head of the industrial-arts department for Arlington Public Schools, the theater has truly become his baby. During the renovation last year, he was on-site every single day, overseeing the project. This year things have calmed down a bit; he's only serving on the board as technical director, set-teching two shows in a row, and designing the set for *Blood Brothers* this spring. He looks young to be retired, has a wiry brown beard, light-blue eyes, a deep voice, and a woodsy look with his plaid flannel shirts, whose breast pockets are perpetually distended by a box of Winston Lights.

"So, now that it's designed," asked Doug, "how do we execute it?" And all eyes turned to Don.

"You take out a shotgun and blow the crap out of it," answered Don, who is not an abrasive man.

"Thank you very much, I just worked on it for two days." Doug emitted a thin laugh through his nose.

"Well, I've just been working on the *Funny Girl* set . . ." offered Don by way of mild apology. Don had spent this entire last weekend building some French doors, only to be informed that they'd been scratched from the set plan.

"Well, this one's simple, at least. It's a single set." Having a single set can be an important selling point for a show when the board is considering the cost of a slate. So is the era in which a play is set: a contemporary piece may be less expensive to costume. So are royalties, which can vary hugely: Tony winners, musicals, and recent hits tend to have greater fees, although this is not always the case. AFD will pay sixty dollars in royalties for producing *M. Butterfly*; *Funny Girl* cost the theater $410 for the first performance and $170 for each of the seven following. For this reason, musicals, despite their immense appeal and general success at the box office, are not typically great moneymakers for community theaters.

"They all start out simple," said Don, with light skepticism bred of thirty years' experience, and then he and Doug began discussing the execution in earnest, tallying sheets of plywood in their heads, and debating the relative merits of one-by-three pine versus strapping, of sized muslin versus crinoline, of masonite versus luan.

"We know from *Elephant Man* how hard it can be to work with masonite. I'd opt for luan," said Don when they got to the subject of how to construct the bend in the ramp, and there were knowledgeable nods all around—this group of people all seasoned enough Friends to be able to bandy show titles about like a kind of code. They evaluated closely the modular aspects of this set, as well as its shleppability, for Doug had had to design it with these factors in mind; the whole thing would have to be broken down and stored, then transported and reassembled six months later, for the EMACT competition.

The Eastern Massachusetts Association of Community Theatres' annual competition, called a festival, takes place on the campus of Brandeis University. Every other year, the winner of this competition goes on to the New England regionals, and the winner of *that* goes on to compete with community theaters nationally. A local win becomes a dubious honor for most small theater groups, who must foot the bill themselves for transporting their shows.

"Remember *K-2*?" offered Don, and others in the group rolled their eyes and eagerly recounted the trials and travails around the transporting of that show's set—a gigantic piece of icy mountain that an actor had actually to scale onstage—first to Brandeis and then, when AFD won first place, to the regionals, held that year in New Hampshire. It had been a wonderful accomplishment and a terrific pain—an expenditure of time and bodies and money that the little theater could hardly bear—and is largely the reason that AFD will only now enter the competition in odd years, when regionals and subsequent nationals do not take place.

Celia listened, dimples carved dark, as Don and Doug mulled and meandered, somewhat philosophically, through the conversation. Her eyes shifted now and then to the clock over the piano. "I'm trying to figure out how much of this we can get donated, so I need a materials list," she finally prompted.

"Great! If you can get it donated!" Doug brightened.

"Psh! We're not paying for all this." Celia made a face showing the absurdity of that prospect, and everyone knew what she meant. It is exceedingly common at AFD for members' employers to make little contributions, knowingly or not, to the theater (from the usual stuff—a little photocopying here, a few donated file folders or rolls of tape there—to actual sums of money).

Don did a little figuring in his head, whispering prices under his breath—"muslin's five ninety-nine a yard for six feet wide. . . . A four-by-eight sheet of quarter-inch luan's fourteen dollars"—and came up with a nice, undaunting cost estimate of four hundred dollars in raw materials for the set. Celia jotted it in red in her pansy-covered book, dimples set at neutral, and Don took his leave, heading back up to tussle some more with the epic-approaching *Funny Girl* set.

Celia offered enlarged bound copies of the script to the rest of the assembled production team. When she got to Doug, he demurred. "I don't need a script. Not unless I'm *in* the show," he added. "I'm still thinking about auditioning."

"I think you should," encouraged Kelley.

"I don't know why you wouldn't," said Celia, a trifle disingenuously, but with the kind of blanket conviction that makes people doubt themselves for ever having thought differently. She has a knack for making what she favors sound inevitable. Nearly everyone who's worked with her has a story to tell, in sort of bewildered, marveling tones, about the time she *informed* them they would be auditioning, stage-managing, producing, running sound, whatever, in spite of their own intentions otherwise—and they wound up doing it.

The others accepted their scripts: Kelley, Mayre, and Stu Perlmutter, who had been recruited from outside the organization to design lights. Stu is fair and low-key, with floodlight-blue eyes and the compact, wiry build of a gymnast. His theater work is mostly for the Vokes Players, over in Wayland, which has perhaps the least clubby and the greatest artistic reputation of any of the fifty-odd Boston-area community theaters. In the American Association of Community Theatres, it is the only "Region I" (New England) theater ever to have won first place in the national competition. Celia approached Stu through his wife, Mitzi ("hoodwinked," she laughs). Mitzi, a performer and choreographer, had first worked with Celia years before at the Wellesley Players, and counts herself among those susceptible to Celia's uncannily persuasive requests. Stu, not necessarily susceptible to Celia, proved susceptible to his wife, and, all being fair in love and onstage, Celia was glad to play that hand.

"It's going to be a tight set to light, to show separate spaces," said Stu, startling them a little as he spoke for the first time. The minimalism of the set means that the lighting designer will be largely responsible for giving the audience the sense of different locales, from a Manhattan cocktail party to a jail cell to a diplomat's office to a Paris apartment, each space distinctly delineated within the fluid, curving black space. "It'll require a lot of shuttering, very focused light," he mused. "Here it shouldn't be too much of a problem, but Brandeis . . . I still haven't got their Web site." Celia, thus cued, whipped out a photocopy of the Brandeis stage plan and light plot (a sort of blueprint of the lights that will be prehung and available for each group's use at the competition), and Stu took it upstairs, to study AFD's stage and house and light booth and light bars, and begin to imagine his design.

Then Molly Trainor walked through the greenroom, and everything stopped. Molly, costumer extraordinaire, was the most desired person not yet signed to the team, and her very presence made the others sit up straight now and lapse into a wheedling game. Doug showed her his model of the set, playing dollhousily, enticingly, with the movable pieces. Mayre, with a goofy, toothy grin, joked, "And it can be any color you want!" Molly laughed at Mayre, sincerely admired the set, and then disappeared again, fast, down the hall. She and her husband, Dave Warnock, had been spending summer evenings landscaping the new front of the building. Tonight they were using a rented stonecutting machine to piece together and lay a brick sidewalk along the Maple Street entrance. Celia first asked her to costume the show in early spring, and was left encouraged but without a definite answer. Molly's job, with a medical manufacturing-and-supply company, has felt shaky for months in light of an impending buyout; the unrest in her professional life has made her reluctant to commit herself to a show this sartorially challenging. Now, with only three weeks until auditions, Molly was going to have to come through with a definite yes or no.

Doug, amid another round of thanks and praise, rose to take his model home, where he would alter and complete it to have ready for the auditions. Celia plugged in a little boom box and began to play Mayre a tape of the music from the original production. Bending, keening notes of Peking Opera music filled the greenroom.

"Does it all have to be like this? Because I have a headache," said Mayre after maybe a minute. "Because if it does I think I'm busy." Her delivery, all flat and punctuationless, elicited the tiniest smile from Celia. They know each other too well to have to laugh at each other's jokes. Celia left Mayre to her listening pleasure and disappeared down the hall to photocopy the music-cue sheet. Mayre made some faces to the music, and chewed a handful of the microwaved popcorn which had been sitting for an indeterminate number of days on the improbably hideous black-and-silver-mirrored coffee table.

"Cee!" yelled Mayre eventually. It was eight-fifteen. She'd promised to be home in Tewksbury by eight-thirty.

"All right. I need to talk with you for a few minutes and then get you the hell out of here." Celia, materializing back in the greenroom, picked up with her same focused urgency: "I'm going to need you to test strength, agility, flexibility. Almost like a gymnastic tryout."

While Mayre and Celia created a format for the movement auditions, Molly slipped back in, looking slightly haggard beneath her poppy-bright bangs, and sat in a tired armchair. She wore a black sweatshirt, black jeans, and white sneakers. She adjusted her little round spectacles and waited.

"So." Celia swiveled to her. "Are you gonna do it?"

"I had a few questions for you," said Molly, slowly. "What are you thinking in terms of the nudity?"

"Basically, we'll know that he's absolutely butt-naked, but we don't need to do frontal in Arlington, Massachusetts."

"What about the pin-up girl in the first act? I wouldn't want her nude-esque if he's going to be really nude. I was thinking she could either be nude, or in a provocative outfit."

"I'm afraid to use any sort of lingerie for anyone other than Song, in the scene where he makes the phone call."

"I don't see Song in any Western outfits at all. I think it'll be harder to maintain the ambiguity. Chinese dress throughout history is more androgynous anyway."

"I'd rather go with nudity for the woman and go with something sexy and flowing for the phone call. Also, her nudity in the first act will help prepare us for his nudity later."

George Rogers, a retired psychology professor who is one of the small corps of regular set-builders, happened through the greenroom with a tape measure in hand and, hearing all the talk of nudity, paused behind Celia with a mock-earnest air, proffering the instrument. "You won't be needing this for auditions, will you?"

Everyone laughed. It was good, amid the general air of essentially covert disapproval, to be able to laugh about the most controversial aspect of the play. Celia and the other board members had been receiving negative comments regarding the choice of play for months (albeit mostly sketchy and unattributed). Despite the negative gossip, there are many who endorse the play and anticipate it gladly. George Rogers, in fact, loves *M. Butterfly*, loves the way it tries to get people to pay attention to the unconscious cultural values that are automatic in them. It's *Funny Girl* he disfavors, it being, in his eyes, funny and nothing else. As far as George is concerned, good theater is theater with a message. But these are not the majority of opinions filtering back to Celia.

"Thanks, I don't think so," she said now with a grin, and George, tall and gently distinguished in his Thoreau Sauntering Society sweatshirt, drifted back upstairs.

"What would make this doable for you?" Celia asked Molly, cutting to the chase.

Molly rolled her eyes. "To not worry about what's going to happen to my job. To know that I'm not going to have to be away on business trips between now and the show."

"Okay. I can't fix that for you." Celia, the quintessential fixer, was palpably disappointed.

But then Molly asked about Gallimard's third-act suicide. "Do you want blood?" Molly and her husband, Dave, who both work for companies that manufacture medical devices, are the theater's resident blood-experts. Dave, an actor and director, is also known as a sort of technical cowboy, called in to design special effects for various shows. A few years ago Dave and Molly together won a special EMACT award for their blood effect in *Agnes of God*, in which they convincingly created the illusion of stigmata, making the actor's palms appear to start bleeding spontaneously mid-scene.

Celia nodded.

"Buckets of blood?" Molly seemed to be getting a little gleam.

"Some blood."

"Well, my philosophy is, if we're going to do it, let's go all the way."

Celia nodded thoughtfully, appearing to take this under consideration. But after Molly left, her dimples radiated as she beamed—her first smile-dimples of the evening—and she looked conspiratorially at the two remaining production staff, Kelley and Mayre. "She's considering it!" More than considering: her specific language and questions told Celia she was hooked. She was probably in the stage of trying to talk of herself *out* of accepting; futile at this point, Celia guessed. From her own experience she knew that, once a show had worked its way under her skin, there was no walking away from it.

But they were far from home free.

"What about scheduling the next production meeting?" asked Kelley, pen poised.

Celia shook her head tersely. "I don't want to schedule anything else now until I'm absolutely sure I can cast it."

"What will you do if you don't get Asian actors?" asked Mayre.

"I won't do it."

"At all?" Mayre shot Kelley a look to see if she knew about this. "Does the program manager know?"

"He knows." The program manager at AFD is the person in charge of obtaining the rights to plays, hiring the directors, scheduling the order of shows, essentially putting together a season. In other words, "the program manager" is another name for the chairperson of the play-reading committee, Jim Grana.

Four

First Rehearsal

FIVE WEEKS AND THREE DAYS TILL OPENING NIGHT.

To the Cast and Crew of M. Butterfly
 *We have enjoyed "using the hall" & know you will too! Fanny
and her "crowd" send their best wishes to BREAK A LEG!!!*
 —the Cast and Crew of Funny Girl

M. Butterfly Cast:

RENÉ GALLIMARD .... James Grana
SONG LILING .... Patrick Wang
MARC/CONSUL SHARPLESS .... Tom Dinger
RENÉE/WOMAN AT PARTY/PIN-UP GIRL .... Carolyn Torrey
COMRADE CHIN/SUZUKI .... Michelle Aguillon
HELGA .... Grace Butler
M. TOULON/MAN AT PARTY/JUDGE .... Doug Desilets
KUROGO DANCERS .... Michelle Estrada, Teri Muller, Orea Nicolls

On September 29 they assemble, *Butterfly's* cast and crew, for the first time. By five after seven, they are all there except Patrick Wang, who's late. Celia, in what will soon establish itself as her rehearsal uniform of denim workshirt and jeans, goes ahead and begins to address the group, first introducing the production team to the cast. There is Doug, at the last minute pulled into double duty as both set designer and cast member. There is Molly, who found herself, to everyone's relief if no one's great surprise, ultimately unable to say no. There is Barbara Horrigan, whom Celia introduces as "the grande dame of AFD," and at eighty-three, with sixty-five years of membership under her belt, one of its most senior members; she has gamely agreed to design the wigs and the complicated, almost trompe-l'oeil makeup the show requires, even though she remains not entirely comfortable with the sexual ambiguities of the plot and makes no secret that she sees absolutely no need for the second-act penis speech, in which Gallimard's young mistress cheerfully and devastatingly deconstructs the vocabulary and symbolism attached to that particular organ. There is David Giagrando, introduced as "Baron's father, and also production manager." There is Debbi Dustin, props manager, who works in police records for the Town of Arlington by day, and manages to carry a little hard-boiled cop edge into her backstage role at night. There are Kelley and Mayre, who will share stage-managing duties once the play goes to Brandeis in the spring. Nods all around. Then Celia, hands in pockets, leans against the upright piano (which is shrouded in heavy cloth and still sporting a *Funny Girl* bouquet of pink-and-white carnations, a jaunty, lingering declaration of that show's success), and lays out in plain terms how much work needs to be done in the next five and a half weeks.

"To be honest, I'm a bit anxious about the compressed amount of time we have to put on a show of this complicated caliber." Her voice punches out with natural force and authority, the voice of a coach in a locker room, pregame.

Patrick comes down the back stairs, tall and serious in his black leather jacket, fifteen minutes late.

"Hey, Patrick, how are you," Celia interrupts herself to say, and he answers inaudibly, with a slight look of deer in headlights, and folds himself into an empty spot on the silvery-green faded couch.

For the cast it's like the first day of school, or the first day back at school after vacation, when some of the kids know each other and some are new to the district. In a matter of weeks, all kinds of private jokes may have sprung up, and a quick, thick bonding among a few individuals, and possibly irritations or animosities among others, but at any rate a common texture, a shared feeling for what they are all working on together. Tonight, even among those who know each other well, a newness hovers. Perhaps the two closest are Jimmy and Grace, who have not only acted before but work together on the play-reading committee. Michelle Aguillon has appeared here once before; she was last seen vamping Jim Grana in the Noël Coward play last spring. Teri has been a member since 1992, although it's been three years since she's done a play here. Carolyn and Orea know each other slightly from Hewlett-Packard, where they both work with Celia. But many are meeting tonight for the first time, and there's an as yet amorphous feeling to the whole endeavor.

The first hour of this first cast meeting is taken up by business: each member of the production team speaks, covering everything from how to buy tickets (cast gets first dibs, with special color-coded ticket-order forms), to what rehearsal clothes people are expected to wear (leather-soled shoes all around; pumps for the pin-up girl; long, loose skirts for the kurogo, a kimono and obi for Song), to whom to call if you can't make a rehearsal ("but you can't miss a rehearsal un-less you're dead"). During all of this, David cleans out the fridge and wipes down the yellow Formica counters in the kitchenette portion of the greenroom, advising that this will be the single time he does so. Overhead, since it's a Tuesday night, the set crew pounds and drills and saws, already piecing together a life-size version of Doug's model, which is perching again on the ugly mirrored coffee table, a by now familiar centerpiece, and almost a lucky talisman, as the one tangible item produced in relation to this play so far.

Then Molly, a blue tape measure dangling around her neck, sum-mons the cast, one by one, into the back dressing room, which some of them approach as if it housed gallows. ("I hate this part." "It's worse than the audition.") Meanwhile, Barbara Horrigan, extracting her own tape from her bag, measures Patrick's and Jim's heads for wigs.

"Jim, is yours going to be getting bigger?" gibes Kelley, for the part of Gallimard is such a desirable one that being cast in it might give any actor a swelled head. Others are quick to amplify: "I don't know if they make them that big. . . . We're not redoing the doorways in the theater again."

Barbara joins in. "I noticed in the script he's supposed to age from twenty-six to sixty-something." She appraises Jim, who's a lot nearer sixty-something than twenty-six, like Sisyphus eyeing the rock. "I can't work miracles, you know."

Jim laughs, apparently delighted. The ribbing is only commensurate with the size and challenge of the role, which he's won, at last, after a year of hoping. Already he has sold ninety-seven tickets to the play, through colleagues at the medical-insurance company where he is a customer-relations specialist. He's also begun running lines at home with his partner of thirty years, John Kawadler, who, although not involved to the same extent as Jim, is a member of the Friends and has offered to manage the box office for *Butterfly*.

The next half-hour becomes an impromptu show-and-tell, for Celia and Molly have brought books on costume and Asian theater traditions, and Barbara has brought a few dime-store masks, which she's already made up, experimentally, for the dancers in the Chinese opera. Celia puts on the tape of the music from the original production, and the new cast members mingle tentatively, and look at the pictures, and begin to fill out the biographical-information sheets David passed around earlier. It's nearly nine when the last people finish getting measured and Celia calls them all back together. She perches on a high red chair in front of the piano and fixes them all in her keen brown gaze. Her eyebrows are thin and almost semicircular, and they leap to punctuate the key phrases in her speech. "First of all, I want to please make sure that tonight's discussion is interactive," she tells them. And then she opens with a familiar theme, one touched upon at each leg of the auditions, and which most of the cast is just beginning to realize poses a real point of concern for AFD. "This production is challenging for me artistically. But it's also Arlington 1998, so it's going to be additionally challenging in terms of subject matter, content, language, nudity."

"Yeah, and some of us have to live in this town," contributes Teri

Muller with a short laugh, although in fact she is the only cast member who does.

"So the best we can do is look at it as an art form. It's all a dance. All curves. All lines. At the same time, it's an intellectual play. It's sometimes regarded as an anti-American play. We all need to be well versed in terms of objective. We need to be working conceptually in unison, to create an end product that's connected in all ways. It's an intellectual play."

She fixes her gaze on the young lead in the black leather jacket who has been so silent, so serious, the most important unknown quantity in the room. "Patrick, you have an incredible challenge in this role. You have to be comfortable as a woman. You can't be a drag queen. It's really important that people walking in absolutely believe that that's a woman onstage. Not a man playing a woman. It's got to be intellectual first. Then the physicality."

Everyone regards him, looking unmistakably large and masculine there on the couch, and listening to Celia with a distinctly unfeminine lack of obliging acknowledgment. Song is the compelling center of the play, the inscrutable black hole to which Gallimard is fatefully, and fatally, drawn; the character whose third-act onstage transformation from woman to man is the agent of Gallimard's unraveling. The script itself is taxing enough on the audience's credulity. Will Patrick tip the scales on the side of willing suspension, or the side of disbelief? Celia seems to be searching for an answer as she scans his beautiful, impassive face.

"All right, you guys," she barks suddenly, slipping her pages of notes and diagrams back into a clear plastic envelope and tossing it on the coffee table. "If I were to ask you what type of a play this is, what would you say?"

"A tragedy," says Tom Dinger, with the confidence of a former professional Shakespearean actor, which he in fact is. Now he writes and markets software.

"Does the hero have a fatal flaw?" asks Grace, equally at home on this terrain. She teaches French and French literature.

"He can't see past his cultural stereotypes," answers Tom, "At any point he could have discovered about Song, but he never does."

"Why?" asks Celia. "You have to constantly ask yourself why."

"Narcissism."

"Fear."

"He's swept up in his arrogance."

"But there's an innocence to his arrogance."

Not everyone participates, but most everyone does, from cast members to costumer, stage manager to choreographer, and this is exactly Celia's stated wish, to create an ensemble in which every person involved in the play has a stake, a common sense of responsibility and ownership. She will speak often about her directorial style's being collaborative, about desiring and counting on the input of others. At times this will seem at odds with the fact that she already holds intractable opinions about the play, formed during her long months of research and planning. Tonight, she sparks discussion with open-ended questions, but does not refrain from sharing with the group the conclusions she has already reached. Noticeably reticent is Patrick, arms stretched out across the top of the couch, one ankle crossed over the opposite knee.

"Fantasy, reality. Role reversal. Yin and yang." Celia leans forward. "If you pull the play apart you'll find that happening, deliberately, from beginning to end. This play is so amazing to me. That the playwright embedded this much stuff." She begins to discuss the different characters in the play. "Why is Marc in it? Don't you answer that," she adds quickly to Tom, cast as Marc, Gallimard's brash and bawdy childhood friend. He grins and shuts his mouth.

"He's sort of an antagonist," says Doug.

"A button-pusher," says Grace, the longtime member who will play the rather thankless role of Helga, Gallimard's cheated-upon and eventually cast-off wife.

"A goad," Tom cannot keep from adding. Tom wowed them at auditions with his professionalism and energetic, comedic presence. They knew right away he would make a strong foil for Gallimard. Two powerful actors onstage equal more than the sum of their parts, for they tend to work harder and bring each other to higher levels of performance.

"And is Marc authentic?"

"He seems to be," ventures Molly.

"I think he's the most authentic person in it," says Celia.

Tom nods very slightly, and smiles. He is handsome in a rascally way, with shoulder-length, graying hair and an actor's strong, articulate features. He has the eyes of a man who knows full well his own cleverness. He is a Siamese cat to Jimmy's golden retriever; they will play off each other nicely.

"He pulls Gallimard to a place in life where he was trusting," says Mayre, feeling her way. "That comfort—he trusts Marc with his nerdiness, his vulnerability."

"What about Helga and Gallimard? What's that about?" Celia's in her *Thinker* pose, fingers at the mouth. She fires questions. "Why doesn't he have a baby with her? Is Song gay? Is Gallimard gay?"

"He's just stupid," says Jim, and everyone laughs.

"He's coming out of Catholic France," says Grace.

"He's questioning himself all through the play," says Mayre. "He sets up those questions in our mind and his."

Celia gathers up her script, reads aloud a few lines from the first meeting of Song and Gallimard, after he has seen her perform an aria from *Madame Butterfly* at the home of another foreign diplomat. "The ultimate question in the play: is Song gay? I don't think it's a gay thing."

"I think it's a power thing for Song," says Molly.

"I think we're supposed to wonder about Song's preference," says Tom. "We should leave the theater arguing about it."

Patrick says, "May I say something?"

"Yes, please," encourage several people.

"That'd be a good idea," says Celia.

Patrick speaks with great deliberation. He makes everyone else in the room seem wildly informal. "Song is just on the edge of being acceptable." The statement, which seems more delicate, ambiguous, and open-ended than the rest of the discussion, occasions a pause.

"Does he get swept up in the arrogance as well?"

"The novelty, maybe," allows Patrick, after a moment of contemplation.

"You're going to have to explain that to me later, in Act Three." At the end of the play, when Song, as a man, testifies against Gallimard at the latter's espionage trial in France, he comes across as cocky, scathing, even bitter.

"Song," responds Patrick, "has lived a very theoretical life."

There is a small, slightly uncomfortable silence. It's as though everyone's trying to figure out whether the new pupil is challenging the teacher.

"Has he ever been with a woman?" queries Celia. "You don't have to answer me tonight."

Patrick considers. "I don't know."

"Good." Celia laughs. "I think we have to leave not knowing."

Around ten, the power tools upstairs grow quiet. The Coke machine hums. The group has discussed everything from gender and sexual politics to Sino-French relations to ethnic stereotyping to the Chinese Cultural Revolution. Celia shuts her notebook and leans forward on it. "Okay. Well, do you see how we have a lot of work to do? Any questions?"

Some of the people here tonight, who were expecting a simple read-through, look dazed.

"The word that keeps coming to mind is transformation," says Teri, the Arlington resident who will play one of the kurogo dancers. "And that's what a butterfly does."

They are dismissed until tomorrow night. From now on, for the next five and a half weeks, this mixture of friends and strangers will never go more than a few days without seeing one another. Patrick shoots out quietly. Celia tells Tom they may have to cut his hair. Carolyn, cast as the pin-up girl, wonders aloud, to no one in particular, "How are we going to do all this in five and a half weeks?" Barbara tells Debbi she's got a couple of *sake* sets at home she could lend as props. Michelle Aguillon, cast as Chin, announces she's going to go home and dig up her old Asian-studies notes from college. (Both Michelles happen to be Filipino, although their physical resemblance is slight at best; for one thing, Michelle Aguillon stands more than a full head taller than Michelle Estrada. In fact, despite people's efforts to come up with more respectful appellations, such as "Michelle A." and "Michelle E.," or "Chin/Michelle" and "Dancer/Michelle," in the end what sticks is "Tall Michelle" and "Little Michelle." "Sorry," everyone always says on the heels of using these labels, but the Michelles are graciously forgiving.)

"Well," says Celia, when the place has mostly emptied out, "I think everyone just took a look at the schedule and had a stroke. I know I did." But as she and Molly begin to discuss palette and budget, they do not seem anxious. Losing themselves in the talk of what each cast member shall wear, what colors and styles shall clothe each of these various people, who will become less and less strangers over the next several weeks of working together, of coming to know each other on and off the stage—in this state of murmuring joint imagination, in which they are summoning a common understanding of the lives of others, they seem not at all anxious, but happy and engaged and edging toward something fine.

Five

Arena of the
Street

SEPTEMBER 19.

At eight o'clock on Saturday morning, a small turquoise car
pulls up in front of the theater and its occupants, a man and a
woman, slip inside and begin assembling what they will take:
a long folding table, two folding chairs, an easel, and the to-scale
model of the theater that adorns the top of the Coke machine. Outside it's still chilly and damp, everything swathed in morning mist so
the sun looks like the moon over Town Hall. They load the goods
into the hatchback, packing everything in miraculously, like the opposite of clowns emerging from a circus car. Then the man, Glen
Doyle, cruises the car around the corner and down the block to Massachusetts Avenue. There is no room left in the car for the woman,
Carolyn Najarian, so she walks down and locates their assigned spot,
No. 17, for which they've paid the town twenty dollars, chalked in
blue on the pavement.

It's Town Day in Arlington, and all up and down the avenue people are setting up booths. Actually, Town Day began last night, with a mime circus, a Dixieland band, pony rides, picnicking, and fireworks at Spy Pond. Today's activities are centered on Mass. Ave.: over two hundred booths of arts and crafts, nonprofit organizations, and local business displays; a moonwalk, a book sale, a road race, trolley rides; ice cream, shish kabob, fried dough, stir-fry, and samosas, not to mention four different performance spaces featuring local musicians and dancers. Arlington Friends of the Drama has not traditionally run a booth (in years past, the Friends have used the occasion to sell old costumes off racks); it was Carolyn Najarian, the theater's publicity director for just over a year now, who came up with the idea to set up an actual booth offering membership information and a free raffle for a set of tickets to each of the season's plays. Last Town Day, the first time they tried it, 350 new people added their names to the mailing list.

Now Carolyn and Glen, who is a member of the publicity committee, unload the car and erect the booth, using lots of duct tape to get the red felt banner in place. The wind is a bit whippy this early in the morning. Already the sun is burning through the mist, and blue sky piercing through in ragged triangles. Beside them, in the space chalked No. 16, another team of workers is setting up, and there are cries of surprise and then hugs when it turns out to be Carole Allen, Carolyn's son's pediatrician, and her colleagues at Children's Health Care. They eye each other's displays with a certain amount of friendly competition. Children's Health Care has a great glass vase of wildflowers on a white brocade tablecloth, but, then, AFD has balloons and hard candies.

Their assigned spot is anyway very good: they're on the corner, for one thing, not hemmed in on both sides, and they're within pointing distance of the theater, which makes a difference when inviting people to come check it out for the first time. Carolyn sizes all this up immediately; she used to do trade shows for BayBank; she knows booth culture. Carolyn stands five feet tall, has long thick brown hair, strong Armenian features, eyes dark and melting as chocolate truffles. She's a single, working mother, an actor and a dancer, and something of a dynamo, having, over the past year, completely revamped the board position of publicity director at AFD. Before Carolyn, the job mostly entailed getting auditions and performances announced in the local papers. She has expanded it to include mounting displays in the public library; getting the town's permission to post an Arlington Friends of the Drama sign out on Pleasant Street; placing advertising sandwich boards on the sidewalk in front of Town Hall; getting local businesses to run ads in the programs; securing talk-show appearances on the local cable channel; successfully campaigning Governor Paul Cellucci to declare last May 9, the group's seventy-fifth anniversary, Arlington Friends of the Drama Day in the Commonwealth of Massachusetts, and obtaining congratulatory letters on that occasion from both U.S. senators, one congressman, the president of the American Association of Community Theatres, and the president of the United States.

Right now she stands in the thin gold of morning huffing up a red balloon, and then it's time to put the finishing touches on the booth. She makes Glen laugh at her perfectionism: rearranging the candy in the bowl to make it heap better, aligning the pens in a diagonal just so, stacking the refrigerator magnets, which boast AFD's current season, and grooming the balloons, tied to the arch of the booth, just as if she were fluffing a castmate's hair in the wings, precurtain. At nine, all at once, the sun burns off the last of the haze and damp, and up and down the street, as if at a signal, people begin shedding windbreakers and donning dark glasses. Glen takes off in his little car to coach a girls' soccer game, but promises to be back by noon. Carolyn peels off her navy Arlington Friends of the Drama sweatshirt to reveal a red Arlington Friends of the Drama T-shirt, with its logo incorporating the ubiquitous masks of tragedy and comedy with a row of mounted stage lights. A man stops by, straddling a bicycle, and says, "I used to do a lot of theater in college. Mostly sound and tech stuff." "Well, you should come down," declares Carolyn, like a doctor telling a diabetic he ought to get on insulin, and she gets him to take a magnet and fill out a raffle ticket. Town Day is under way.

Now a fife-and-drum corps composed of eight men in full colonial dress wends its way down Mass. Ave., like a sudden shot of undistilled Americana, to the flagpole outside Town Hall. A musket cracks twice, and "The Star-Spangled Banner" is played on fife while the flag gets raised. Not a large crowd gathers for this, and the eight knickered men, in their tricornered hats and billowy shirts of homespun, return in narrow fashion along the sidewalk instead of down the avenue. Carolyn, as they thread behind her booth, claps loudly, publicly, her hands held high and prominent before her, and people nearby follow her lead, and the men grin sweetly, modestly, at this applause as they beat their retreat.

Arlington is a town proud of its identity, which draws heavily on its role in Revolutionary War history. Its main artery is Massachusetts Avenue, which spools through the center of town and connects it on the east to Cambridge and Boston, and on the west to Lexington and Concord. Mass. Ave. in Arlington constituted one leg of Paul Revere's ride, and it was the route of the redcoats' retreat after the famous battles in Concord and Lexington that officially started the revolution on April 19, 1775. The Jason Russell House, which stands one block west of AFD's Town Day booth, preserved as a historical site and museum, was the site of one of the bloodiest battles between the retreating British regulars and the American militia. The greatest casualties and the most savage fighting on that seminal day occurred in the town of Arlington (then known as the hamlet of Menotomy); twenty-five Americans and at least forty British were killed. The combat here was house-to-house, hand-to-hand, and the British plundered and burned houses, taverns, and churches. The Old Burying Ground, one block east of Carolyn's booth this morning, holds a mass grave for the colonists who died in the fighting, and the town holds a host of commemorative activities, including re-enactments, every year on April 19.

A century after the revolution, Arlington had become a thriving market garden town, supplying Boston with its famous "pure white" celery and clear blocks of ice cut from Spy Pond. It boasted gristmills, carriage makers, woodworking and blacksmith shops, knife- and saw-manufacturing concerns. Spa hotels in Arlington Heights attracted wealthy Bostonians during the summer months, with the slogans, "Noted for Ozone," and "Unrivaled for Health." At the end of the nineteenth century, telephone lines, free postal delivery, electric lights, and trolley cars all reached Arlington, making it attractive to people who wanted to move out of the city. The town population got further increased and diversified by waves of Irish and Italian immigrants. But notions of exclusivity still governed and shaped Arlington's upper echelon. The official town directory at that time listed only property owners, and among those, only ones residing at the right addresses.

Arlington, five and a half miles square, is today a town of forty-four thousand. Its population is still overwhelmingly white—nearly 94 percent, according to the 1990 census—but the demographic is economically mixed. Sociologically as well as geographically, Arlington occupies a midpoint between the city and its more tony suburbs. Neither as urban and ethnically diverse as the former, nor as exclusive and homogeneous as the latter, Arlington is like an early rung on the ladder of upward mobility, a town where Boston accents are still ample and thick, and housing options range from sprawling Victorians on shady streets, to two- and three-family homes with aluminum siding and concrete stoops, to dull-yellow brick cubes of low-income housing.

It's a town that may be somewhat ambivalent about its proximity to the city; on the one hand, it's a piece of cake to head in for a Red Sox game or to see the ballet; on the other hand, it's just as easy for city dwellers to make their way out to Arlington, where affordable housing might even lure them to set up camp, and not everyone in Arlington is eager to encourage such an influx. As recently as 1982, a recommendation in the official report on Arlington Town Day read, "No publicity in Boston media is a good idea. We did not have the problem elements."

But the face of Arlington is changing, if slowly. Just six years ago, in spite of considerable defensiveness and resistance from some residents, the town established a Human Rights Commission to educate citizens about the benefits of diversity and to work with the police in dealing with instances of intolerance such as racist graffiti. Among Arlington's public-school children, more than two dozen different languages are the primary tongues spoken at home, from Japanese and Spanish and Haitian Creole to Hindi and Dutch and Mongolian. And a couple of years ago, the annual Christmas concert in Town Hall metamorphosed into a multiethnic Winter Celebration instead, offering Cambodian dancers, African drummers, a Klezmer band, Irish folk music.

And just as the town is evolving toward a more varied mixture of people, Arlington Friends of the Drama has been emerging from its socially exclusive roots. In its earliest days, becoming a member was by invitation only, and as late as the 1960s, a new member had to be "sponsored" by two existing ones. Although it was never written policy, Jews and people of color never used to audition, on the general assumption that they were unwelcome at the Friends. For the bulk of its seventy-five years, the Friends did little if anything to publicize themselves; they had no need to, operating like a social club whose membership regenerated itself effortlessly. In fact, for all the years it has been sitting in the same spot, right behind Town Hall, strikingly few town residents are even aware of its existence. It's only very recently, with membership having slipped and loyal members aging out, and the new mortgage to worry about, and a growing contingency who believe it's the theater's responsibility to reach out to a new and more varied population, that AFD is really turning outward and making a conscious effort to appeal to those beyond its immediate family.

As the modest fife-and-drum corps disappears in the direction of the Jason Russell House, the final view of them swallowed up by a pushcart tentacled with Mylar balloons, a far larger regiment, with far greater draw—the Arlington High School cheerleaders—sashays with chewing-gum finesse down the avenue to get ready for their performance on the sound stage outside Town Hall. This reminds Carolyn it's time to collect AFD's Town Day performers, scheduled to go on directly after the cheerleaders. She leaves the booth to another volunteer and heads up Academy Street to the theater. The day has turned really gorgeous: cold and hot at the same time, like a baked Alaska. Around the back of Town Hall, she notices the local cable people have set up their mobile unit. Carolyn wanders over and says hi to a couple of the guys she's worked with before. It's not an idle stop; pressing palms never is for a publicity director. The cable guys and Carolyn all look over as a squadron of the more advanced cheerleaders practices a towering pyramid formation under a black-walnut tree nearby. Straight-backed and light-footed on each other's shoulders, they are willowy and powerful at the same time, like horses, or muses. Carolyn, at her height, could pass for one of them. She looks as if she would have been the top girl in high school, little and nimble and capable of belting out the cheers with surprising force. She also gives the impression she would have been president of the peer-counseling organization, warm and empathetic, a good listener and a candid adviser. Really, she was neither of these things: she spent all her extracurricular hours doing drama.

Maybe the reason Carolyn Najarian is able to pour so much of herself—already stretched thin by work and single motherhood— into the drudge work that accounts for most of her hours at AFD, is that theater has long been a kind of haven for her, the place where she feels truest. In her childhood home, a full palette of emotions was frowned upon; all but the middle tones were deemed histrionic and unsuitable. But she saw that in one arena more feeling was permitted; this was the arts. Carolyn had a grandmother who'd been a flapper and danced the Charleston, an uncle who'd worked with the chore- ographer Jerome Robbins, a mother who did oil paintings and would coax her husband into jitterbugging with her around the living room. In the context of these endeavors, rules governing composure did not apply. When Carolyn began to wend her own way into ballet and school plays, a part of herself became unsquashed. Here, onstage, under lights, she could feel everything at last, her emotions at large, and she was not chastised but applauded for it.

All this was well and good until she declared her intentions to carry her theatrical pursuits beyond childhood. Then she ran into for- midable opposition, twice, from two men. The first was her father, who forbade her to go away to college and major in theater, as Car- olyn's high-school drama teacher encouraged her to do. Instead, she would live at home and attend community college, banned from vis- iting anyone's dorm room or apartment, expected home every night by eleven. From this arrangement she fled into an early marriage, which, for the first few years, managed, barely, to tolerate her involve- ment in community theater. But it was a troubled marriage, and fif- teen years into it, lonely at home with a small son, Carolyn made up her mind, or realized with a kind of health and clarity like that old feeling of being free and herself under the stage lights, that the thing she must do was theater again. Her husband said he couldn't support that. The marriage ended.

Now the man in her life is Jonathan, aged ten, and in his own way he, too, comes between her and theater, unwittingly limiting the roles for which she can audition (they must be small enough that she can squeeze all her rehearsals, with the cooperation of an understanding director, into Tuesday nights, when Jonathan stays with his father), but this limitation of course is different: there's no sting to it, no bitterness or grudge. When Jonathan does accompany her to the theater, for an evening of stuffing envelopes or the odd extra rehearsal, he is sweet about it, sweet about his inevitable boredom. Petite as his mother and darkly handsome, he'll do yo-yo tricks backstage, or flop on a balding velvet sofa with a Game Boy and a soda, resigned to the visit with the patient familiarity of a theater kid. And all too soon, Carolyn knows, he'll likely be off on his own in the evenings, and this world, which has all these years coursed beside her but out of reach, like a brook running parallel to the train she's been on, will become available for her full immersion.

In the meantime, she contents herself with singing the national anthem at meetings of the Rotary Club or Chamber of Commerce now and then, and volunteering to make up actors before a performance. Two months ago, she had her first role in an AFD show in five years: a sort of cameo appearance as Carmen Miranda in the musical-revue summer fund-raiser, *Stage Door Canteen*. She got to wear skimpy frills and a saucy turban and roll her eyes and croon a campy little number that went, "Ai, ai, ai, ai, ai I like you verrrrry much!" Jonathan would practice singing it with her in the car. But mostly she is biding her time being the best publicity director she can; it's not what she'd most like to do with the theater, but it's what she's able to do, and as she says, she'd work with this group in virtually any capacity, just to get to be down there at the Friends with all those other people who love it like she does, making plays together.

Now it is ten, time for the cheerleaders to perform, and AFD is scheduled for the slot immediately following—a happy coincidence, as far as marketing-savvy Carolyn is concerned, a perfect opportunity to capitalize on the naturally large audience gathered for that ever-popular act. Carolyn heads into the theater to collect the performers, members of the *Funny Girl* cast who have been called into extra service this morning. For months, Carolyn had envisioned a healthier showing. A full chorus of tap-dancers, maybe, or at least an appearance by the lead, the woman playing Fanny Brice herself, who for all intents and purposes *is* the show. She was miffed when the director, Barbara Tyler, reluctant to overtax her cast and especially her leading lady right at the start of the show's two-weekend run, decided to deliver only three performers: Ellen Kazin, playing Fanny's mother; Bill Allsbrook, as Fanny's dance coach; and Michael Hogman, who choreographed the show and then wound up dancing in the chorus as well when someone dropped out. Carolyn's understanding, ever since the slate was voted on last winter, was that whoever wound up directing this first show of the season would make clear to the cast from the outset that their commitment would involve performing on Town Day. Her series of pleasantly firm appeals did not budge the director, however, and Carolyn has chosen to keep her disgruntlement over the matter mostly private. She's still part of the new, younger wave of Friends, and is canny enough to see little sense in alienating one of the old guard.

Now that the hour has arrived, Carolyn projects only good cheer as she rallies the little group from their exhausted poses in the greenroom. It's Barbara and the three performers and Ellen's husband, Stu, all kind of sprawled and wry and draggy after last night's opening party. They greet Carolyn's arrival with sardonic stabs at enthusiasm and little moaning references to hangovers and sore feet. Stu Kazin, who performs the role of Florenz Ziegfeld in the show, is along this morning simply for moral support, or equal penance, or something. He has a kind face, full of laid-back, philosophical humor, and a black walrusy mustache. Ellen, prostrate on the far sofa, complains freely but with no trace of annoyance that she shouldn't have bothered changing out of costume and makeup last night at all.

Carolyn shepherds them onto the street, into the fever-bright day, and they stagger a little, giving weight to the old stereotype of actors as being not quite fit for the society of clean, upstanding early risers who keep the wholesome life of town running smoothly. Michael, a tall, slender, sweet-tempered young man, squints darkly and alternates between coffee and a cigarette as they cut down Academy Street. "Sunglasses would've been good," notes Ellen, holding her tap shoes in one hand and shielding her eyes with the other. She's a compact woman, crackling with pert retorts and a sense of fun. Irrepressible freckles wink through her pancake base in the sunshine. The cheerleaders, lithe and spiffy in maroon and gray, are going full-force on the sound stage, with some sort of music emanating through speakers which have been tuned so that all that comes through is pounding bass.

"What ever happened to simple cheers?" queries Stu, as the girls pile onto one another's shoulders in a series of dazzling geometric formations.

"I don't like following animals or children," Bill decides darkly. Yet another regiment of cheerleaders takes the stage; they are performing in waves, in squadrons, with a kind of pumping vigor and intensity suggestive of military maneuvers.

"Gee, it's a lot of enthusiasm for ten in the morning," drawls Barbara, who has a way of barely moving her lips when she speaks, and keeps her eyelids generally at half-mast, so that nearly everything she says comes out with a sardonic spin, as if she were playing a gangster in an old movie. Tall and still mostly svelte, in jeans and heels and a bright-red belt, she cuts an imposing figure. They are playing their fatigue for great comic effect, all of them, enjoying themselves in a sly, communal way.

Eventually it's time. Ellen and Bill and Michael slip round to the back and put on their taps, and then they come out and do two short numbers, one of them heavily abridged from its regular ensemble of a dozen. They don't flop, and neither do they shine. The acoustics of Mass. Ave. are not exactly optimal for musical theater, nor does the gigantic, empty stage, which has, after all, just accommodated seemingly every pubescent and prepubescent girl in town, exactly showcase the three to their best advantage, but it's something else that really alters the act, that drains it of its polish. It's the incongruity, the anomaly, which translates as three parts embarrassing and one part affecting.

If the idea of community theater alone is enough to make a considerable portion of the population smile into their sleeves, then tearing off an actual little piece of it and plunking it down unsupported in the midst of autumn sunlight and roast-lamb smells and milling pedestrians and dispersing cheerleaders and local politicians and popcorn machines and baby strollers and sand art and crafts vendors—plunking it down, in other words, in the midst of noisy, rough-edged reality—seems to point up its wistful failings, its striving, self-important inadequacies. In this light, all the skepticism of those who balk at the idea of adults' donning costume and makeup and pretending to be other people seems natural and correct.

Perhaps for everyone except children, there is an inherent fragility to the willing suspension of disbelief. What just might magically transport within the dark box of the theater strains and suffers in the broad, untempered arena of the crowded street. Just as the fife-and-drum corps earlier was diminished, rendered somewhat odd and pathetic by the louder reality of Disney-character balloons and kids clamoring to get into the moonwalk, so, too, is this raw sliver of an old-time musical made trifling and foolish by its surroundings.

But the same elements that show up the act in a softly embarrassing light are what make it strangely affecting. The sheer improbability of adults' doing this, of a couple of grown men and a middle-aged woman standing up before a town and singing "Rat-a-tat-tat!" while executing the intricate and clicking steps of an ersatz Follies routine, the very folly of the act, anachronistic and thin as it seems on that giant sound stage in front of Town Hall, makes it brave, and rare.

AFD is not alone in bringing costume drama to Town Day, however. Down at the Jason Russell House, great numbers of men and women are working as costumed docents, guiding batches of guests through the historic building, and re-creating through storytelling the battle that transpired there on the eve of the American Revolution. An even better costume drama is probably that of the town's teenagers, who are today outdoing themselves gloriously. A great number are roving around in shaving-cream-induced, spray-paint-enhanced Mohawks (an impromptu beauty parlor apparently having established itself in the bushes between the library and Town Hall). They are not re-creating past events, except of the most general and timeless nature: rituals of courtship and self-identity, hard-wired, perhaps, into our culture or our very genes. Then, too, there are all the little ones running about with stars and rainbows and fish and cherries and automobiles applied to their cheeks at the face-painting booth.

The whole town is decked out, caught up. Reality and heightened reality dodge in and out of each other's shadows along the avenue on this ritualized day. Even the cops keeping the peace, rerouting traffic at either end of the blocked-off street; even the environmentalists and human-rights activists, earnest and sweaty at their booths; even the open-air cooks, heaping Styrofoam plates as fast as the customers demand; even those who are doing nothing but lying in the grass of the library gardens, eyes shut, listening to the music of the classical violinist playing under a fat old maple there—all are playing parts in the day, if only in the dramas of their own imaginations. We play public roles all the time, and we tell the day back to ourselves in the evening, to our families at table, or to ourselves in dreams, making narrative of it, making pattern and sense. We rehearse tomorrow and practice some of our lines, and then we go on and improvise, with the pages of yesterday's script in our back pockets, playing out the next act for an audience of our neighbors and our consciences.

By late afternoon, the hard candies, replenished many times, have dwindled terminally in the bowl, and the AFD banner has been reduct-taped twice after gusts of wind knocked it down, and several shifts of booth workers have been and gone. When Carolyn and Glen return to take the last shift of the day, they find the booth practically swarming with unofficial AFD representatives. Everywhere now people are straggling, weighted down by impulse buys. The pace along the avenue has slowed, and the sun is cutting a fierce apricot angle as it lowers. T-shirts are smeared with ice cream and ketchup, cheeks are sunburnt, children are crying or passed out, floppy-headed, in their strollers.

But at the AFD booth, attendance has not slackened; more and more Friends wander up for idle gossip and a candy, and the theater group is sprawling past its allotted boundaries, with people clustered in front and along the curb in back, the booth itself drawing members like a satellite clubhouse. Even Michael Hogman, so bleary-eyed before this morning's dance routine, and due at the theater again in only a few hours for this evening's performance, can't resist swinging by for a while, although he declares he's ready to take a break after

Funny Girl closes, and his feet go into an unconscious little tap number on the sidewalk as he listens to other members discuss which upcoming shows they're considering auditioning for or working crew on. Five people pass around two cans of soda, remembering to interrupt their own conversations periodically to field questions from people who stop at the booth to inquire.

Over and over again, longtime Arlington residents express puzzlement and surprise to learn that Arlington *has* a community theater. Some confuse it with the Capitol Theater, a renovated old movie house that shows second-run, foreign, and independent films; others with the Regent Theater, a historic motion-picture house where, more recently, children's plays have been produced. Others say they have heard of AFD but always thought it was a professional theater. "I didn't realize it was open to, you know, just the public," is how one woman puts it.

The booth workers are well accustomed to such confusion, and politely point up Academy Street, again and again, to identify the building. Part of the renovation included painting the exterior, so the building looks newly smart these days, its gingerbread painted contrasting colors in a colonial palette of sash green, terra-cotta, and downing straw. That AFD does not have a higher profile is no one's fault but its own, since for most of its years it operated rather exclusively; still, the depths of the general public's ignorance of the group can be sobering. A recent report on Arlington by the Metropolitan Area Planning Council identified one potential category of development as such: "The Capitol Theater could be the ideal centerpiece for an arts and entertainment district. . . . Street-level development could include a community theater. . . . [This] would not only attract local residents seeking edifying activities for their leisure time, but has the potential to draw people from neighboring communities." Quite absent from the report was any indication that the authors realized a community theater already existed in Arlington.

Today winds down with the promise of new members—new audience members, at the very least. The raffle basket is overflowing with new addresses for the mailing list, and Carolyn's easel advertising the upcoming season draws notice as well. A number of people have inquired whether it's too late to buy tickets for the second weekend of

Funny Girl. Others brightened at the prospect of the upcoming Neil Simon comedy this winter, or the British musical *Blood Brothers* this spring, and a few asked curiously what *M. Butterfly* was about. "That's that opera?" asked one man, dubiously. The poster for that show bears a prominent warning regarding its subject matter, which raises its cache among a certain set. One teenager, sporting braids and lollipop, enthuses, "I want to see that one!"

Now, as up and down the avenue other booths are folding up, and the police are removing the traffic barriers, and the sun slips another notch in the sky, a few more Friends wander over to say hello, to sit on each other's laps in the folding chair, to snap each other's photos standing underneath the felt banner. And if at times one of the public has to wait an extra beat to get someone's attention, even clearing a throat to alert one of the booth workers, all so punchy and full of self-referential laughter by this hour of the day, perhaps it doesn't come across as off-putting so much as alluring, and perhaps some of the thickness and passion of the group is conveyed.

"Right up the street," says Carolyn for the hundredth time today, as brightly now as she said it this morning, pointing the way up the aisle of elms, where the theater, in its fine new hues, stands waiting to be entered.

Six

Stage Business

OCTOBER 2. FIRST BLOCKING REHEARSAL.

And they are into it, suddenly and all at once, after months and months of planning and plotting, after months and months of the play's living in shadowy, idealized form in the participants' minds—the rehearsal process is under way. And although a few silver-glittered flats and the ticket booth from the *Funny Girl* set remain propped against one wall of the house, waiting to be picked up by, respectively, a church group and a community theater out in Springfield, the *Butterfly* people inhabit the space with a strangely effortless ease, and the theater accommodates this new conglomeration of workers without missing a beat or batting an eye; it is as though they have been here rehearsing always.

Tonight, at the first real rehearsal up in the house, everybody already seems quite hunkered in. Jim and Tom sit in the third row, running lines. Kelley, the stage manager, is up onstage fixing Roman numerals of masking tape to the floor, to identify where the five distinct segments of the ramp will be. Celia has made a station for herself on the edge of the thrust, with her script on a dented old music stand. One of the most piddling yet simultaneously profound signs that people have lodged themselves unequivocally in the theater is that snacking has already begun. Bringing food into a space is no small signifier, and the sorts of food that people snack on during the rehearsal process can even function as a barometer of the overall mood. Some productions develop a familial, nurturing atmosphere, and cast and crew members have been known to bring in homemade Linzer tortes, and Tupperwares of hand-picked blueberries, and hard bread and soft cheese, and deposit these things casually on the edge of the thrust for general consumption. Tonight, Tall Michelle is slouched in the front row, crunching baby carrots; Grace, on an aisle near the back, nibbles saltines; Carolyn fishes a Ziploc bag of almonds from her nylon briefcase; Kelley has set a bottle of Poland Spring water next to her script.

Celia brings everyone onstage, explains the point of the Roman numerals, and then begins walking the cast through the blocking from page one. Directors are vastly different in how they structure rehearsals. Some let the actors feel their way into their characters for a while before they start issuing direction. Others give very specific character direction from the start, and allow the actors more input and creative latitude as the process goes on. One AFD director, years ago, got replaced a week before opening night when the board learned he'd had the cast do nothing so far but improv games. Most directors, of course, fall somewhere along the spectrum. Celia has spoken to everyone assembled about the collaborative style she values, but tonight, by starting the process with blocking—a rather dry task, in this case, that involves one-way communication: her instructing the actors where and how they'll physically move through the play— she sends another message: business first, with a single executive director.

Last week, on a rainy night in an otherwise empty theater, Celia and Kelley and Mayre had gathered on the greenroom sofas and worked out a rehearsal schedule based on all the various conflicts that different cast and crew members had written down earlier. It had felt like piecing together one of those fantastically difficult 3-D jigsaw puzzles, Kelley wielding her Wite-Out and Mayre hunched over her bulky, much-filled-in engagement calendar, and the two of them had grown visibly frustrated with the task. It was Celia, for once, who served as the leavening agent, agreeing to all sorts of juggling changes with soothing shrugs and bright "okays."

But at rehearsal she is different: all the energy is still there, but tightly coiled now, not so playful and loose. She has been blocking this play, in the concentrated arena of her own mind, since last winter, working with eyes closed, listening to the audiotape she purchased of the original Broadway production, seeing every step, every turn, every glance, and as she instructs the cast now, they are kept very busy penciling all the details into their scripts. So already the process is vastly different from that of the previous production, in which Barbara Tyler's general modus operandi was to say, "Come in that door," "Go out that door," vaguely regardless of whether a door would actually be there at all: frustrating at times, but liberating as well. Some actors appreciate the opportunity to find their way into their characters' movements and physicality on their own and in collaboration with their fellow actors. Under Celia's governance, there is little room for such exploration, at least this early in the process. She is entertaining no discussion tonight. When Jimmy and Carolyn do the pin-up-girl scene (in which a pubescent Gallimard, poring over his uncle's stash of porn magazines, fantasizes that one of the models is coming on to him), Celia blocks him lying on his stomach, facing the audience, with Carolyn behind him, upstage, and still his instinct is to twist around and glance at her.

"No, you deliver it all *out*," corrects Celia.

"So I'm not looking at her?"

"No. Remember it's a fantasy."

"I know, I—"

A bit sharply: "The focus is not on her, to answer your question."

And they move on.

She instructs not only major moves and orientations around the stage, but the minutiae as well.

"Jimmy, I want you to think about your diminished stature in this scene," she says of the opening, when Gallimard is an old man in jail, convicted of treason for having passed French state secrets on to his

Chinese lover, who has turned out to be not only a man but a government spy. "Take small, deep inhales on the cigarette. I want small-
ness."

"Song, run your fan up Gallimard's arm."

"Song, fix his tie as you say that."

"Okay, gentlemen, then you toast."

"Tom, you're going to do something suggestive with the tennis
racquet on that line."

And Kelley notes it all assiduously in her stage manager's script:
"Fix tie." "Clink glasses." "Tennis racquet & crotch." Later, when the
cast is off book, she will have to cue people, feeding them not only
their lines but their blocking. To that end, she has photocopied the
diagram of the stage set dozens of times over, and every time the
scene shifts very much (every other page or so), she tapes a fresh one
into her script and notes the location of the actors and major props.
Her copy of the script, more than anyone else's, will become a sort of
bible for running the show.

An hour passes and ten pages have been blocked, and still the actors haven't done any acting as such, only walked through their
scenes as per Celia's notes. For her part, Celia, in her rehearsal uniform of blue denim jeans and workshirt, keeps them corralled with
her own purposeful intensity. Her style is clean and blunt and brisk.
A common criticism of Celia as a director is that her priority is not to
create a sense of fun. A common compliment of Celia as a director is
that her priority is turning out a finished product with excellent production values. Already her style is making a strong impression on the
Butterfly cast. Some—Patrick chief among them—find themselves
bristling at her terse, imperious commands. Others are drawn to her
sense of purpose and control. Everyone plays, in varying ways, to her
style.

Jimmy is more than ever acting the sweetly magnanimous ham
with the rest of the cast, already trying to make people laugh, put
them at ease, welcome them warmly into the life of the Friends. He's
a kind of slap-happy goodwill ambassador, shaking hands or hugging
his scene-mates at the top of each scene. When Tall Michelle, sitting
in the front row, sneezes, Jim, onstage, broadly mimes wiping himself
off before he winks and says, "Bless you." By some collective misun-

derstanding, everyone refers to the kurogo dancers as kurogis; already Jim is calling them, cutely, "pirogies." He is bounding and earnest, and when Celia eventually pauses to inquire generally whether she's going too fast, he effuses, "Oh no—this is terrific!" and it feels genuine and ingratiating at once, as though he's truly thrilled to be sinking his teeth into all this blocking so quickly, and as though being recognized as diligent and kind and good are all part and parcel of the community-theater experience for him.

Patrick, in contrast, appears reserved, poised, sober. He has beautiful posture and almost surreal composure. When Celia, after chewing her thumbnail over the height thing again, suddenly crosses to him and shows him the crouch his character is always to assume, slapping his thighs with her gym-teacherish authority as she instructs, "You've got to really get used to this exaggerated position. So that your quads start to hurt," he neither looks at her nor responds, except to copy the note dutifully into his script. His affect tonight functions like a barrier, and neither Jimmy's eager friendliness nor Celia's blunt direction pierces through it at all. His face is sort of luminous, like a deer's or the moon's, and he carries himself with a stillness and maturity that belie his age, which is twenty-two. He graduated from MIT only months ago; he's the baby of the cast, much to everyone's surprise when word trickles round.

It becomes clear, as they move through the act, how much the show rides on the two leads, Song and Gallimard, Patrick and Jim. Jimmy has eschewed the larger, Celia-provided script in favor of the original pale-aqua booklet, which can be easily held in one hand, and in which he has already highlighted his lines; a flip through the pages shows a daunting amount of the acid-yellow ink. Patrick is working with the enlarged reproduction, more cumbersome but with larger print and more space to jot notes, which may in part account for his circumscribed movements; he cradles the bound sheaf in front of him in both hands, and gives it a great deal of attention.

The rest of the cast mills between scenes, finding backstage perches or exploring the rest of the theater. The three kurogo, Teri, Orea, and Little Michelle, must be on fairly constant call, gliding in and out for subtle scene changes or the handing off of props (mostly mimed, for now, making it all the more confusing), and they create a sort of station for themselves by the baby grand offstage left, on the wider of the two shallow wings. Teri and Orea are in their forties; Little Michelle is twenty-eight but looks sixteen; two are from Greater Boston; one is from upstate New York by way of the Philippines; two are wives and mothers; one is single and childless; they work, respectively, for Boston Beer Company, Hewlett-Packard, and Children's Hospital—but in spite of these differences the three are a seamless unit, largely due to what soon emerges as their shared thankless status, for they have more to do than almost anyone, arguably even the two leads, and yet they speak virtually no lines and perform the most subservient supporting actions. Their scripts quickly become riddled with complicated pencil marks, and they consult each other softly to confirm stage directions. They are needed, in small ways, in nearly every scene.

But the others—Tom, Grace, Doug, Carolyn, and Tall Michelle—are needed rather sparsely, and the evening drags somewhat for them. This is the nature of most plays, and the basis for the whole side-culture of secondary pursuits that often spring up in the theater's off-stage hallways and hollows. These pursuits may be individual, from knitting, to grading papers, to listening to sporting events on transistor radios with the sound turned low; or plural, from playing poker, to playing practical jokes, to serious flirting and romancing. Just what these pursuits will turn out to be on this show it is also too soon to say, but the possible groupings, based on who has offstage time and who doesn't, are becoming clear.

At ten minutes to ten, they finish blocking Act One, and as some of the cast members begin reaching for their jackets and bags, Celia says, "Okay, that wasn't hard. Now let's run it."

"Is it my imagination, or is she getting more energy as we go along?" asks Carolyn, flopping back into her seat, half aggrieved, half impressed. Carolyn is here entirely because of Celia, whom she met last winter while assistant-directing another play of Celia's, at another community theater, several towns over. As a result of that contact, Carolyn wound up applying for and getting a job at Hewlett-Packard with Celia as her immediate supervisor, and as a result of *that* contact was persuaded to audition for the part of the pin-up girl in *Butterfly*. Carolyn is in her early thirties, tall, with smart blue eyes and very short blond hair. She has performed in lots of musicals, but this is her first-ever role in a straight play. Her ambition is to direct, and she is here as much to observe Celia's technique and oddly matter-of-fact charisma as to act.

"Does anyone need time? To pee or anything? No?" Celia climbs off the stage and takes a seat in the front row. "I can't sit here," she immediately announces to herself, and pops up and moves back to the middle of the house, where she chooses another seat.

Now the show is the stage manager's, and from her spot at the edge of the thrust Kelley speaks the dry cues that will eventually translate into real action: "Music music music, kurogos exit, lights up on Gallimard."

Molly appears in the wing with a celery-green rehearsal kimono rummaged from the costume room downstairs. She beckons Patrick over and fits it around him during Jim's opening monologue, fastening it with a wide, bulky towel to substitute for an obi. He is in stocking feet now, and about a half-inch shorter than Jim, who is wearing rehearsal boots with a chunky heel.

Every so often, one of the actors does something that doesn't correspond with the blocking in Kelley's book, and she turns around and makes a squinchy face at Celia. But Celia is thinking, Celia is concentrating. She gnaws heavily on her perfect nails, mocha-colored tonight, and a muscle in her temple flashes. She paces, and comes back down to the front of the house, and sits, and buries her face in her hands. She looks like a brain surgeon, like a homicide detective, like a senior Pentagon official in the war room.

"Are you okay?" whispers Carolyn, done with her scene and sitting back in the audience. Onstage, Patrick is speaking in the cool, gliding woman-tones he is cultivating for the part.

Without lifting her head, Celia replies, "I'm just listening to his voice." Though, with her bent there like that, fingers half hidden in her short brown hair, face obscured, shoulders deeply rounded, what she might be hearing is anyone's guess.

Celia Bartolotti Couture came to theater a little bit in spite of herself. As a child in Lexington, Massachusetts, she'd been exposed to a musical extended family—at gatherings, someone would always be whipping out a guitar—and she danced on scholarship at a nearby ballet studio, and made occasional theater trips to New York with her father, who enjoyed a weakness for Broadway. But essentially Celia was a jock, and at Lexington High School, jocks didn't act. So theater stayed a closet love, and by the time she was studying English and secondary education at Florida State University, it had become an old and all-but-forgotten love, so much so that, when a couple of dormmates persuaded her to accompany them to auditions for the school's production of *Oklahoma!*, she went only to watch, and had to be cajoled individually by the director actually to climb onstage and audition, whereupon she was quickly cast.

After that experience, it was, as they say, all over. She'd been bitten by the bug. Celia became a high-school English teacher as planned, but also directed the school's dramatic club, and soon decided to study for a master's degree in fine arts—specifically, in directing for secondary education and for community theater, a program she found at Emerson College in Boston. People began to notice Celia's work with high-school students, and soon she was being invited to direct at community theaters as well. In the early eighties, budget cuts obliterated the arts in many public schools, and Celia changed careers, transferring into the business world at Hewlett-Packard. But in a way, she didn't change careers, or she didn't change the career that mattered most: her work as a director of amateur theater, the work of taking a piece of literature, bringing it to life, and sharing it with an audience. That work remained constant.

Besides being president of AFD, Celia is currently a member of three other community theaters, and directs plays for still others. To a surprising extent, she has bridged her seemingly incompatible theater and business communities. About twenty Hewlett-Packard employees have become members of AFD because of Celia, including one security guard who himself sold two memberships to his son and daughter-in-law. She has opened up Hewlett-Packard conference rooms for AFD board meetings and even occasional rehearsals, when space in the theater is tight, and has gained such a reputation at AFD for drawing on her Hewlett-Packard resources that some members have grown obscurely resentful. "Oh, *M. Butterfly!*" snorts one of the old guard. "That's not a real AFD production, that's just Celia bringing in her Hewlett-Packard stringers." In fact, although Carolyn and Orea are fellow employees of Celia's Burlington office, no one else related to the company will work on the show. But even if they were to, the resentment would be lost on Celia. As far as she's concerned, that's exactly the type of connection that community-theater members ought to facilitate—especially in this day, when the word "community" has come to mean less a geographic neighborhood than a broader, sketchier network of colleagues and kindred spirits. The way Celia sees it, the future of AFD, the perpetuation of the organization through the attraction of new members, will depend on its branching out and making connections any way it can.

The effort to open up AFD, or at least to acknowledge and address the perception held by a substantial number of those outside the group that AFD is exclusive and exclusionary, has surpassed even the expensive renovation project and resulting burden of mortgage payments to become the signature controversy of Celia's presidential reign. All community theaters, just like all communities, have their politics, and Celia, without exactly planning to, has become deeply embroiled in AFD's. She didn't set out to be a maverick or anything; she didn't even exactly set out to become president. She had been Marion Desilets' vice-president. Then Marion and Doug adopted Jeneane, and Marion decided to resign a year early, and Celia was sort of left holding the ball. As a businesswoman, she was seen as an ideal person to lead the group through the renovation project Marion had begun. What members didn't expect was all the other ideas for change she would bring with her.

"Leave it alone," people told her last January, after the renovation was finally deemed a success at the ribbon-cutting ceremony and gala reopening celebration. "Let it be," even her closest friends advised her. "This is an old group. You've already pushed them enough for one presidency. Ride out the rest of your term quietly." Such suggestions are not quite anathema to Celia, but she does not seem constitutionally capable of letting go of an issue she's passionate about, and the membership issue is just such a one. It would be a lovely mark to leave on the group, too, a sort of philosophical renovation to go along with the physical one.

At the very beginning of Celia's term, the board mailed out a membership survey in order to gather information on everything from members' ages to how people truly felt about the theater. The responses this garnered were varied and eclectic and not infrequently contradictory. Regarding play selection, for example, suggestions had ranged from "More classics," to "More contemporary plays;" from "More shows with parts for my age group," to "No English comedy," to simply, "Better shows." General comments ranged far and wide: "Attract younger people." "Valet parking for older/infirm." "Old timers are too critical." "It was hard to find out how to join." "Wish we had more loyal members as years gone by." "Felt very welcomed." "Currently not fun; no smoking is hard." "Lighten up. We take ourselves too seriously."

The comments that interested Celia most were those addressing the subjects of cliques and exclusivity. These included, "AFD is clique-y," "Even with Friendly [committee] there is a cliques atmosphere," "AFD is an 'In-group'; others feel excluded," "Crew is not treated as part of production," "Less factions and more unity," "Value the people;" as well as the baffling, "Non-members were abusive to older men." Except perhaps for this last, these comments did not come as a shock to most board members—not that they necessarily agreed that AFD *is* exclusive; the response simply reinforced an already dimly (or not-so-dimly) sensed impression that many people *perceive* it to be. And Celia, every time she raised the issue, first with the board and later with the general membership, took care to stress that distinction. She was not chastising the group for *being* exclusive, just trying to get the group to acknowledge ways in which it might be inadvertently sending that signal and alienating potential members.

Her proposal—which anyway wasn't her proposal, being generated very properly through a committee set up to make a recommendation based on results of the surveys, but which the membership at large, in any case, and with a certain degree of correctness, attributed personally to Celia—was this: do away with the archaic and hierarchical system of membership that divides members into the categories Sustaining Member, Active-Waiting Member, and Active Member, only the last of which has voting rights, and the other tiers of which can be transcended only upon the event of what has become a rather sporadic and mysterious board vote (the elevation of members from one category to the next is traditionally announced, with the air of an unveiling, at the annual election meeting each spring), and in their stead implement one category of membership, to be termed, unfussily, Member. The idea was that here was one, essentially symbolic, way to broadcast a different message to potential members, a way of saying, "Join our group and you'll be welcomed immediately, not on a lower rung but on the same level as everyone else." Taking a long view, it was also a way to alter radically the course that had been set when the ladies of the Arlington Woman's Club in 1923 made membership by invitation only, and then naturally proceeded to issue such invitations only to those of a similar social background as themselves. The proposal was, in a sense, an attack on the last vestiges of a club that had once been a bastion of white gloves and silver tea services, of propriety and the best families in town, and of careful, narrow definitions of art.

The response has been ugly. Most of the members of long standing have been vehemently opposed, reacting as if Celia had hurled personal epithets at them. The June membership meeting, at which the proposal was first made public, practically ended in fisticuffs. The next general meeting, at which the proposal will come to vote, is scheduled for October 4, this Sunday. Celia and the other board members are bracing for it with some trepidation. At the last board meeting, the matter lurked heavily in the background, although there were plenty of sharp and irreverent cracks made, too: a kind of gallows humor prevailed.

The meeting had proceeded according to protocol, opening with "Friendly news," and progressing to correspondence. The big news here had been the letter from President Clinton congratulating the group on its seventy-fifth anniversary. The hand-signed sheet got passed around the glass-topped conference table, and there were the requisite Monica jokes: "That's no watermark!" "Should we have this dry-cleaned?" Then Celia read aloud a letter from Nancie Richardson, AFD's librarian and one of its most devoted members, recommending that some of the officer guidelines in the board books be rewritten and updated. "Can you believe she wrote this on July Fourth?" said Celia, noticing the date. "She's whacked. And where were *you?*" she demanded of Nancie's husband, Don, on the board this year. At least one of the Richardsons, AFD's godparents, seems always to be on the board. "On the golf course, probably," decided Celia before he could answer, and Don smiled enigmatically behind his beard.

Next came a letter from an Arlington teenager trying to raise money to attend an acting competition in California.

"She lives around the corner and she never did anything with us?" said Jim Grana. "She gets bubkes."

"No, no, we can turn this around," raved Carolyn Najarian, the publicity director, a gleam in her eye. "I can see the headline now: 'Arlington Friends of the Drama Supports Local Talent!'"

"I say we give her a free ticket to *Funny Girl* and call it a day," said David Giagrando, breaking off a piece of his NutriGrain Bar to feed Baron, who was sitting at attention on his lap.

The meeting rolled along in its usual fashion, the briefest items made long by detailed and non-sequiturish digressions, the driest items enlivened by quips and often bawdy repartee. Every so often someone would get up to peruse the refreshment table, which Celia managed to provide through her company, and invariably there would be some unbusinesslike contact as a result—one board member rumpling the hair of another, or throwing a bag of chips across the long table, or getting into some comic shenanigans with Baron, ever on the lookout for a morsel—so that, in spite of their gleaming, professional environs, no one could ever mistake this ménage for a gathering of actual corporate employees.

Eventually Celia brought it up: "We have a very controversial list of ballot items for the October meeting."

"How many copies of the ballot do we need?" asked Stu Kazin, who had just come on board as vice-president. It is generally understood that he is next in line for the presidency, when Celia's term expires in June. "Two, three hundred? Is that going to be enough?"

"Oh yeah. A hundred'll be enough," said Celia, mindful of the pitiful turnouts at membership meetings over the last years. The old guard talks about the old days, when every single membership meeting—and there sometimes were ten a year—drew over a hundred people. Now there are three membership meetings a year, and attendance hovers around twenty or thirty.

"It depends on what the entertainment is," suggested David. Every membership meeting features some kind of musical, comic, or dramatic act after the business meeting has ended.

"*This*'ll be the entertainment," predicted Stu, a little ominously.

"The only agenda item I have for the meeting, frankly, is this vote," continued Celia. "I don't intend to bring up anything else controversial." She sounded grim and weary saying this, as though she were talking not only about the upcoming meeting but about the rest of her presidency.

"What about the five-show-four-show season?" somebody asked. At one point, Celia had planned to address the long-simmering possibility of modifying the yearly slate from five productions to four—another issue that to anyone outside the group would hardly seem incendiary, but that within the group would be, at least to some members, tantamount to sacrilege—but, as she answered now, "You can bet your ass I'm not dealing with *that*. I've done enough controversial things."

"I've been given to understand that two or more members are planning to object to the ballot on the grounds that the bylaws weren't followed exactly," said one board member.

Celia replied that she'd asked an attorney to be present, as parliamentarian, just in case someone threw a curve ball, like a last-minute amendment, or in the event that all the points of order start to get trampled and confused, the way they did last June, when tumult and tempers erupted and several people ended the night privately in tears.

"To be perfectly honest with you guys," said Celia after the brief, anxious silence that followed this announcement, "if the item doesn't pass, I'm not losing any more sleep over it. If you don't like it, vote no, and let's move on." This was not an entirely faithful account of her feelings. Celia cares deeply about the group's viability's continuing into the next millennium. In her view, if the proposed change goes forward, however grindingly slow and fraught the process has been, it will have been worth all the sleep she's already lost over it.

But, taking their cue from her outward shrugging pragmatism, the board members launched almost giddily into the lighter subject of planning the entertainment for the postbusiness portion of the meeting. A staged reading from an original play? An evening of love duets? Test out the nude scene from *M. Butterfly*?

"Yeah, right," snorted Celia.

Someone told Stu he should call up one talented and busy member, currently in the professional touring company of *Evita*, and delegate the entertainment to her.

"And when she tells me to be fruitful and go multiply?"

"I know!" cried Carolyn, punchy now. "We can have that teen girl come and perform!"

"And she can pass a hat," put in Stu.

Carolyn announced the headline, " 'AFD Gives New Teen Terrific Break!' "

"Nude or New?" Don pretended to wonder.

"That word is in our vocabulary for the rest of the year now," groaned Jimmy.

And the meeting drizzled into the most pleasant and lighthearted and irrelevent minutiae, and no more mention was made of the difficult vote ahead.

OCTOBER 4. MEMBERSHIP MEETING.

"Come to see the fight?" one member blithely greets another in the shallow upstairs lobby just before Sunday night's meeting. Longtime members still tend to use this Academy Street entrance, rather than the expansive new downstairs lobby entered via Maple Street, and tonight they keep trickling in up the old concrete steps. Kelley O'Leary is passing out ballots to all voting-eligible members as they pass by and find seats in the house. Tonight, as at most meetings, this translates into virtually everyone; few active-waiting and fewer sustaining members ever attend.

The ballot contains four items, three pertaining to rather simple housekeeping-type questions, the fourth reading:

> *Create one class of membership.*
> *A FOR vote would eliminate the three classes of membership:*

"Active," "Active-Waiting," and "Sustaining" in favor of a single class called "Member." There would continue to be "Student Members." A member would be entitled to attend one performance of each production, vote, and hold office.

An AGAINST vote would retain the current classes of membership.

Celia paces slowly down the house-left aisle, moving her lips silently as she counts bodies, trying to get a sense of whether the vote will take place. AFD bylaws require a quorum of twenty-five. She is dressed for business tonight, not in her denim rehearsal outfit or in the casual polo shirt she wore to last June's fiasco, but in a neat, sedate pant suit. Her husband, Gerry, is here, sitting a few rows back from where Celia and the rest of the board members have planted their belongings. He doesn't ordinarily attend these meetings, but he's an active member, with voting rights, and each side has worked to bring out bodies tonight.

The weather outside is sweet, with a soft chill and the reddening October trees now dimming their wattage as the light slips from the sky; Maple and Academy Streets are quiet and still, and the houses, all with their gracious setbacks from the curb, are curled up like cats for the evening. But inside the old church-turned-clubhouse-cum-theater, frenetic particles seem to be dancing invisibly and spiritedly over the population's heads, which are decidedly weighted toward the gray or graying, the bald or balding. Though everyone is pointedly friendly and carefree while taking seats (each deciding, in swift, scanning calculations, with whom to sit and how to align him- or herself with or apart from apparent factions that may be distributed throughout the rows of seats), awareness of the main course on the evening's agenda has everyone a bit tense. The eight-by-ten ballots flutter white around the room.

At five past seven, Celia stands at the front of the house and taps a pen on the black metal music stand she is using as a podium. "Good evening, everyone," she calls brusquely, and her powerful, blunt cadences carry cleanly through the theater.

"Good evening, Miss Celia," choruses back a little crew, in goofy mock-obedience, and Celia dimples.

She begins the meeting in the normal way, with "Friendly news": mention of the member who's in the national touring company of *Evita* is greeted by applause and a few whistles. Barbara Horrigan, grande dame and longtime chair of the Friendly committee, stands to announce that a former member is now a regular on the television show *Dharma and Greg*; more applause, politer this time, for no one seems to have heard of the woman. People shift in their seats and look over their shoulders to see who's here and who's seated next to whom.

"Before we get to 'the' vote in question," says Celia, with a little wry dimpling, "many of us who have been in and out of the theater over the course of the summer have noticed the incredible landscaping and brickwork that have appeared out front." She holds up a small plaque and reads it aloud; it's a tribute to Molly Trainor and Dave Warnock and all they've done to beautify the grounds of the newly renovated building. Celia walks halfway back in the house to present the plaque and give Molly a kiss. "I don't know how you do it, Molly, with the amount of work you have." Again, everyone applauds, and if it's a little rushed-sounding that's because they all know what's coming next.

Celia introduces the attorney, who stands briefly to look around and wave. "He's here to answer any parliamentary questions, should that become necessary," she explains, to a small stir—this is not a customary measure. "Kelley, do we have a quorum?" Celia calls next.

"We have forty-one," replies Kelley, from the back of the house, where she has numbered each ballot as she's passed it out. Forty-one: not a bountiful turnout, but as large as any they've had recently, and obviously enough to let the vote go forward. First, however, the floor is open to questions, which start out mildly enough.

"What will the number required for a quorum be?"

It will stay the same.

"What happened to the alternative proposal?" (One member at last June's meeting had proposed yet another idea for restructuring the membership categories.)

It was never submitted.

"Will student members still pay a reduced fee?" (Half the regular rate of fifty dollars.)

Yes.

After a few more of these straightforward questions, points of inquiry begin to segue almost imperceptibly to points of opinion.

"Without a separate list for active members," declares Dot Lansil, frowning, "then *everyone* will be getting calls to come down and help with the lights and ushering and whatnot, and people will get annoyed if they only want to come to the shows, and they won't join again next year."

"We have the list down in the greenroom of people who are interested in getting involved in specific areas; we can refer to that when we need to cold-call for volunteers," suggests a man with a British accent.

Barbara Horrigan rises from her seat in the front row, sassy and resplendent in white pants, a turquoise top, and gold earrings shaped like the masks of comedy and tragedy. She angles her body with great stage presence in order to address everybody—the board up front and the membership scattered all around behind her—at once. "My yearbook"—the annual directory, which organizes members by category—"is a bible. To have to come down here to look for a list is an inconvenience."

A warmly and vivaciously pretty young woman, very bright-eyed and plump, stands and gives an alternative view almost apologetically. "A few years ago, when I was trying to recruit ushers for the shows, I wound up calling people from the list of sustaining members, and a number of them were very happy to get the call."

"But did any of them come down?" fires someone from across the house.

"Yes, yes, some did!" confirms the bright-eyed woman, popping up again to respond, her brown hair bobbing with all the activity.

A gray-haired man in a camel cardigan rises. "In a nutshell," he says, projecting his voice beautifully, and with a certain elegant disdain, "what is the reason for this? What is the advantage?"

Celia dimples, and it's not a smiling sort of look but a biting-something-back sort of look. "We've gone over this at the two previous meetings."

"But I still don't get the picture."

She sighs, and launches into a succinct rehash of all the motives and rationales they've been beating into the ground since forever now, it seems.

"The basic thrust," chimes in Nancie Richardson, "is that every member should have the right to vote. You should not have to earn the right by participating in shows."

"Why not? *I* had to earn it," someone grumbles loudly from the back of the house.

A small woman in a plum-colored hat stands. "I still remember when I was elevated to active status and it was announced at the meeting. It was a very special—I felt touched, and proud, that people had recognized my work."

"I still have my letter," someone else agrees. Upon the announcement of a member's elevation, a board member used to read aloud a letter citing all that the member had done to merit the change in status. "It's not about being elite, it's about being special."

"I don't see what's so bad about the word 'elite,'" says another longtime member. "If we have a reputation for being 'the elite,' it's because we put on quality plays; we should be proud of it."

The board treasurer, an affable, beaming sort of man, tries another tack at conveying why the change would be beneficial. "It's really about opening up a whole new world to us of talent, to make us grow and prosper."

"Anyway, the categories wind up being meaningless," says Carolyn Najarian, less affably. "There are people in the directory listed as active members who I've never heard of. And then there are people"—she names a few truly involved, dedicated members—"who have been on the active-waiting list for years. I mean, it's embarrassing!"

"But that's not the fault of the system," Ellen Kazin pipes up sharply. Her short red hair and pert features seem to send sparks, and she stands with dancerly posture. "It's very easy to fix that."

"It's the fault of the board," puts in Lorraine Stevens in her throaty, decisive voice.

"Excuse me, I was speaking. I recognize my voice," Ellen snaps at her old friend, and some laughter ripples as shades of the previous meeting's tensions are recalled. Ellen breaks into a hearty laugh at herself. "It was a real stretch playing a pushy member—I mean mother—in that last production!"

"I'm concerned about changing the structure at a time of fiscal responsibilities and debt," observes a roundish man near the back, in a slightly petulant tone. "The current structure protects us. You can say, 'Oh, goodie, we'll have more ushers!' but it's going to make us more vulnerable."

"I don't like the idea of outsiders coming in and having a vote and making changes overnight," agrees another member.

Stu Kazin rises and retorts with one of his exaggerated philosophical shrugs (plenty of eyebrow, plus a mustache lift). "I've said it before: those are the words of elitists. If you're so worried about the barbarians at the gate, about takeover by some evil empire"—and he puts such a mocking spin on the words that people laugh—"then it's in our best interest to *get* our bargaining base larger, to *give* more members a vote."

Once upon a time, married couples were not allowed to sit simultaneously on the board, the theory being that they would vote as a block. Stu and Ellen Kazin have given the lie to this belief many times over the course of their long involvement with the Friends, and the ease and good grace with which they (frequently) differ is admirable. They chalk it up to their ability to keep things in perspective, not to let AFD issues cloud their relationship outside the club. It's no secret that tonight their votes will cancel each other out.

"I'm just concerned about the lack of interest," says Barbara Horrigan, with feeling. "Look at the number of people here tonight. It's disgraceful." And she sounds truly, deeply disgraced.

"It's the nineties," says Celia gently, or as gently as she is wont to say anything, which is to say frankly and without sarcasm or bite. "People are more transient. We know, we've had a hard time getting people for the past two shows. Our hope is that opening up the membership will help." She is looking out over this rather smallish collection of people giving up their Sunday evening to be here in this windowless room. Every one of them, by definition, is here out of love. Some of them, in their love and nostalgia, are certain that change will hurt the club, detract from it in some possibly inarticulable way. Some of them, in their love and idealism, are certain that change will strengthen it.

In spite of so many ominous remarks and warnings that have buzzed about the theater in the weeks leading to the vote, the prevailing mood seems more of weary disgruntlement, dubious pessimism.

Those who don't want the change worry about the decline of the theater in any case. Numbers are down; camaraderie has waned; the rosiest days are gone for them, and will likely never be equaled. Those who do want the change know that the theater will nevertheless carry on without it, as it has for three-quarters of a century. They expect to see many changes anyway, in the course of their association with the group, and believe that most of them will be for the better.

However much those two views are in opposition to each other, the people themselves are strangely united. When it comes time to work on a production, they will find themselves, like Ellen and Stu Kazin, once again side by side wielding paintbrushes or scripts, sewing needles or gels, their philosophical differences taking a back seat to the cherished, beloved work at hand. All of them have adopted, or chosen to be adopted by, this clubhouse, this old wooden edifice which is the vessel for something utterly unlike anything else they find in the course of their daily lives. In some ways the building, for all its renovations, remains every bit as much the church that it was constructed to be nearly 125 years ago; in some ways this assembly gathered here tonight is a spiritual congregation, a fellowship of kindred souls, each one moved to seek something beyond the worldly.

"Any more questions?" asks Celia, and when, after a beat, no one rushes in, she quickly calls the matter to a vote. Pencils scratch. Two board members move down either aisle, collecting ballots. Now there are voices and laughter, and a moment later Celia taps her pen on the music stand again and says, "Okay. Thank you very much, everybody," and the lawyer slips out, happily unnecessary, and even though no one yet knows how the vote turned out, the mood is almost celebratory, as though the real victory is in having the matter behind them; now they can move on as a group once more.

Carolyn reports on publicity, and Celia on fiscal matters, and David Giagrando on the box office. Doug Desilets, as the new technical director, delivers his report, announcing who's agreed to serve on the stage committee this year, all the while holding three-year-old Jeneane in his arms, her red shoes dangling. Stu names all the people who have agreed to head up AFD's numerous "special" committees for the coming season; Kelley reports on the number of new members; and Don rattles off the names of the house-committee members—"Thanks to these folks, the place is clean and neat,"—and asks people to be better about locking up behind themselves. Downstairs, the night's entertainment—the Liberty Bell Chorus of Sweet Adeline, a cheerful and polished a cappella group of about three dozen mostly middle-aged white women—is audibly warming up.

Just before they perform, the results of the vote are announced. Everything has passed. The membership item, with twenty-four FOR votes and nineteen AGAINST, has the smallest margin, but there it is—a clear majority—and as the lights dim and the Liberty Bells launch into their first multiharmony standard, twenty-four people in the house are delighted with the heralding of a new direction for the Friends.

But after the concert, as everyone begins wandering downstairs for refreshments, Don Richardson makes his way quietly to the front of the house and tells Celia that by his reckoning the motion didn't carry after all. A bylaw change requires a two-thirds majority; they've missed it by four votes. No official correction is announced; more board members need to consult the bylaws and confer with one another before the mistake will be officially recognized and acknowledged. But by the end of the evening word has gotten round to most of the people milling in the lobby around the blondies and punch, and before the lights are turned out for the night, nineteen people are delighted with the news that the Friends is proceeding unaltered.

OCTOBER 5. REHEARSAL.

At the following night's rehearsal, no mention is made of the failed initiative, but an air of gloom prevails. At seven o'clock, Patrick, cocooned in his leather jacket, is reclined stage left on a dingy gold couch (which has finally been deemed too decrepit for the greenroom and is on its way out to the curb for garbage pickup). Celia, at her music stand onstage, looks deeply preoccupied, her dimples as pronounced as if etched in stone, and a wince marking her brow. Kelley leans against the thrust, her stage manager's binder spread open before her. Orea, Tom, Grace, and Carolyn all come down the aisles and pick their ways across rows of seats, as if heeding invisible homing devices; they plant themselves quietly, following the tone that has been set.

Only Jimmy, tall and relaxed in a black-and-tan warm-up suit, is his bounding and exuberant self, walking about, greeting everyone warmly and by name, most often with a cuddle or a kiss as well. Theater has been his milieu, his haven, for over forty years, ever since he played Applegate the Devil in a Christian Youth Organization production of *Damn Yankees* as a teenager in East Boston. He'd once dreamed of going off to New York to try a life on the boards, but caring for a diabetic and manic-depressive mother kept him at home, and kept him from finishing an Emerson College degree in theater arts as well. So theater became his avocation. Rarely does he pick up a book to read that isn't a play; he's even a member of a monthly book club that deals exclusively in scripts, and revels in his work as program manager, collaborating with the play-reading committee to create excellent, exciting slates. But there is nothing he likes so much as being onstage himself, and hearing the quiet of an audience held entirely in his grasp; more than applause, it's that quiet he loves, and the experience of having occasioned that quiet again and again on the Friends' stage makes him inhabit the space with a certain air of friendly entitlement.

Now he ventures over to Patrick, who does not rise from his prone position, and bends down to say something cordial and inquisitive. He is apparently rebuffed. In a moment Jimmy's voice floats very brightly into the house: ". . . Okay, well, I better let you get your rest, then."

Doug is missing entirely tonight, unable to make it. Tall Michelle slips in a little past seven, with her nine-year-old daughter, Gabbie, in tow; Michelle is a single mother, and Gabbie is well accustomed to doing her homework in the greenrooms and lobbies of various community theaters. Teri comes in a half-hour late, pink-cheeked and-nosed, smelling of the woodsmoky evening, apologizing that on Mondays she teaches aerobics and can't get to the theater until seven-thirty. But they haven't even begun yet, and when they do, it's with a lagging sort of energy. Carolyn notes that Celia seemed stressed at work today. Hewlett-Packard is undergoing restructuring, and the latest development was the sudden announcement that morning of voluntary severance packages. Patrick has still not smiled in anyone's presence. His seeming remoteness has unnerved some of the others, and there have even been a few surreptitious inquiries as to whether it's too late to call in one of the other actors, the man who'd been everyone's second favorite for the part.

Rehearsal is plodding and grim. They're all off. The kurogo seem put out each time they are directed to perform what in any other play would be the job of the stage crew. Celia speaks sharply to them when they confuse a cue or a bit of action. They carry on, silent, nonplussed, unsmiling. Jimmy seems to be trying to make up for the general sobriety by clowning.

When Kelley asks Celia, for purposes of recording the exact blocking in her book, "What's he sitting on?" he interjects in a golly-gee voice, "My ass!"

"So it's the low chair?" Kelley attempts to verify a moment later, again speaking to Celia. "The hung-low chair," Jimmy cracks, but no one is joining in, so his cheerfully dopey jokes fall flat, and the mood doesn't shift one bit.

An hour later, when Celia announces a short break, Patrick glides wanly back over to the couch, near the unofficial kurogo camp, whereupon the three women gather near, and Teri presses a motherly hand to his brow and pronounces him feverish. Kelley is informed, and aspirin produced, and Patrick dismissed with many faintly acknowledged wishes to feel better soon, and they try to resume, but now Celia is standing in for Doug, and Grace for Patrick, until Celia says flatly they're not getting accomplished what she'd hoped. "I'm not very happy right now," she adds, unnecessarily.

The intensity with which she works makes her look often as though her tooth hurts: she cups her face with one finger at the temple, a row of knuckles by her mouth, one tip of one fingernail resting on a tooth. It's a sheltering kind of pose; she appears cryptic and learned and pained all at once. It's broken often by her need to move—either into the scene at hand, in order to manipulate one of the actors physically or demonstrate a stance, or else out into the far reaches of the theater, in order to see and hear the thing from someplace afar, or simply to pace. At times she most resembles a caged tiger with a toothache. Really it's her stomach that hurts, though.

She's skipped supper again; no one here knows it, but she's been having chronic abdominal pains, and they seem to be worsening.

Even though they are not scheduled to be off book for more than two weeks from tonight, Jimmy, who has by far the most lines in the play, is already working hard on getting his part memorized; as the evening progresses, his calls for "Line!" become increasingly frequent, and are often accompanied by a rather theatrical gesture: he whacks his thigh, or slaps his forehead, or clutches several times at the air. Eventually he goes back to using his little pale-aqua script. Grace, by his side as Song for the moment, repeatedly snaps her gum in a delicate, rhythmic way. Carolyn changes into pumps to rehearse her pin-up-girl scene. Tom, just finishing a scene, slips offstage and takes a seat again in the dim house. Everyone appears to be treading on eggshells, as if informed by an unspoken awareness of Celia's very high expectations and her displeasure at anything that falls short.

The tension that has established itself so early as being an inevitable component of *M. Butterfly* rehearsals cannot be attributed entirely to the nature of the script. As many members who have been involved in all manner of AFD plays over the decades are quick to clarify, just because a play's content is heavy doesn't mean the rehearsal process has to be. It's more a function, they say, of the director and how she or he feels about community theater. Just as Celia, in her president's hat, has been criticized for treating AFD more like a business than a club, in her director's hat she is sometimes accused of treating the aesthetics too seriously, not focusing enough on people's need to enjoy themselves.

But for Celia, and for many of the people who rave about working with her, the enjoyment is all *bound up* in the intensity, in the hard work and the hard-won accomplishment. Even some of the *Butterfly* cast members who will eventually refer to her as a "hard-ass," and "the toughest, least warm-and-fuzzy director I've ever worked with," will say in the same sentence that they've never before learned so much about acting, and about making meaning of a script on every level. That *M. Butterfly* will go to competition this spring is not incidental to both the felt challenge and the extra tension accompanying it.

The issue of competition tends to split people into camps, with one group more interested in having the rehearsal period yield a sense of belonging and joyful collaboration, and the other more interested in having it yield a fine production with the ability to touch an audience. But both ideals, in the end, are about using theater to make an impact on a community, whether it's the community of volunteers who make up the theater, or the community at large in which the theater exists. And most shows probably manage to do some of each. It's not an on-off switch but a spectrum of possibilities, and community theaters can slide along the spectrum from show to show, continually crafting and recrafting their own identity and purpose. No community is a fixed thing, baked in the kiln and done. Communities live and breathe and are constantly in flux, and no attempt to define them can ever be more than a quick-frozen slice, snatched from one moment, already less than the whole evolving story.

Gabbie, homework done, pads down the aisle in Kelly-green sandals and helps herself to a mini chocolate-chip cookie from the plastic container Grace brought in. Celia, standing above at her music stand, turns at the slight rustle, then breaks unexpectedly into the softest, warmest beam; children do this to her, melt her. Gabbie, self-possessed and moon-faced with earlobe-length hair, regards the director and smiles back in only a qualified sort of way. Celia grins at the honesty of that and swivels loosely back to the actors onstage. It's Tom and Jim again, doing one of their male-bonding scenes. The feeling of the grin carries over. "All right, guys, don't get shticky on me," she barks, but with a lift of good humor in her voice, and then she sets off on one of her paces round the house. "You're better actors than that!"

A hundred times a night the dynamic can shift, the players all like living kaleidoscope pieces, clicking together and apart unpredictably, forming pattern after pattern as they move slowly forward in the surprising and beguiling way of actual life.

Seven

Behind the Scenes

OCTOBER 8. FOUR WEEKS, ONE DAY, TILL OPENING NIGHT.

At Thursday night's rehearsal Patrick smiles for the first time, and it's as though someone has taken the kaleidoscope and given the knob a mighty twist, and everyone laughs, delighted, because his smile is so delighted and lovely, and all the colors for a moment are orange and yellow and rose. He is still on the quiet side in general tonight, and dressed, as usual, in gently formal attire—light-gray trousers, belted, and a blue-gray plaid shirt with the sleeves rolled up—but his manner overall seems lighter, both between scenes and during, as he has begun to inhabit Song somewhat more openly and playfully. When everyone else's laughter makes him throw back his own head and laugh, he looks suddenly fourteen years old. Or eight. He looks as if he should still have baby teeth, his laugh is so sweetly gleeful and unchecked. And everyone breathes a little easier; maybe what earlier looked like aloofness was only shyness plus being under the weather. Maybe now some chemistry will blossom between the leads.

As for Jim, he is working hard, still trying valiantly to get off book early in the game, which effort leads him often to cry, "Shit! I'm sorry," and punch himself in the thigh. He is working hard, too, on establishing connections with the others in the cast. Every evening, every person he sees receives a special greeting, each time with a new rush of bounding energy, a "*Hey*, you!" as often as not accompanied by a hug or a kiss, and always a smile which makes his whole craggy face light up. He is just self-deprecating enough to broadcast the message that he's a *regular* guy, affable, approachable, no prima donna. Something about his Boston accent, too, seems quintessentially *regular*, and therefore cozy, inviting. A hundred times over the next few weeks, Celia will correct his speech, barking out from the back of the house the standard pronunciation of a word from which he has subtracted the letter "r," and every time it happens a couple of other cast members will smile at each other; it's endearing, after all.

Celia roves the theater, vibrantly in her element. She calls people "honey," "friend," "kiddo," "sweetie," "gentlemen," "ladies," "dancers," "you guys." She curses easily and meaningfully, to indicate both extreme pleasure and displeasure, as if in this environment a kind of *de rigueur* primal coarseness is unleashed. She paces and rubs her facial bones and bites her blood-red nails. Somewhere out in the dim aisles of the house, she'll drop suddenly to the floor, experiment with a reclining pose, then leap up again and transfer herself to the stage, where she'll insert herself, mid-scene, and demonstrate the position for one of the actors to take. So much has been worked out ahead of time— down to the exact line on which an actor is to establish eye contact— but she cannot be still, cannot stop tinkering, improving, perfecting. Everything she does is physical, even when all she is doing is listening, even when all she is doing is thinking, as if her cognitive wheels turn more noticeably and kinetically than other people's. And as much as she interacts freely with the actors and production staff, she gives the impression of essentially working on a huge solitary project. Sometimes, when she inserts herself onstage mid-scene and manipulates one of the actors, or uses her own body to work out a piece of blocking, it's as if she's literally strategizing a life-size game of chess, with playing pieces that just happen to live and breathe.

At a point when many directors might be content just to have their cast begin to learn the blocking and experiment with characterization, Celia is precise about demanding several things at once: intricate intellectual understanding of the scene, perfectly timed speeches to the blocking, the shedding of regional accent and personal shtick, the picking up of cues cleanly and without messy seconds of pause. When at one point she is giving notes and Jimmy murmurs something to Kelley, Celia cuts quickly and evenly to the chase.

"Are you listening?"

"Yes," says Jim, charming, contrite, slipping into the role of a chastened but essentially doted-upon schoolboy.

"Okay. Why do I feel like I'm losing control?"

"Because I was distracting him," says Kelley. *Mea culpa.*"

"Okay. Jim, you're going to move from platform six to four to five. . . ."

The whole exchange is relatively easy, but broadcasts a strong message, and the reactions of the cast, like the tiniest rustling of leaves, make clear that some sort of wind has just swept through. The message is plain: Celia won't tolerate the least loss of control. Her tone was not harsh but it wasn't tempered with humor, either; she was perfectly serious, even though Jimmy, who is after all the lead, a fellow board member, and an AFD member of very long standing, was hardly cutting up. Another director might have ignored the murmuring. Not Celia.

At this point in the rehearsal process, everything is trust—all any of them is standing on, the thinnest translucent sheet of trust. The actors must trust each other to be good, to support them onstage, to be strong enough to make the reality of the world they are creating hold solid. And they must trust Celia, her vision and her method, her game plan and her recruits; they cannot follow her direction without deciding to trust her not to let them look like fools. Celia, in turn, has to trust not only the cast—with everything from interpreting the characters as she desires to memorizing their lines—but the production crew as well. She has to believe that Doug's gorgeous model of a set will in a few weeks stand reproduced, full-size and functional, on this stage. She has to believe that Molly's sumptuous costuming ideas will come to pass as actual fabrics, that each stitch will really get sewn. She has to believe that each team member will get her or his job done as planned.

No matter how much control a community-theater director might ideally like to have over a production, it is the nature of theater that volunteer hands, amateur hands, must do the work, and that these hands are also busy with daily life. No written contracts have been signed, no cash exchanged, no professional reputations put at stake to help ensure that the promises are kept, the goals met. All they can do for the moment is skate along on that sheer, fine surface of trust, waiting for a firmer base to form beneath it.

The following week, on a fickle, hazy day when the sun can't decide whether to hide or to shine, Molly Trainor takes an official vacation day. She gets three weeks of vacation a year from her job as associate product-manager for a company that makes blood pumps for open-heart surgery and emergency heart-lung bypass machines. She will spend nearly two of those weeks on preparations for *M. Butterfly*. (She already took off last Friday to research kurogo dancers at the library, on the Internet, in various Harvard Square bookstores, and at a Japanese import store in Porter Square—all to no avail.) A great number of the key figures involved in the production will wind up taking some time off from their day jobs. The amount of work is too great to be crammed entirely into weekends. Molly knew full well when she accepted the role of costumer that she would necessarily be making this sort of sacrifice; it was one of the reasons she weighed the decision so exactingly.

Molly and her husband, Dave Warnock, live in a one-story house in Malden, thirty minutes north of the theater, with two large cats, a raucous, rambling garden, and a jade-painted picket fence. The entire basement has become Molly's workshop, teeming with dress models, fabrics, costume racks, washing machine and dryer, ironing board, work tables, sewing machines, tubs for dyes, endless cupboards and shelves and bins filled with buttons, sewing patterns, fabric paints, scads of trim. The cats pick through it with catly bemusement. They and the radio keep Molly company while she works.

But today is for foraging, for hunting and gathering, a day when luck had better be with her—or, as Molly puts it, a day when she must throw herself on the mercy of the gods of the closet. She's been allotted five hundred dollars to costume the cast, a sum that she knows from experience will be wont to disappear as quickly as a lump of sugar in hot tea. In professional theater, assuming anything resembling a real budget, the costumer wouldn't be remotely so dependent on the whims of fanciful deities. On the other hand, the financial limitations of most community theaters are part of what makes costuming a show there uniquely challenging and satisfying. At best, it's like composing a poem within the rigid, formalist confines of a sonnet or a pantoum. Of course, at worst, it's like banging one's head against a wall. Molly drains her mug of ginger tea, pardons herself to the cream-colored cat, who has been using a library book on Japanese dress as a throne, and gets in her Toyota wagon parked out front.

Her first stop is the library, where she returns the book, one of several she's consulted in her research thus far. She often begins her research a year in advance of the production date, and has accumulated quite a library of her own at home, with books on theater, design, sewing, and history currently overflowing the bookshelves in two rooms of their small house. Next she's off to Cambridge, to Central Square, which has the happy distinction of being home not only to Pearl Paint, the area's largest artists'-supply store, but also to a handful of eclectic shlock-and-dreck discount shops, and to Yoshinoya Inc., a Japanese-import store. These shops constitute only the first major stop of the day; as ever, there's much to do, and scant time. Molly guns it a little as she drives down from Malden, speaking with gentle impatience to the cars on the road around her: "Hello? Come on. Yes, you, honey. What are you doing? Thank you very much. Hello, wake up."

She scoots expertly into a rare parking space off the avenue and, grabbing her costume bible (a fat white binder containing script, measurements sheets, contact sheets, general calendar, and "French scenes," which are basically a breakdown of blocking within scenes that lets her know exactly who's onstage at any given moment, how much or how little time characters have between entrances, and whether she'll therefore need to slit any suits up the back and apply Velcro, etc.), she walks briskly to Pearl Paint and straight downstairs to the cavernous craft department. She's searching primarily for cheap white face masks, which Barbara Horrigan will make up in the style of actors in the Peking Opera. The sales help, who all seem to be about sixteen years old and sport multiple piercings and blackish lipstick, apologize dolefully and tell her to come back closer to Halloween, but Molly does find some iridescent cord, perfect for making the tassels that she wants to put on the kurogo headdresses. Pearl or purple? Or orange? She cups the different colors of looped cord, brushes them with the back of her hand. Pearl. Done.

Molly herself is a pleasantly arresting amalgam of artist and pragmatist. There is her rather elfin cap of poppy-bright hair, offset by the sensible discs of her neat round glasses; there are her dancingly bright blue eyes, offset by the measured purse of her lips as she calculates costs and yards and such. Today she is wearing a red tank top, jeans, and sneakers. Her earrings are long metal rectangles with holes punched out. She has a white pencil stuck behind her ear. Her business side comes across in her clean, take-charge manner, in the thoroughness of her paperwork and research, in the way she has a tendency to refer to the audience as "the customer," even in the rather flat, matter-of-fact cadences of her speech.

But there is nothing pragmatic about the devotional, near-obsessive manner in which she throws herself into her theater work. Once, for a production of *Les Liaisons Dangereuses*, she built the corsets from muslin and boning, just to see if she could. If a costume is meant to be weathered, she'll weather it: drive over it with her car, leave it out in the sun, stain it, throw it through the wash a couple of dozen times. People who've worked costume crew with her whisper about her passionate perfectionism: whereas other community-theater designers might slap and baste garments together (after all, who's going to get close enough to inspect a hem?), Molly works overtime to render couture-worthy stitches. For her, the integrity of a costume is part of the overall integrity of a production; like any other design element, costumes elicit emotional responses from the audience, and contribute to the actors' kinesthetic sense of their characters.

Molly grew up in a one-room house on the South Shore, wanting to become an artist. Her mother did paste-up work at the local newspaper, but also made her own greeting cards, and a four-story shingled dollhouse for Molly's birthday, and fantastic Halloween costumes for the children every year. Her father did bits of what seemed like everything. He was trained in forestry, taught math, worked as a tool-and-dye cutter and then as a stock analyst—but at the same time he used to make shoes for the family in his basement workshop, and raise cows and chickens, and weave his own cloth, and carve nudes out of blocks of wood (so many that they were used all over the house, as doorstops, to prop up windows, hold cookbooks open, etc.)—so that, between the two, Molly's childhood was informed by what she calls an "undertone of the aesthetic in everyday life."

In 1969, upon graduating from high school, she studied painting and drawing at the Museum School in Boston, but withdrew after a short while, frustrated with what felt like the clumsily anarchic, naïvely self-celebratory culture of the program at that time—and privately fearful of being mediocre, besides. She worked at a bookstore, and then, driven largely by economic realities, trained to become a profusionist, someone who works the cardiopulmonary machine during surgery. It was in this capacity, while working at Massachusetts General Hospital, that she met Dave, and it was through him, years later, that she was drawn into theater, tapped to costume a play he was directing for another community group. With that first play a floodgate opened, and something enormous and unstoppable swept Molly loose from her moorings. Now, fifteen years later, her work in theater—her basement life, as it were—is threatening to move right upstairs to ground level, and she is—slowly, scarily—beginning to contemplate drafting a real business plan with a colleague and having a go at making the leap from amateur to professional theater.

For now, though, it's the likes of Maxi's Ninety-Nine Cent Store for Molly, not that she minds. She peruses the aisles with an open mind—briefly lulled by a bin of plastic flowers; amused by the display of rubbery horror masks ("I don't think these would quite do. It'd be a whole different show," she murmurs); pleased with a big box of $1.99 Chinese slippers, from which she rummages pairs in the right sizes for Patrick and Little Michelle (she verifies the fits by holding them next to actual sole tracings she made and stuck in the costume bible); and all-out delighted by the jet-black super jumbo braids hanging near the door, made in China with "100% synthetic hair." "I wonder how long they are. . . ." At ninety-nine cents apiece, they ought to be perfect for adorning the Peking Opera headdresses.

Around the corner, at Yoshinoya Inc., Molly finds a few of the items she's looking for (toe socks, fans, Japanese sandals), but all are too expensive. Are the gods with her today? They don't feel entirely remote, but neither are they quite lined up in her corner. The pearl cord and jumbo braids go into the car, and Molly heads off for a fabric warehouse in Chelsea. She never remembers exactly how to get there, but always manages to feel her way along the puddly, potholed, one-way streets that make up this anonymous gray industrial area on the edge of Route 1.

Sure enough, she zeroes in successfully on one completely indistinct building, goes in through the heavy metal door, and finds herself on familiar ground, the territory of Barry-David Fabrics, an old and well-circulated secret among community-theater designers and no-frills fashionistas both. It's a warren of rooms lit by wan fluorescent lights, with portions of the ceiling and walls and floor missing. Pieces of cardboard are laid over holes in the linoleum floor. Pieces of ceiling panels hang in shreds like kudzu. The bolts of fabric stand so densely, one nearly has to bushwhack to get by. Here treasures lie within reach to the expert eye. Molly's gaze starts working the rooms with uncanny efficiency; without a little strategy, a whole day could easily be squandered here. "Do you take checks?" she asks the small, middle-aged man moving among the boxes and loose bolts. "American?" he asks, with a vaguely comic lilt. "Because I once took a beating on a check from Vietnam." She smiles. A trio of Portuguese women comes in, and he goes to assist.

Molly fingers the fabrics, plain and textured, cottons and polys and blends. The formaldehyde commonly used to finish fabrics at the factory begins to trigger her allergies. She presses on, throat itching. There are literally hundreds of bolts of white and off-white, and she lingers for a long time over these, weighing the differences, seeing the show in her mind's eye. She decides on a sheer eggshell cotton with sizing, and the man hefts it back into another branch of the warren, where a second worker loads the bolt onto a huge industrial rewind-machine that rolls and measures at the same time. Molly chats with them, obviously and animatedly interested in the machine, which is half a century old, and in the men and their business and the whole obscure world of this place, so eccentric and dusty and commanding.

She barely has time to glance at the most amusing offerings (cloth printed with hot dogs, Monopoly money, stethoscopes, pink hippos), dedicated now to searching for the right red for Song's initial appearance. There are silky cherries and crimsons, brick-colored corduroy, a ketchupy poly. She pulls out a bolt of fire-engine-red twill to examine in the light, trying to gauge how it will read onstage, how it will absorb light, how it will move. She likes the color but not the texture. Nevertheless, she asks to take a small sample of that one. In the front of the shop, embroidered ribbons and tassels and such overflow from a metal storage unit, and she fingers some of these lovingly. A beautiful green-and-bone brocade catches her eye; she's impelled to splurge on five yards of it for an obi. In the end, all she buys is that, plus thirty yards of the white sized cotton to make banners and the giant fans that are part of the stage set.

She stashes the receipts in her costume bible, stashes the fabric in the back seat, and, though it's one-forty-five and she hasn't brought a snack, she heads straight off to Boston, to Chinatown. Far from slowing down, she's moving faster now, aware of time seeming to slip away more quickly as the sun begins its descent. The air has grown drier, more sprightly and cool, and Molly clips along the narrow, winding streets, stopping in stores and popping out again without allowing herself the luxury of really browsing. She grows more focused as the afternoon wears thinner, zipping down aisles, scanning left and right, fingering the odd piece of merchandise, moving on. She checks the notions stores for Chinese slippers and fans, the fabric stores for reds. All around her, businesspeople and mothers with strollers and tourists and students and delivery-truck drivers are going on about their real-life, daily business, and the sun shines in vivid patches over the buildings and through the alleyways and the small branches of sidewalk trees, and Molly goes searching, searching for the perfect red for Song Liling to wear in her opening scene, and the perfect fan, decorated on both sides, large and bright and cheap enough to fit both the budget and the Arlington stage.

Chinatown abuts the theater district, and Molly's last stop is at Boston Costume, a big, rather glitzy store across Beech Street, with a brash funhouse air. Masks galore. Lady Di masks, Nelson Mandela masks, gorillas and monsters and severed-neck masks, feathered masks and sequined masks, glitter covered, Day-Glo and fluorescent masks. None to fit the bill. The only plain white masks are full-face, instead of the forehead-to-nose, Lone Ranger style that they had discussed. Mayre, in particular, had been worried about the danger of dancing in masks—down the curve of the ramp, no less. Molly tries one on and regards her blank white face in the countertop mirror. She tries to evaluate how freely she can breathe through the nostril slits, and how easily she can see through the eye holes, and how readily her breath forms into condensation on the interior wall of the thing, and then goes ahead and buys four. Perhaps they can be cut.

And now it's time to collect her car from the parking garage and head home. If the gods of the closet didn't exactly loft her high on their shoulders today, neither did they desert her. Masks, Chinese slippers, tassel cord, fabric—the rear of the wagon is gratifyingly cluttered with the early materials of construction; she has embarked. Tomorrow she'll be back at her day job, but right now her costume-designer brain is clicking, turning over the objects she's found, piecing them together with ideal mates she has yet to discover. Today may not have been a revel at the shore, not a vacation well spent by other people's estimations, but it was the vacation day of Molly's choosing, and she comes out nourished by it, sustained.

OCTOBER 12. THREE WEEKS AND FOUR DAYS UNTIL OPENING.

At the next rehearsal, Patrick grows shorter and Celia and Mayre are beside themselves with glee. It's a dance rehearsal; everyone has the night off but the kurogo and Song, and they spend the better part of the first hour warming up and listening to Mayre talk about Chinese opera. In the play, Song is a star of the Peking Opera—which has a real-life tradition of men playing female characters and sometimes, as with Song, extending their feminine role-play to life offstage—and at various points in the script, scenes from the opera are re-created. Mayre clarifies first that they will be striving for an *idea* of Chinese opera; that she herself has no training in the art, other than what she has gathered from books. She has brought in a couple of these, having picked them up at the Drama Book Store on a recent trip to New York. All through the rehearsal process, people will continue to bring in books, to share their personal research with the others. Celia has brought in a few more of her own tonight; later someone will plunk in the greenroom for general perusal a book on the real-life transgender spy story on which the play has been loosely based; Doug will share his daughter's Chinese picture book that inspired part of the design element; Little Michelle will bring in an anthology of short plays all dealing with the duality of being Asian-American.

One of Mayre's books, a thin volume on the Peking Opera, is loaded with pictures, and the dancers—Teri and Orea and Little Michelle, as well as Patrick—still stretching out their hamstrings on the floor of the stage, pore over its pages, studying the masks and makeup, the fans and swords, the flexed feet and hands, the costumes and headdresses. In particular, they examine photos of a real-life male opera star famous for portraying female characters and for maintaining a female appearance offstage. They scrutinize pictures showing the audience pressed close to the stage, with their own cups of tea resting right on the apron. They study the pictures of musical instruments, too: a *pipa*, or Chinese lute; a moon guitar; a clapper; drums; a two-string bowed fiddle; and a seven-string zither. The extreme foreignness of the Peking Opera is transmitted through these images in a way that words alone cannot convey.

"The movements and music will be unusual to you," advises Mayre. She speaks in a kindergarten teacher's voice, patient, with round, warm syllables deliberately enunciated. "It'll seem weird. It's not how we normally move in this culture. In the end, with the makeup, costumes, music, you will have really shed anything Western in your movement, facial expression, affect, everything."

Celia interjects. "You guys open the play. You're going to signal right away to this audience in Arlington, Mass., that this is something different. We want them to know right away this is a Chinese play."

And they practice walking then, because it's a special walk they have to learn first, with the knees always bent, and the shoulders and hips quite still, and the gait tiny and smooth, so that in their rehearsal skirts they seem almost to glide across the stage, to and fro, again and again, some more smoothly than others, and all at different rates, with the result that they look like contestants in a strange relay race, or ducks in a shooting gallery. And this is when Mayre tiptoes to the edge of the stage and whispers to Celia, standing below, "Are you watching 'em?" Celia nods. "Watch *him*," hisses Mayre. They watch Patrick and are psyched. His physicality is radically altered. He looks both smaller and more feminine. Then Mayre has him begin moving his arms as he walks, gesturing fluidly out to the side, folding and unfolding the sleeves of his celery rehearsal kimono around his forearms, and Celia talks to herself in a private register, her voice ringing with vindication: "Yeah, see, he has beautiful arms, very graceful. Very graceful."

What drew her to cast Patrick in the first place was her sense of his intelligence. She often speaks of how much easier it is for her to direct an intelligent actor, by which she means an actor who can approach the material intellectually, and from the first audition, before she knew he was an MIT grad, or that he now works as an analyst for an economics think tank in Cambridge, or that he is a classically trained singer with experience speaking seven languages, she knew that he was bright in a way that would make all the difference to the role. What she did not know was whether his instincts would develop symbiotically with her vision, and what she still does not know, but has hope in, is that he will come to connect emotionally with Jim and the rest of the ensemble. Tonight that promise seems high.

Mayre presses PLAY on her little boom box, and the tape of the Broadway production's music begins. Bells shiver and drums cleanly snap, and something almost whiny and piercing begins a plaintive, kneading melody, and the dancers improvise, working to shed their Western movements and feel their way into something foreign. Although Michelle's family moved to the States when she was only a baby, she grew up exposed to Filipino culture and took Filipino folk dance in college; perhaps for this reason, or perhaps just because she is naturally graceful, she adapts to the movements beautifully. Orea, at forty-two and doing her first play since high school, is more halting in her efforts at first, but her concentration is intense, almost childlike in its earnestness, and soon she is walking the walk, too. Teri, the aerobics instructor, has the most trouble integrating the stylized movements into her own tall, athletic frame; she is the eldest and most experienced performer of the three, but will have to work the hardest at separating herself from her Western skin.

Patrick is the one Mayre and Celia can't take their eyes from.

"Look how short he looks!" whispers Mayre. "No one's gonna believe he's six two."

Celia grins. When the music ends, she delivers the ultimate compliment. "Patrick, you were at least a foot smaller."

He smiles modestly.

"This is good for me!" says Celia, and her relief is so bluntly evident he tips his head back and laughs, a happy waterfall of sound. It's infectious, not just his laugh but also the momentum of Celia's and Mayre's pleasure at what they see taking shape onstage. From scratch these actors are carving out personas, beginning to submerge themselves into another way of being; the feel of something foreign has already been evoked, and in itself this has transformative power and weight.

Patrick was born and grew up in Houston, the oldest child of traditionally conservative Taiwanese parents, a mechanical engineer and a computer finance expert. Neither parent encouraged him to find a life in the arts. They saw no need, purpose, or justification for it, and made their disapproval understood through a quiet, blanket omission of support for Patrick's theater work. He had to go all the way to Argentina, where he was a fifteen-year-old exchange student, in order to fall in love with performing. With his host family, who were musical, he discovered that he could sing. Patrick, his host brother, and another young man wound up touring the country in a pickup truck, performing Argentinean folk songs in discos, cafés, small performance halls; the following summer, he went back and toured again, this time in a political play with a group of Argentinean students. Back in Texas, he eschewed high-school plays and gravitated toward theater work with small, experimental, semiprofessional groups, to the bewilderment if not outright displeasure of his family. He had tasted something novel and found it essential to his diet.

Patrick's love of performing doesn't approach his love of the *idea* of theater. His curiosity, his marveling excitement over the whole concept of people getting together with the full knowledge that what they're going to see is not real, and yet delivering themselves to the material, trying to believe it anyway—it is this that compels him more than anything. His pleasure in theater is as much philosophical, even quizzical, as it is visceral and ego-bound.

He and his partner, Brett Conner, live on the ground floor of a beautifully kept Victorian house in Cambridge, where they host a Monday-night theater group of readings and discussions with theater friends. With Brett, who is making a go at a career in theater, Patrick has started a small production company, Pet Brick Productions, whose first project, they hope, will be an evening of Beckett. Patrick has recently become a board member at the New School of Music in Cambridge, where he has sung as a featured soloist and directed musical revues of the compositions of Kurt Weill and Leonard Bernstein. He has worked with the Theater Offensive in Boston, a gay-and-lesbian theater group, and has tried his hand at playwriting, as well as light verse. With such sophisticated and far-reaching artistic interests, Patrick might stand out in any community-theater group, even if he did not also give the impression of constantly reserving a piece of himself from being swept into the moment, of considering events from a gently musing distance. Such qualities lend him at times a lofty, also an angelic, air, and it is this, more than his nonmembership status at the Friends, his ethnicity, age, or geographic background, that renders him to some degree a perpetual outsider. Even as his friendships with cast and crew members progress, he will remain so, forever standing slightly apart, one foot in the margin, head cocked in contemplative regard.

Now Celia disappears downstairs while Mayre begins to construct, with the dancers, the bones of the actual choreography. The kurogo will appear one at a time through the sliding doors at the top of the ramp, glide to their various places onstage, and freeze as Song appears, framed by the same half-circles of the sliding doors, and performs ritualized motions with her arms. It is an awkward process, with Mayre trying to feel her way through what is essentially a simulation of Peking Opera choreography. "Thank you for hanging in there," she says at one point. "This is not typical of how you choreograph a piece, and I appreciate your input."

When Celia returns, it is with props for the dancers, scavenged from the costume room: a cane for Teri, in lieu of the sword she will eventually wield; a length of yellow chiffon for Orea, which will be replaced by a pink silk swath; a clutch of magenta feathers for Michelle, standing in for what will later be two gold folding fans. At first the props are things to fool with. Teri clowns with her cane, spinning it like a baton major. Orea gyrates a little with her scarf. Michelle can barely practice with her ersatz fans, so busy is she trying to keep from tripping over the hem of her assigned rehearsal skirt. She finally just steps out of it and dons her own skirt from home, fastening it around the hips instead of the waist in order to approximate the desired length. But they finish all this business, and Mayre coaches them to allow more stillness in their faces—"Like Patrick, watch him"—and more controlled movements, more precision of placement—"Less frantic, less American." Then she presses the button on the boom box and they take it again from the top; the props seem to help them move deeper into the sense of it all, and they focus and glide and rotate their wrists and wield these totems, looking more and more swept into the tableaux they are creating.

Without knowing it, they are learning to question the obvious. They are dancing their way into something foreign, something imagined, and such a journey affords an opportunity to regard the familiar with a fresh eye. All successful theater creates this situation. But staging a production that deals explicitly with the otherness of a foreign culture heightens the response. The theater is filled with a presence that did not enter through any door; it was born here, onstage, in a collaboration of bodies, ideas, music, movement, images. The materialization of something palpably *other* charges the house with a sense of wonder and excitement. Or, as Celia puts it, whispering to herself as the keening notes of the *pipa* unspool and she watches the dancers glide again through the choreography, transformatively cleansed of affect, elegantly brandishing their props (she may be exacting, but when she's pumped she's pumped), "This show is going to kick ass."

OCTOBER 13. THREE WEEKS AND THREE DAYS LEFT. SET CONSTRUCTION.

The next night, Tuesday, the actors stay home but the theater is not dark. Tuesday and Wednesday nights, and Saturday mornings, are always reserved at AFD for set construction. This happens on every show like clockwork, and like clockwork on every show it is the same small band of techies who show up. That the band is small and its members are virtually identical on every occasion is both a sore point among them and a point of closeness and pride.

On this night, Don Richardson is the first to arrive. He leans against the cloaked baby grand that resides in the wing for a little standing-up supper of takeout Chinese food. While he eats from the carton, in comes George Rogers, the septuagenarian psychology professor who lives in the neighborhood and joined AFD a few weeks after his retirement. The rest of the core group trickles in soon after: Dennis Fitzpatrick, who heads the English department for Belmont Public Schools; Florence Gedzium, a mechanical and computer engineer; and Tim McMahon, a retired supervisor for the Federal Aviation Administration. Other people float in from time to time on other nights; there is a psychiatric nurse who manages AFD's paint shop, a retired architect who helps with construction and also runs sound, another computer engineer who lends his hand in every which way, from set construction to lighting and sound design to serving on committees of the board to acting onstage. These and other faces appear from time to time, but the core group has consisted, for the past decade or so, of the above-named five people, who show up three times a week as much out of fondness for each other's company as for love of the theater. They come together, one woman and four men, from their disparate backgrounds, to use power tools and sweat and ingenuity, to chat and laugh and construct a small world that will exist for a few weeks and get torn apart again, and they meet on a kind of common ground detached from everything else: from the rest of their daily lives and from the rest of the theater, too, for they are, this thickly joined and quirky minority, not exactly ostracized but largely ignored, or unnoticed, by the rest of the Friends.

Not on the face of it. On the face of it, everyone remembers at certain appropriate moments to acknowledge the hard work of the techies, without whom no show could be produced and the theater could not function, blah blah blah. But the perception within the core group, whose members are, in varying degrees, notably unshy about voicing this, is that by and large such mentions are lip service. This needn't be the case. Some community theaters require every cast member, as a condition upon accepting a role, to put in a given amount of time on set construction. At AFD it is a source of pride that actors are never asked to pitch in this way. The organization's tradition of being technically self-sufficient frees actors from ever having to pick up a hammer or paintbrush, and it's widely held that AFD appeals to actors for precisely this reason. Some of the overworked, undervalued techies, however, argue that the whole essence of community theater is pitching in, and that requiring the so-called artistic component to help construct sets would only strengthen their investment in and commitment to the group, not to mention furthering their appreciation of the larger artistic process.

Techies used to hold somewhat higher status at AFD than they do today. Once, they took their own curtain call after performances. Once, their pictures were taken and mounted in the lobby alongside the cast photos. Once, the traditional closing-night festivity was called a "production party" instead of a "cast party," and the cast presented gifts of appreciation not only to the director and more visible or higher-status production-staff members, but also to the techies. These customs have fallen largely by the wayside. Such is the lack of real regard for the work of the techies, even among board members, that meetings of the board and its various subcommittees are almost invariably scheduled for Tuesday or Wednesday evenings, even if that precludes participation by techies or takes them away from an evening's work of set construction.

So the bonds among the five are tight and somewhat textured by a shared sense of non-grata status, which leads to a certain amount of in-joking, a certain defensive pride, a certain protective warmth toward each other and salty humor aimed outside their small circle. That their circle is so small is cause for concern, as they are sharply aware, not least because they reflect the age demographic of the larger membership, all of them falling between fifty and seventy-six years old—heavy lifting, operating certain tools, and bounding up and down ladders are no longer as easy for some of them as before. If the problem of attracting new, younger members has become critical to the theater in general, it's that much more urgent among the technical crew, who are already stretched thin. It's a dilemma that goes unresolved. One particularly devoted techie did throw in the towel a few years back, finally fed up with the lack of respect and support; he no longer comes down on crew nights. The others more or less alternate between advocating bluntly and often rather testily for their interests in the presence of the general membership, and going about their business with a shrugging, good-natured dedication in the relative invisibility of set-construction nights.

Work begins this night with a parsing of a set of instructions left by Doug Desilets about a change in his set design. Doug, like a lot of designers, tries to be on hand while his set is being built, to help with the construction as well as to clear up any misunderstandings about just what exactly the thing is supposed to look like in real life, but now that he's accepted a role in the play as well, he's finding himself more swamped than usual, and won't be able to make it tonight. The change refers to something that seemed to work beautifully with the little bits of foam core Doug had cut out to make the model, but which doesn't translate so fluidly to actual sheets of plywood several feet long. The note says that the highest segment of the ramp now ought to be split in two, with the first of these no longer sloping but parallel to the ground, in order to make the angle less treacherous for the actors as they round the corner.

Much deliberation follows as they discuss what exactly Doug means and how to carry it out. There's a great deal of head scratching, and mentions of algebra and geometry, and calculus, too, and everybody takes turns flourishing a pencil and sketching things out on the back of Doug's note. The model is toted over and consulted, and everyone weighs in again, except for Dennis, who declares, "I'm

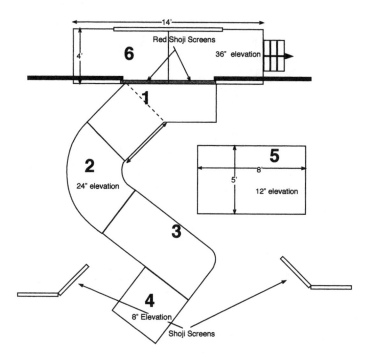

an English teacher," by way of excuse. But when a consensus has been reached, in an unhurried, democratic way, they all move into action equally, easily, as if the tasks were prerehearsed.

What's sort of remarkable is that there's no leader, no lieutenant giving the final opinion or approval. Even though Don in many ways ranks highest in the group—or could be expected to, being a current board member, the official set technician for *M. Butterfly,* the most senior AFD member present, as well as of course bearing that unofficial "godfather" title—he never asserts himself as such. The degree of collaboration is almost uncanny. No one issues directions. With the barest of utterings, they all move into operation, picking up tools, assigning themselves roles in the overall effort to get the ramp built. The distribution of work seems to occur on a subverbal level, as if they were honeybees dancing the route to pollen, or acting students performing a mute ensemble exercise. Tools are located in the shop, which is really just a corridor running below the wing, connecting the house to the backstage stairs, and periodically someone will leap down off the wing (or, increasingly, use the little flight of stairs) and come back with an orange coil of extension cord, a level, a wrench, a handful of screws, or a mallet.

They do not play the radio; they barely discuss their days. Some of the crew come to the theater precisely *not* to discuss their days, but as a kind of antidote to the outside world. Occasionally someone will tell a joke. George, who though trim and distinguished-looking could not really be called buff, is wearing a Gold's Gym sweatshirt, which he jokes Gold's pays him *not* to wear. Dennis tells a very mildly off-color joke involving a kindergarten student and his teacher. Don says something amusing in his low voice, so close to his chest it's barely audible, and Frances guffaws in her great loud way. But mostly there is very little talk. Mostly what there is, is bodies working in proximity, and in tandem. Somebody power-drills legs onto an inverted platform, and somebody else hops onto the platform to steady the plywood with his weight. Somebody switches on the circular saw to slice a length of wood, and somebody else helps guide the piece through the blade. Somebody needs a pencil to mark a two-by-four, and somebody else removes one from behind his ear and hands it over.

Several times, the power drills are set in reverse as the techies decide something must be undone and refigured, and no one gets rattled or exasperated; these are not mistakes per se, but part of the inevitable process of bringing an idea from paper to life. If anyone did get exasperated, he might as well go home and eat a bowl of ice cream and catch up on the evening news or something; anyone with something better to do might as well go do it, for nothing but desire compels anyone to be here. This is what they all know and share, and this more than anything gives them ownership of the place. Someone has brought Dunkin' Munchkins and left the box on the baby grand. The techies help themselves and lick the sugar off their fingers. The stage smells of sawdust.

Around ten, they begin to pack up their tools. One sheet of plywood, stored for too many weeks leaning up against the paint-shop wall, has become ridiculously bowed, and they decide to flatten it using the decrepit gold sofa that's on its way out to the curb for garbage pickup. Two people place the plywood center stage, and two others heft the sofa, and they leave that job to gravity and the span of a day; in the casual way of family members leaving home for a bit, knowing they will all meet up again in a little while, they say good night and go into the snap of the autumn evening.

All of this is as unwitnessed as every telephone call and car trip Debbi Dustin will make to track down props, and the visits Barbara Tyler will make to her hairdresser to have the wigs dressed, and the hours Dot Lansil will spend cleaning the toilets on the mornings of performances. At the next rehearsal all the sawdust will have been swept up, and the portions of the ramp will seem to have been built and assembled by elves, and the actors will simply begin to use them, to tread up and down the smoothly angled segments that have been magically calculated and fitted together by hands they never saw, by people they would not know if they were to pass one another on the street.

OCTOBER 16. THREE WEEKS TO GO.

When Celia's back goes out and she has to miss the next rehearsal, no one takes it as a major crisis, but it does seem a little early (only the third week of rehearsals) for people to start getting sick. Patrick's cough won't go away, either, and Kelley's coughing now, too, and then Jimmy has some oral surgery and shows up for rehearsal with his mouth gauze-packed, jaunty as ever but a little sore. Injuries and ailments accompany productions not uncommonly, but ideally don't hit until the *end* of a run, when defenses are down from the good kind of exhaustion, that of having spent all one's energy on the play. Early during the rehearsal process, they might be seen as a manifestation of something less productive, some kind of tension or gloom hovering over a show.

Certainly no one would accuse this production of being a great deal of fun so far; cast members have already begun commenting on this, and searching for explanations. The cast, first of all, is smallish. The script is neither particularly heartwarming nor light. Even the comic moments are dark and rather biting. There are almost no moments of tenderness or caring love between any of the characters. The play is tragic in an unforgiving, unrelenting way. All of this might well account for some of the general grimness which has marked the process so far.

But it's Celia, too. Celia, in her intensity, fired by all her high and fierce expectations, is driving this production hard, with no detours for picnics and only the most fleeting pit stops for fuel. When she returns, stiff-backed, and still suffering privately from increasingly acute abdominal pains, they've three weeks until opening. She announces this tersely, sitting on a purple stool before the music stand onstage, and there's a silent ripple of apprehension, as though the news has taken people by surprise. Then there's a little gaping silence. They're waiting for Patrick, who's late.

Another shadow: the chemistry between Gallimard and Song still isn't coming along. Individually, both actors are developing nicely. Jim's scenes with Tom and Grace, his old school friend and wife, respectively, are going to be good, Celia can tell. And Patrick's work on the physicality has enhanced his already nuanced, provocative portrayal of Song. But in their scenes together nothing is clicking; Patrick maintains an almost insulating composure, and Jim winds up coming across as a bit desperate and bumbling beside him. This close to the opening, a couple of people are still murmuring things to Celia about calling that other Song from auditions.

Now Patrick arrives, twenty minutes late, unsmiling, coughing, a bit wet from the rain which has been falling outside. The others know by now that he is without a car, and depends on the No. 77 bus to get here from Cambridge. He slips out of his leather jacket and mounts the stage without hesitation, immediately available to work.

Jim, with his broad Boston twang somehow exaggerated by the gauze in his cheeks, cries, "Hello, Monsieur Patrick!"—indefatigable in his cheer.

Mayre, in the army-green raincoat she hasn't bothered to remove, gets a nod from Celia and clicks on the boom box. For the first time, the rest of the ensemble will see the opening Peking Opera number, which has hitherto been rehearsed on nights with just Patrick and the kurogo. Bells, and a strange, stirring, crashing sound, and then the wavery, piercing melody fills the house. Little Michelle swoops down the newly constructed ramp, graceful and strong, with two real straw fans now in place of the Day-Glo feathers. Orea glides down, late on the count but managing a few nice poses with her scarf. Teri follows her with militaristic intensity and precision. Now comes Patrick, showing no residue of the bus and the rain and rush hour, just clear and calm inside the enigmatic person of Song, moving with a gait unlike his own, using his arms and hands in a way that transforms him. The others watch from the audience, apparently rapt. Celia gauges their silent reactions.

"Orea," asks Mayre, clicking off the boom box at the end of the short piece, "what was your count?"

"One, two, hundred," Orea responds, with appealing conviction.

"No: one one thousand, two one thousand—go!" Mayre laughs. Orea is quickly emerging as a kind of Gracie Allen character, adorably, unwittingly funny in her earnest cluelessness. She is perfectly up-front about both of these qualities: her almost disbelieving joy at being in a play, and her great void of experience with the same. Others among the cast have begun to pick up on what a stitch she is, and how genuinely thrilled she is to be here, and they have started quietly to help her along, show her some theater ropes, right her when she stumbles.

They don't know the story of how she came to be here in the first place. As a child living in the depressed mill town of Lowell, Orea, who was named for an Iroquois grandmother, delved into the plays organized by the nuns at school in order to escape the reality at home. At home was her father, at least some of the time, sleeping in a tape-patched leather chair in the living room, a row of dark bottles at his feet, a cigarette burning between his fingers. Her mother worked in a diner, where Orea and her four siblings were expected to help out after school, and while the family struggled on and off welfare for years, Orea fastened all her dreams on graduating from high school and going off to New York City to act. During senior year, she found out her Catholic school was going to award her a theater scholarship—two thousand dollars!—and a talent scout had spoken with her mother about letting Orea go to New York.

Then, one day, the principal called Orea into the office and told her that, because she hadn't paid her book bill, the scholarship as well as the part of the lead in the school play were being revoked. Soon after that, Orea's mother had a breakdown, and the five children were all sent to live with different relatives. Instead of graduating with her class, Orea got a GED, and a job at a diner, and married at eighteen. And for the next twenty-four years, while raising children of her own, she read about theater in the paper and went to local performances when she could, usually alone. Then, one day last year, shortly after becoming a sales coordinator at Hewlett-Packard, she noticed a clipping on the bulletin board about a play that was being directed by Celia Couture, and Orea felt her heart skip a beat. Here was the business branch manager, whom she admired so much already—educated, professional, strong, smart, advanced—and now it turned out she directed theater on top of all that!

A few months later, Celia and Orea were scheduled to go out to lunch for a performance evaluation, only they never got around to talking business. Orea, feeling shy and ridiculous, nevertheless immediately blurted out to Celia her decades-long desire to be involved in theater, and Celia, instead of taking them back to the office after lunch, drove Orea from Burlington all the way down to Academy Street in Arlington, where she extracted a set of keys from her purse and opened the theater door. Inside, she let Orea explore the place on her own a little. When Orea was pretty sure Celia wasn't looking, she stole up on the stage and stood there, and the wonderful audacity of that action, of planting herself in the middle of the raised, dark platform and looking out into the empty house, made her eyes fill with tears and her throat fill with ache, and when she got home that night she wrote Celia a card, thanking her for bringing back such memories and hopes.

Celia's the one who pressed Orea to audition last spring for the final show of AFD's season, *Kiss Me Kate*, and Orea almost did; she drove all the way down from Dracut and sat in her car outside the theater for an hour, watching people go in and out, trying to work up the nerve. The next day, when Celia asked her what happened and the story sort of hemmed and hawed its way out, Celia said, "You're going to the next audition," in her Celia way, not exactly pushy but so flat and firm you don't quite realize you've been bulldozed. Orea did attend the next auditions, for *Funny Girl*, making it as far as the back row of the theater this time, though not quite actually up onstage. Once again, the next day at work, Celia wanted to know what had happened. By the next round of auditions, which were for *Butterfly*, Orea had persuaded herself to see it all the way through (and of course, with Celia herself running these auditions, Orea had little opportunity to duck out unnoticed). And then the fantastic thing happened, and she was cast.

No one involved in rehearsals would ever guess their connection. Orea does not hang around Celia, expecting to be taken under her wing or presuming any special promise was implicit in that initial introduction. And Celia offers Orea no special encouragement or even acknowledgment. In fact, she snaps at Orea on more than one occasion, on nights when she's particularly impatient with the newcomer's lack of experience. The candor and generosity, the unusual reaching out both women did on the afternoon of Orea's performance evaluation some months back, remains one more invisible story behind this production.

Even now, as Mayre chortles again, shaking her head at the thought of Orea's improvised count, and Patrick does one of his magical light-ups, and Teri lets out a hoot, Celia is curtailing the merriment, keeping the rehearsal on track. "Okay, you guys." A gorgeous opening is nice, but there's another sixty-two pages of script to get through. "We don't have time to do this a hundred times."

Mayre presses PLAY again. The dancers dance the opening; then they recede; the music switches to Puccini's *Madame Butterfly*, and Jim, seated on a box stage right, launches into his opening monologue.

There are more people here tonight than just Celia, Kelley, Mayre, and the cast. Debbi Dustin and the two other women working on props sit in the audience, conferring quietly and itemizing things they'll need to procure. Molly, who looks as though she's wearing a costumer's costume—a swatch of stenciled orange cloth is pinned to her shirt, and a grosgrain ribbon around her neck dangles a little pair of scissors from one end, a pincushion from the other—meets in the back of the house with Stu Perlmutter, the lighting designer, to show him fabric samples before he decides which colored gels to use in his light plot. Barbara Horrigan is working on the wigs down in Horrigan's Hideaway, the makeup room that was officially named for her during the renovation last year. She surfaces periodically in the house, looking a bit like Salome, clutching a white Styrofoam head with a great floppy bun of black hair.

Celia kneads her temples, then grimaces while she chews the very tip of a fingernail. "By the way, people better be off book *soon*," she interjects in the middle of a scene. "Just thought I'd mention that. Go on." The calendar has them off book starting next Wednesday; at present, Jimmy is the only one who's making an obvious attempt to have his lines down. He has by far the most lines, of course. Great chunks already he is delivering without script in hand, although occasionally this still forces him to call "Line!" so often that Celia again has to suggest he go ahead and use it for now, in order not to slow things down. Meanwhile, out in the house, little pockets of sound gather and die as the other actors, scattered about, memorize their lines by themselves, whispering in reverie, or not even whispering, just mouthing, with the tiny delicate noise of lips and breath and rustling pages. It sounds faintly ritualistic, like prayer.

"Patrick, honey, you need to be off book soon for Act One," Celia says later, during another scene. He acknowledges her with a slightly brusque nod. Except for the opening dance, he has yet to come on-stage without the big floppy script encumbering his hands. He says nothing but is annoyed by her prodding; he is well aware of the off-book deadline in the calendar; it's not as if he's overdue.

They are working one of Gallimard and Song's early scenes to-gether, when the fledgling courtship is highly mysterious and brittle and charged. They are supposed to be strolling arm in arm through Beijing on a summer night, one of the few places in the script where Celia can't easily conceal Patrick's height through creative blocking. "Get those knees down, Patrick," she reminds him, sharply, mid-scene. She lets them continue a few seconds. "Patrick, you need to be more animated, flirtatious. Jim, you're more confident, enjoying it. This is more conversational, gentlemen. It's not *dramatic*." She sighs, drops her pen, massages her eyes. "He has to *like* you, Patrick."

Patrick neither nods nor makes eye contact but jots in his script.

"Okay, people," says Celia at the end of the evening. "We have three weeks. That's the reality. And until you have your nose out of your book, there's very little I can do." She has faith, still, in Patrick's intelligence and skill, but she wishes he would give her a little more indication that he's getting her notes. She detains him a few minutes tonight, tries to convey that to him, puts her hand on his knee and asks for some sign, some signal that the transmissions are getting through.

Looking into the middle distance, he nods.

For all of the connecting that does go on—after all, that knee she has touched belongs to someone who only a few weeks ago was a total stranger—more connections are missed, more layers never guessed at or glimpsed. Celia will never experience one of Patrick's Monday-night theater groups; she'll never wait for the public bus with him late at night; she'll never hear how rude and abrasive he is finding her. Patrick will never see her defending the production to irate community members; he won't know about the abdominal pains she's concealing every night; he will not hear how much she appreciates and admires his mind and his work. And only Jimmy will witness his own nightmares about forgetting his lines onstage; the others won't realize how anxious he's growing, not for a while yet, anyway; and they will never know how angry, how wronged he'll feel in the end.

People fetch their jackets, shake keys metallically out of their pockets. The nights are getting cold.

The production snack of choice has emerged. It seems almost too perfect. Not home-baked goods, or crackers and cheese, or fruit or nuts, or even lollipops. From now on, virtually every night, someone from the cast will pass around a tin of Altoids, those hard, bracing, test-of-endurance little breath mints.

Eight

The Guard in the Poet's Tree

By the time I entered high school, I was besotted with theater. Or with "the stage," as I probably would have said at the time. I was determined to become an actor—not determined in a clear-sighted, ambitious way, but in a hopelessly, soggily lovestruck way. It seemed the only thing.

I had begun to watch myself almost constantly, trying to analyze, as I led my life, what exactly *constituted* living a life: what it was that constituted emotions, actions, reactions. It was not uncommon, in the molten, shifting, sharply felt days of adolescence, for me to find myself wet and pulpy with tears on an afternoon, standing in front of the mirror, trying to parse, even as I sobbed genuinely ragged sobs, the components, physical and emotional, that went into a hard cry. I wanted to learn it to use later on the stage. If adolescence is a time of heightened self-consciousness, I watched myself doubly, once through my own teenagerly self-obsession, and once as an act of near-clinical practicing and preserving, for later application to a character in some play.

For all of my life that I can remember, certainly since long before I could have phrased it so, storytelling has seemed to me the most basic and essential part of being a living person. I mean, food and shelter are very nice, but without stories to hear and tell, we might as well be the walking dead. During the heyday of my romance with theater, being *inside* the story was the pinnacle of my desires. Walking around inside it, speaking the lines, feeling the feelings, committing the actions, taking the experience into my marrow—this all seemed like the fullest, fattest, richest way to live, to have my own life and a thousand others besides.

Not to say that I wasn't swept up by the vanity, too. I loved makeup and costumes, hot blinding lights, the knowledge of eyes on me, accolades. Sad to say, this was the era of *Flashdance*, and there I was in T-shirts with the collars scissored out, and legwarmers, and ripstops, which were a kind of baggy dance overall made of lightweight, checker-stitched nylon. I used black eyeliner and the kind of lip gloss that makes you look as if you've just come up from getting a drink at the water fountain; sometimes I wore knickers or scarves or a wide-brimmed felt hat. I took lots of dance classes and adopted from the older dancers every affectation that I possibly could. They all had beautiful, wistful eyes, and smelled of talc and mints and cigarettes. I developed contessalike posture; I could run up a flight of steps as noiselessly as a cat; every movement I made, I kept myself lifted from the pelvis, open across the chest; the most prosaic actions I made rarefied and theatrical—I used to lace the fingers of both hands around a cup when drinking, artfully childish, as if it were too great a burden for me to heft in only one. It was all very delicious and sickening.

Chafing at the bit to get on with a more extraordinary life, I completed my junior and senior high-school years in one, and became an acting major at New York University's Tisch School of the Arts at age sixteen. I moved into a dorm in Greenwich Village, a few blocks from Washington Square Park, and began training three days a week at the Stella Adler Conservatory of Acting. The other two, nonstudio, days were for academics—a course in Greek drama, something called Intro to Theater, and a freshman writing seminar. There was a lot of traipsing about the city. Our voice and movement classes were held in a shambling, warehousy loft building on lower Broadway, and occasionally in another loft, in the meatpacking district. Our academic classes met on the main campus, around Washington Square. And our technique class was held at Stella Adler headquarters, at City Center, in midtown.

Well, it was all very exciting, very glamorous. We were kind of a tribe, we drama students, all of whom had been farmed out to one of five different acting studios in the city. Those of us at Stella Adler spent our studio days together, meeting each other bleary-eyed in the mornings before the heat really got going in those neglected buildings whose elevators were forever breaking down. Our voice teacher, a sardonic taskmaster who once gave the homework assignment, not exactly in jest, to "go out and get laid this weekend," instructed us on the first day to procure pocket mirrors and corks, which we were to bring to every class, and we spent a lot of time looking at the reflections of our mouths pronouncing vowels around the obstacles of these corks—I forget why exactly—and also lying on our backs on those cold and dust-mousy floors, learning to say "Mmmmaaaaaa" from the proper place in our diaphragms. Our movement teacher was a preternaturally peaceful man who taught us how to massage our own feet and each other's bodies, and helped us explore negative shapes and group rhythms, and to do "femur bounces" and make "arcs" across the room. Frequently he would say, "Take a moment for yourselves," which was the signal that we were supposed to close our eyes and reconnect with our alignment, I think.

Our technique classes were terrifying and thrilling. We'd take the B, D, or E up to the Seventh Avenue stop, walk over to City Center, and take a dark, grimy elevator upstairs to our classroom. A smallish room, with gurgling radiators and theater "blacks" (heavy, soft, black drapes) secured over the windows, it was crowded with chairs and appointed at one end with a tiny stage that we were under no circumstances allowed to set foot on. Real grown-up actors took classes at the Stella Adler Conservatory—some of them had parts in real plays—and of course there were tales of all the legendary stars (Brando, De Niro, Beatty) whom Stella Adler had famously coached. We NYU freshmen of course did not study with her; we were taught by one of her disciples, a remarkably and, one suspected, studiously classy woman who must have been in her late fifties. She always wore pumps and knee-length skirts, which revealed her extraordinarily shapely calves; in fact, she always stood just so, with one foot angled out from the arch of the other foot, showing off her legs to their best advantage. She held a cigarette in one hand, and gestured with it mesmerizingly as she spoke; her smile would flash brilliantly across the surface of her face with little warning, and vanish again just as abruptly. She had a chronic sniff that was more of a snort, a little guttural sinus-clearing sound that ought to have wrecked the overall effect but instead mysteriously enhanced it. She informed us on the first day that she was aware we all referred to her behind her back as the Dragon Lady, and from this we learned to do so.

Her classes were inscrutable and oddly compelling. I'm not sure any of us had the least idea what "technique" was supposed to mean, and nothing the Dragon Lady said directly elucidated us. Our classmates at the Actors Studio were apparently already honing their sense-memories, and rumor had it that those who'd been assigned to Circle in the Square had actually begun scene work, but those of us at Stella Adler had to be content mostly with listening to the oblique and riveting discourses of the Dragon Lady. She talked about "excess insides," "strong actions" versus "weak actions," and learning to be "private in public."

Very rarely, we were asked to speak. She was interested in our ability to "see" with our imaginations and to describe in detail, with truth and specificity, a variety of given subjects. These subjects never included anything so rich and complex as an event, say, or a feeling (we were, after all, merely freshmen), but tended to be very simple objects or sensations: a bottle, for example, or the feel of sweat around one's waistband on a hot day. However, the Dragon Lady had little patience for our unpolished stammerings, and no matter how lovingly and precisely we tried to conjure the imagined subject, she tended to cut us off witheringly after a few sentences in a way that managed to suggest that Konstantin Stanislavsky would roll over in his grave before any of us would ever be actors, and that she would never, if she lived to be a hundred, fathom why we weren't all accounting majors.

The truth is, there was something marvelous about the Dragon Lady and her passion for truth and her passion for serving the hugeness of life and the complexity of the human experience through theater. If she was scathing in her estimation that we all fell desperately short of the mark of even understanding it all, then she was also essentially correct. And if she wasn't exactly the educator to guide us ably into a deeper understanding of life and the power of theater to interpret and explore it, then she was at least someone to rattle us alert to the incredible depths of what we had yet to learn. In this regard, she was a brilliant teacher, not because she actually taught us anything, but because she made us hungry, or made me hungry anyway, made me ache with desire for everything invisible I hadn't suspected—made me ache with the immensity of the possible.

None of which is to say that the baser qualities of vanity and self-importance, those frequent handmaidens of the theater world, never intruded upon this magnificence. As we all scrambled over ourselves trying to please the Dragon Lady (an impossible task; the rare times she was satisfied with something one of us did, the effort was generally quite inadvertent), we one day witnessed just how entrenched and ridiculous the ego-stroking could be. Our class had just ended, and some twenty-five of us were scraping back chairs, gathering knapsacks and jackets, converging on the door, when said door swung open and the great lady herself loomed—surprisingly tall, with a stiff blond coif that made her even taller. Instinctively, we all froze. I had pictured her, for some reason, tiny and beautifully wizened, but she cut a ferociously imposing figure. She was in her early eighties.

It appeared she was attempting to enter the room to teach an advanced class, only to find her way obstructed by the motley lot of us NYU kids. This had never happened before; perhaps there'd been a scheduling change. She did not deign to glance at us, and addressed our teacher without a smile. Her projection was practiced and imperious and riveting. She might have been doing Lady Macbeth. "Miss————. Haven't I told you always to have your students exit through the other door?"

"But, Miss Adler," the Dragon Lady replied, and it was shocking to see her suddenly deferential, even kowtowing, though her delivery was as polished as Miss Adler's and beautifully timed, "there is no other door."

Amid all the codified, posturing grandeur of the Stella Adler Conservatory and, to an extent, of the Tisch School in general, with its

rigorous if inscrutable methods of instruction—perhaps "indoctrina-
tion" is the more fitting word—I gathered that my experience in
community theater was ranked insignificant at best, detrimental at
worst, to developing the real craft of a serious actor. This was partly
because real (that is, professional) theater had necessarily to be something inaccessible to the masses. The masses could buy tickets and be
entertained, of course, but they could never fully understand the mysterious, laborious process by which theater was achieved. Theater
professionals are often exasperated by the sentiment, possessed no
doubt by the vast majority of the public witnessing an actor's performance, that "I could do that"—and understandably so, since that
belief is generally naïve, and demeaning to the training and skill of
the professional. But that exasperation can breed haughty disregard,
which in turn demeans the human drive to imagine and play-act, and
that drive will never be the exclusive property of the professionals.

Nevertheless, every week in our Intro to Theater class, quite
renowned guests from the professional theater world would address
us all in a gigantic lecture hall, and always the tone was important and
insiderly, with a little requisite fawning on the part of the school's
moderator, and not once did anyone show honest irreverence for or
sincerely question the assumed paradigm. It was the culture of the
school to pay homage to the great, rarefied world of professional theater, whose secrets remained beyond the grasp of the laity. For any of
us seriously to question that culture would be a dead giveaway that
we were crass impostors, accountants manqués, who would never understand and, more important, never make it.

I'm sorry to say that some of us felt so lucky and grateful to have
been admitted, however provisionally and on however low and wobbly a rung, to such a thrilling and exclusive sanctum, that we bought
into the culture with little reservation. So a lot of black was worn, and
a lot of coffee borne about in paper cups printed with those ubiquitous representations of the Acropolis, consumed in exaggeratedly
world-weary sips, or, alternately, herbal teabags and special health-
food-shop throat lozenges were consumed and discussed, and names
of massage therapists and chiropractors exchanged, and outlandish,
actorly garments purchased from tiny SoHo boutiques, or Lower East
Side thrift shops, or, preferably, from the men who sold clothes and

record albums and the occasional busted toaster from blankets they spread out on the sidewalk by Astor Place. We were all so busy gathering the proper accouterments to be Young Artists in Greenwich Village, and tending to the development of our instruments—that is, our bodies—that we could hardly be expected to have other pursuits. In fact, outside interests might function as a sign of insufficient dedication to our training.

Partway into the semester, the situation struck me as gross. Here I was, sixteen, knowing so little of anything *outside* the tiny sphere of my own existence, spending an inordinate number of hours a week concentrating on my own breathing, peering at my cork-blocked mouth in a pocket mirror, learning to massage the various bones in my foot—all in order to be able to fly someday into the hearts of characters whose histories, cultures, and experiences were foreign to me. I don't mean to ridicule the training as being invalid or unuseful to actors developing their craft, but for my part, the whole equation was a little unbalanced; here I was at college, hungry to come into contact with the larger world, and instead I'd entered a course of study that required nothing so much as focusing inward.

It was 1984. There was fighting going on in Lebanon, Ethiopia, Yugoslavia, Cambodia. AIDS had gone mainstream and scientists had just identified HIV. Republican welfare cuts were having an enormous impact; acid rain had been discovered; the Moral Majority was on the rise; a presidential election was around the corner; and of all of this, I had only the vaguest, rushing-importantly-past-the-newsstand-on-my-way-to-the-studio inkling. In spite of my self-involvement, however, some shred of responsibility for being engaged in the world had led me to start volunteering at a little nonprofit called Madre, which worked to support the victorious socialist Sandinista revolution in Nicaragua against the right-wing U.S. government–backed contras. It was an ad for volunteers in the back of the *Village Voice* that alerted me to this particular group, but the story was one my family and I had been following in the news, and the idea of engaging in some sort of activism—indeed, of being *active* in the world, a player on more than just a theatrical stage—was true to my family's culture, so it was not surprising that the little ad caught my eye and shattered my myopia.

This was a few years before the Iran-contra scandal broke, but everyone at Madre seemed to know that our government was up to something fishy, and the atmosphere at the boxy office was quintessentially irreverent and questioning of authority—a far cry from the rather desperate obeisance over at the drama school. I spent a night a week at Madre, photocopying articles or stuffing envelopes, and one night, on my way out, a flier on the overcrowded bulletin board caught my eye. Across the top was hand-lettered "Arts for a New Nicaragua," and below that followed a call for musicians, photographers, performers, and fine-artists to join a Boston-based "arts brigade" that would travel to Nicaragua the following June.

I had dinner with my parents on my seventeenth birthday and informed them that I was going to transfer to another college next year to study writing instead of acting, but that I hoped first to spend a month stiltdancing in Nicaragua.

Arts for a New Nicaragua was a tiny, fledgling grassroots organization. I applied, auditioned, and was accepted to be on the second brigade it ever sent. We were sponsored in Nicaragua by the Ministry of Culture, a branch of the government under the FSLN (Sandinista National Liberation Front), whose purpose was not so much to cultivate professional artists as to bring culture to the people by making it available on a local level through CPCs (Centers for Popular Culture) in towns all over the country. It struck me as amazing that even in its war-torn condition the country allotted the arts such an important and active and grassroots role. Camus has written, "Beauty, no doubt, does not make revolutions. But a day will come when revolutions will have need of beauty." The very existence of the CPCs at this time of intense contra fighting, and the Sandinistas' recognition of the arts as a vital part of the society they were trying to build, seemed evidence of an uncommon national health and sanity. One of the popular *consignas*, or political cries, that our audiences often spontaneously broke into, went: *¡Cultura es el fusil artístico de la revolución!* (Culture is the artistic tool of the revolution!).

As for the "brigadistas," we went in support of the revolution, which, although it had officially been won six years earlier, felt new and charged with spirit and urgency, not least because the contras were still trying violently to overthrow it. We were deeply conscious that our own government was inflicting much of the damage. Our purpose was partly to show solidarity with the government and people of Nicaragua by bringing artistic supplies difficult to obtain there (paint, musical instruments, film) and engaging in an intercultural exchange; and partly to bring back information and experiences to share with people in the United States.

We landed in Managua on June 3, eleven other brigadistas and I. Seven of the group were visual artists, and would spend the next three weeks stationed in different towns, making murals and masks with townspeople and local artists and giving photography workshops. The four musicians (two women, two men) and I were to spend the time traveling around the country, performing in various towns and settlements and army bases. Our program included songs in Spanish from Nicaragua and other Latin American countries, and songs in English by George Gershwin, the Beatles, Holly Near, Woody Guthrie, and a few that had been written for the occasion by the musicians in our own group. I danced to one of the songs on my stilts, and to another song on my feet—a sort of interpretive modern dance that told a story—and the musicians taught me to play a little backup percussion on the claves for some of the others. We'd rehearsed our act together a few times before going down, but except for Willie, who had organized the brigade and gone the previous year, we had little idea of what to expect. We just showed up at the airport, with the rolls of toilet paper and the hot-pink antimalarial pills we'd been advised to bring packed carefully into our small duffel bags, and our eclectic and cumbersome carry-ons (saxophones, guitars, paints, stilts) raising eyebrows among the other passengers.

In Nicaragua, the musicians and I traveled with two *responsables*, CPC representatives who were our chaperons and guides, and a bus driver named Tonio, who wore a black beret and a black mustache, and sometimes drove bare-chested so that he could simultaneously swat at the wasps that flew in the open windows with his rolled-up T-shirt. No one in our group, including Tonio and Carlos and Cleo, the *responsables*, was over thirty, except Willie, who might have been just over, and we were all very casually companionable. We gringos spoke varying degrees of Spanish. The Nicaraguans spoke no English. But it seemed as though we were always talking with each other; we were full of conversation, jokes, questions. We ate together in various one-room wood-and-tin houses, and at schools and army bases and union headquarters, and we drank *refrescos* and beer together in the hot afternoons in the shade of some roadside shelter, and we danced together at the evening music sessions that seemed to materialize wherever we were, the local people pulling out a few instruments to jam with the gringos, and pretty soon a few crosscultural romances blossomed, and although we were officially being sponsored by the Sandinista government, the whole trip felt incredibly nongovernmental. The relationships seemed to grow between us the way spiderwebs form silently in the night and in the morning meet the eye sparkling and inevitable, and the music and song and dance that passed among us everywhere we went seemed to spring forth with equal inevitability, as though constantly flowing just beneath the thin crusts of all our lives, and they provided the most natural means of connecting to each other across the language barrier.

Our first performance, the evening after we arrived, was at a three-room cinderblock school building in a barrio of Managua, and it seemed very festive and spirited, with the audience breaking into rousing *consignas* in between our numbers, and applauding us noisily and happily. When we finished, the same audience gathered into a procession outside and asked us to lead it—to the wake of a man who'd been killed two days earlier by contras up north. We processed, four people across, about twenty rows long, to the man's house. There were people all around in the dark street and yard, playing cards, drinking, children playing. We approached the house, whose walls were boards loosely nailed together; slivers of reddish-yellow light shone through from the inside, so that it was like glimpsing into the hot heart of something. The house was packed with people. There was a coffin with the red and black FSLN flag draped over it, and a huge wreath of flowers the FSLN had sent. Inside the house some people were crying, and inside the house some people were laughing. A man approached us afterward in the street and told us this was what Yankee imperialism did. He said it was good we were taking pictures to show people in the States.

We often performed two or three times a day, at schools, police stations, CPCs, army bases, farming collectives, in the street, on tobacco fields, in barns, and once at the foot of a short, steep mountain with cows behind us. As we traveled farther north—near the border with Honduras, where the contra camps were—we got closer to the war zone, and sometimes abandoned the little soccer-team bus for transport in the backs of tarpless army trucks. Tonio still accompanied us when we did this. It turned out he was our guard as well as our driver; as a member of the militia, he carried a gun at all times, although I'd never noticed it on the bus. We would share these truck rides with soldiers, and with any other hitchhikers they stopped for, too: old people, children, a woman with a couple of live chickens under her arms. Sometimes the roads up into the mountains went from packed dirt to rocks and dust, and we had to get out and push. Sometimes we ran out of gas and had to wait for one of the *responsables* to get another gas ration. Sometimes we stopped to wash our hands and faces in brooks, or to shake mangoes from a tree, or to let Tonio climb into a tree and break off a branch of a fruit called *mamones*, which were sort of like grapes with tough skins you split with your fingernail and didn't eat. Once, we stopped at a waterfall and went swimming.

After we performed, we almost always became the audience in turn: some children would get up and do a folk dance, or a CPC theater troupe would put on a short play about the revolution, or a group of soldiers would set down their rifles and borrow our instruments to offer us some songs back. In one town, a civilian ran back to his house, returned with a shiny white electric guitar, and launched into "Twist and Shout." We performed in Managua, Matagalpa, Masaya, Sebaco, Darío, San Ramón, Bonanza, La Laguna, Jinotega, Estelí, Ciudad Sandino, Jalapa, Ocotal, Juigalpa, Santo Tomás, Villa Sandino, Boaco, Jipi-Jopa, Camoaco. We often ended the evenings dancing together—the Nicaraguans a smooth, supple sea of salsa, the gringos jouncing around like popcorn in their midst. We laughed at each other and ourselves. We talked with the people we met—sometimes haltingly, across the language barrier—about art, revolution, literacy, pacifism, truth, power, killing.

One rainy night in Ocotal, near the end of our trip, we were performing for some soldiers in a dank cement building with bullet holes all over the walls, when suddenly almost the whole audience picked up and left. Tonio helped me untie my stilts and I asked ¿Qué pasa? and he said Nada. I said No te creo, and he said something about a mobilization, but not to worry. Then, while we were packing up the instruments, the lights went out, and a soldier told us to move our stuff to the far corner of the room, by some sacks of flour, and sit still and be quiet. Another soldier came and lit a candle and sat with us. Tonio and Carlos, who was also in the militia, got their ammunition vests and their guns and went outside. Two soldiers stayed with us and told us to move into the barracks, stay quiet, and be ready to lie on the floor with our heads down if the word came to do so. If anyone approached we were to ask, "¿Quién vive?" and if the answer was Arbol then it was okay, but if not, we should lie down and be quiet. Nothing like this happened, and after a while Tonio returned and sat with us, and the soldiers smoked and joked softly.

Eventually, some tension eased. The electricity went back on and the soldiers turned off the bare bulb again and told us to lie down on the cots and get some sleep, which I was unable to do. After a long while, I realized Willie was still awake, too. We found Tonio and asked if we could take a walk. He and another soldier put their ammunition vests back on and got their guns and we walked through the town. The streets were empty, but there were lights on at the FSLN office. We stopped and learned that twelve soldiers had been killed in combat with contras a few kilometers away. The next day, we learned that the roads were closed to Somoto, which was where we were to have performed next, because of contra action there.

Once, after a performance for some soldiers, they showed us American canteens, ammunition vests, and belts they'd taken from contras in combat. We all knew that the bullets that killed their compañeros were financed by our tax dollars. Then they gave us some biscuits and red soda and borrowed the instruments so that they could play for us. After we left, one of them came running out into the street to present us with a big framed poster of Sandino. The frame was made of nailed-together sticks. On the back the soldiers had written a message of thanks to us.

In general, there were shortages of everything in Nicaragua—

largely the results of a U.S. embargo. We had been advised to pack small, basic utilitarian gifts in our duffels—things like pens and crayons and T-shirts—but by the time we left, we had gotten a better sense of how much was difficult to obtain, and we wound up leaving nearly everything behind, giving things to friends we'd made and people who'd hosted us in their homes. We left soap, toothpaste, shampoo, clothes, sandals, bracelets, notebooks. I left my stilts, packaged them up for Carlos, who had family in Matagalpa, to bring to a couple of students I'd met at the Center of Training for Theater there. The Nicaraguans gave us presents, too. In Boaco we were presented with small bottles of the local rum, Morir Sonando (Die Dreaming). Fernando, a young dancer at one of the CPCs, gave me a little burlap bag he'd sewn and hand-painted with my name and the Nicaraguan and FSLN flags. Bayardo, one of the CPC workers, gave me sketches he'd made of me dancing. Zobeyda, a girl my age in Matagalpa, gave me a handwritten booklet of original poetry, which she'd decorated with red-penciled flowers. I later learned she'd killed a contra; she'd been on a student coffee-picking brigade, and it had been her turn to stand lookout; a contra came through the forest and she shot him. I learned Tonio had fought in the revolution and killed someone in hand-to-hand combat, with a knife. He gave me a dozen "Nicaragua Libre" postcards that the CPC had produced from children's paintings, and he'd written a small message on the back of each one.

On that trip there was no separation between art and life, or if there was a separation it was perforated, so that the two flowed forth and back and into one another. Art—song, dance, murals, masks, plays, poetry—was a natural and necessary part of being a participant in life. In our home country, the richest in the world, theater and art resided permanently in the margins, a citizen of the border lands of frivolity and fluff. Here in Nicaragua everything—every little task and commodity I took for granted—was difficult to accomplish or obtain on a daily basis, and yet art was considered a central, intractable thread in the fabric of the struggling society. Art and life were useful to each other, and neither was more valid or essential than the other; they were simply complementary parts of a larger thing, a great revolving wheel of experience.

In Nicaragua we performed without lights and sets and makeup and costumes (other than my stilt pants: four-foot-long columns of cloth sewn to an old pair of shorts). We performed without illusion—without the illusion of a magical divide between performers and audience, without an aura of unbridgeable separateness between what went on within and without the playing space. The performances themselves, peppered with *consignas* called back by the audience members, were a kind of active dialogue that continued in different fashion once the instruments were packed up, or handed off, as was so often the case, to audience members who wished to reciprocate. That speeches and stories often followed performances at first seemed odd, but after a few weeks felt only natural. As for the idea of "community theater," in Nicaragua the phrase sounded ridiculously redundant. Theater and art were by their nature of and for the community; to classify them explicitly so would've implied otherwise.

I don't mean to suggest that this cultural view precluded or dismissed professional or great art. It seemed, rather, to incorporate it. Professional art and folk art and popular art and amateur art—keeping these categories separate had little importance. Professional art was celebrated, but not with a lot of fawning and fanfare, and not by erecting strict hierarchies, with the Public paying noisy homage on one side of a red cordon, and the Artists sipping nectar and spooning ambrosia on the other.

One day we were in the town of Darío, named after the internationally recognized Nicaraguan poet Rubén Darío, about whom the *New York Times* had coincidentally published an article only a few months earlier. (I remembered being struck by the article, mostly because I'd never heard of a U.S. town's being named for a poet.) We visited his birthplace, which had been restored into a landmark: a one-room house and a garden in which a little open-air theater had been built in his honor. We visited on a Monday, when the place was officially closed, but the guard let us in anyway, and after we toured the tiny house, the guard said to wait and he climbed a tree and broke off several branches of *mamones* for us, and we all sat in the grass and ate those for a while, talking about the deceased poet and the ongoing war. No image of the trip stays with me more than this one, of the guard himself in his army greens scaling the great poet's gnarled old tree, snapping off branches, and then sitting in the hallowed garden with us as we all shared the tart fruits, just as if we were all people, which we all were.

Did I swallow up everything I saw and thought I saw in Nicaragua with the same aching, adolescent seriousness and lack of ironic distance with which I had found fault at NYU? Maybe. Maybe that seriousness and lack of irony is part of the job of being seventeen. It is difficult, in any case, to imagine a year bookended by two such disparate experiences of performance. I learned a lot from both. Ultimately, those weeks with the arts brigade interested me more, and I was glad that every certainty I had learned in New York that autumn got broken down, swept away in Nicaragua by the unstoppable flow of life into art—song to sketch to story to meal to embrace to testimony to tears to dance to arms.

Nine

Cue to Cue

OCTOBER 17, SATURDAY. TWO WEEKS AND SIX DAYS TO GO.

It's only Jim and Patrick tonight. They've been blocking the scene at the end where Song strips, confronting Gallimard once and for all with the fact of his maleness. The audience has learned the truth, and so has the public, Song having testified in French court and the whole sordid story having broken in the international press; only Gallimard, now on shaky ground psychologically, willfully rejects the truth, and continues to believe in the illusion of his perfect lover, his Butterfly. The blocking of this scene has been put off until now, and Patrick's height is proving a challenge. Celia had wanted him down center, facing upstage, but she can see now, as she roams stiffly about the house, her back still sore, that he's too tall—sight lines will be cut off if he stands there.

"Try it down left a little."

He moves. They begin again. It's just a blocking rehearsal, scripts and pencils in hand, Patrick staying clothed, but Jim emotes fully anyway, going down on his knees at the top of the ramp, his face turning red as he breaks into hysterical laughter on the line "You're a man!"

"That's not going to work," Celia interrupts, and Jimmy pulls out of it instantly and goes off to sharpen his pencil. Celia chews the inside of her cheek. Patrick regards her and waits, patient, statuesque. She tries him down left and down right, and she and Kelley take turns scrutinizing him from respective corners of the house. They're worried about him tipping a profile to the audience and exposing any frontal nudity.

"All right, try it down right, but closer in to the platform."

Patrick obeys, a chess piece. Celia takes an Advil.

After a five-minute break they come back to work the early courtship-and-seduction scenes from Act One. Patrick has donned his celery kimono and obi and removed his shoes. He practices Song's glide: bent knees, baby steps. His stocking feet scritch over the platform. Kelley, Jim, and Patrick are coughing.

"Gee, we sound like we should all be in *Camille*," says Jim.

"Patrick, how are you on lines?" asks Celia, squinting and dimpling at once.

"Pretty good," he replies, giving nothing away.

They plunge into the first flirtation scene. Celia interrupts a hundred times—"It's too slow. This has to move. . . . Take it back for rhythm. . . . We need to see a big smile there, Song. You're *flirting*. . . . Outwit him. . . . You're nervous around her, Jimmy. . . . Beats, beats, beats." She has them drop all emotion and blocking and just deliver their lines as an exercise in pacing, and she cups her whole face, intent. "Don't wait for each other's lines."

"Even if it doesn't make sense?" queries Patrick.

"It will, trust me. Again." This time she turns her back, only listens.

Patrick and Jimmy repeat the sequence, rapid-fire, and something indeed is happening, changing, an electric dynamic that seems to have grown out of speed alone, but whose effect suggests an interior urgency, the heady tension of possible infatuation. Celia comes down and perches on a chair, stirs her fist in the air to indicate the even quicker pace she wishes they would take, and pats a little speeding tattoo on her knee. Jimmy flubs a line and roars, "Shit!" They zip through it again, and again, and finally Celia says, "Okay, let's take that scene from the top."

For roughly the millionth time, they go back to Gallimard's line about wanting to "pamper" Song.

"Or Huggies," murmurs Patrick, and Jim looks up quickly: it's the first time he's cracked a joke.

They run it, and Celia gives notes. "Make the blocking part of the story, Patrick, when you kneel. . . . Don't pick up on each other's tonal quality. I need to hear two separate speeches there. . . . During his talking there's an inner monologue, and I need to see what that is." Jimmy registers every note broadly, screwing up his face in contemplation, nodding affably, apologetically. Patrick fans himself and coughs, softly and repeatedly. His posture coveys an extreme civility. "Do you have any plans for me to do that scuffing on the platform without making a ton of noise?" he asks.

"It may be okay once it's sanded and painted and you're in slippers."

They go to the next scene, the stroll after the opera, and Jimmy tosses in the "pampers" line from the earlier scene. Patrick corrects him and Jim says, "I *know*," and whacks Patrick's shoulder playfully with his script. Later, rounding the end of the platform, Patrick stumbles, and Jim catches his arm. Under the barrage of Celia's exacting notes and comments, a little camaraderie is growing between the two leads. The later the hour, the easier its expression.

They run the scene five, six, seven times. The sense of Arlington just beyond these wooden walls grows faint, and the small black playing space seems to swell and develop a distinct aura, an impression of place and time, phantom smells and sounds and Beijing night air, all a function of the energy between these two men, not Patrick and Jim, but Song and Gallimard, who are beginning to shimmer up more convincingly through their real-life counterparts on this stage.

OCTOBER 18, SUNDAY. TWO IN THE AFTERNOON.

It's an amazing day, mid-seventies, sunny, varicolored, with fresh hatchings of ladybugs all over the place. People arrive in shorts. Little

Michelle comes straight from rollerblading. Tall Michelle comes with nine-year-old Gabbie. Doug comes with three-year-old Jeneane, wearing tiny red cowboy boots and a red bow in her hair.

Inside, the theater is dark and dusty and cool as ever. The two six-foot halves of the round jigsawed element which will adorn the sliding doors at the top of the ramp have been painted bright red and at the moment are laid out like a giant mandala on sheets of plywood across three rows of seats in the audience.

Jimmy is greeting everyone by name, blowing kisses, squeezing shoulders, calling out "Bless you!" whenever anyone sneezes.

Jeneane and Gabbie sit on an aisle and examine the littler girl's rehearsal gear: a white squeaky bear, large white sunglasses, a sheet of bubble paper, Chicken McNuggets, a lollipop.

The actors themselves are juggling more props this rehearsal. Patrick fans himself with a gold-foil fan. Jimmy paces offstage, trying to get comfortable with a cigarette, on which he puffs cautiously, coughing afterward. He holds it in every combination of fingers except that which a real smoker would use: like a stick of incense, a pencil, a bug. He peers at it occasionally as if to make certain it isn't doing anything it shouldn't be.

The partygoers today rehearse with real (empty) wineglasses. Carolyn does her pin-up girl scene in pumps. Tall Michelle delivers a length of scrap lumber to Tom mid-scene.

"What is that?" Celia barks from the back of the house.

"It's a tennis racquet," says Tom, twirling it sportily.

"No—"

"I just mention it." His demurral is witty, debonair. Tom alone in the cast seems utterly sure of himself with Celia. He is wearing an AACT T-shirt today, a relic of his triumphant trip to Knoxville, Tennessee, to participate in the American Association of Community Theatres' national festival a few years back. The group he performed with, the Vokes Players over in Wayland, is the only Region I theater ever to have won the national competition.

"There are tennis racquets to be used," instructs Celia. Teri finds one backstage and holds it out to Little Michelle. The three kurogo spend all their spare time in the wings, conferring in whispers over pages of notes on who's doing what in which scene. Their three trade-mark motions have become penciling, erasing, brushing eraser crumbs away. Their tasks seem to change at every rehearsal, and all Celia seems to do is order them around like servant women, and act as though *they're* the ones forgetting the blocking. Teri, the most experienced of the three, is also the most frustrated. She's been fantasizing about quitting.

Debbi Dustin and the two other props people, Lauren Cochran and Leah Ktono, watch and take notes from the audience. They spent yesterday rummaging through Chinatown, searching for a restaurant that might be willing to lend the production a few small black lacquer chairs in return for a mention in the program. One had the right size chair but the wrong style seat covers. Other props have been located successfully, and are accumulating on a sagging folding table in the shop. The trappings of the set will grow in quantity and verisimilitude, but for now consist of: a stack of old porn magazines Debbi borrowed from one of her co-workers at the police station; a bottle of French wine dutifully drained by Leah (its contents to be replaced by grape juice); an Asian Cabbage Patch doll belonging to Lauren's adopted Korean daughter. Also an empty picture frame, lensless eyeglasses for Tall Michelle, a matchbox, a coffee can of water in which to put out cigarettes and cigars, a hairbrush, fake roses, and a tea set, which for the moment consists partly of a couple of Dunkin' Donuts Styrofoam cups.

OCTOBER 19. MONDAY-NIGHT THEATER GROUP.

Patrick and his partner, Brett, started the group just over a month ago. It meets in its founders' apartment, and it meets on Mondays because Mondays are half-price nights at Mike's Pizza. Members begin drifting in around seven-thirty, and sit around the big blond dining table, on which have been set two bottles of red wine and a cobalt vase filled with red and pink roses. Tonight there are eight people, some of whom have never met before; the membership is informal and ever-changing, in part because people get cast in things and drop out temporarily (Brett is away at a rehearsal tonight), and in part because Patrick and Brett are constantly inviting new acquaintances to come; the group is the antithesis of exclusive.

Eventually Patrick returns from picking up four pizzas, and he takes off his leather jacket and shoes, and everybody loads up a plate and retires to the living room, where the plays are. Patrick and Brett have most of a bookshelf devoted to plays and anthologies of selected scenes, and everyone chooses a book and for a while sits and reads and chews and sips, and then gradually people begin inviting others to read scenes with them. A tiny sunroom off the living room makes a natural proscenium, and Patrick jumps up and dims the lights in the former and turns up the lights in the latter, with great flourish, and everyone oohs and then laughs, Patrick especially. He is warm and unassuming with the people in the room; each separate person, it seems obvious, occasions his real and specific affection. With the stage now established, he flops back onto the couch, and the actor-friends take turns performing for each other.

They are mostly in their early twenties, and some of them have grown-up day jobs, like the woman in the maroon suit who works on a trading floor at a bank, and some of them have loony patchwork-type day jobs, like the woman with the piping high voice and blue nail polish who gets called to do promos dressed up as a box of Parliament Lights, or as a Godiva Chocolate girl. Some of them have almost no acting experience at all, like the woman who did one play in college, and some of them have written scripts and made films, like the man with the cell phone who's on his way to Hawaii soon for a screening at an independent film festival. But they all have in common a distinct lack of tortured self-importance. When they take the "stage" to read their scenes together, they are serious and committed and not a little talented, but the scenes are followed by a bare minimum of critiquing or reviewing or chin-waxing of any nature; they are instead received with delight.

There is an overriding sense of possibility among the group, which may partly be a function of youth, and partly a result of the fact that several have participated in new and experimental theater projects in the area, but must surely also be attributed to happiness. The group seems so happy to be here, not as a step along the way to something bigger, or realer, but as a pleasure in and of itself. And, in a Zen-like paradox, just when the moment is happy and full, one's sense of possibility swells accordingly.

This group has no agenda, no bylaws or hierarchies, and although several of its members have pooled and continue to pool their energies to stage independent theater projects in and around Boston, the goal of the Monday-nighters is not to grow into a production company or community theater itself. The group is more verb than noun, more process than product, more inquiry than answer.

Late in the evening, the filmmaker's cell phone rings and everyone necessarily falls silent while he answers it. "Hi . . . No . . . I'm actually at an actors' play-reading . . . group . . . meeting . . . thing."

The others break up gleefully, Patrick, as usual, looking suddenly like a child.

"We've got to get a better name," one of them says, but it seems a safe bet they probably never will.

OCTOBER 20, TUESDAY, CREW NIGHT.

Stu Perlmutter is hanging lights along with a couple of pals—a skinny guy called Mikey, who works for the electric company, and a big guy who goes simply by "D" who works in architectural lighting. None of the three are part of AFD's regular band of techies, Celia having gone outside the club to get the lighting designer she most wanted to work with. ("Oh yeah, Celia's stringers," one of the regular techies will later snort, but none of this animosity is directed at the lighting guys themselves.) The trio most often do their theater work at Vokes, and in fact none of them have ever hung lights here at Arlington, and they're a bit stymied. The problem is, the extension ladder looks decidedly shaky against the truss, which hangs up near the top of the vaulted ceiling. There are two of these trusses out in the house, with electrified rods on which the lekos are hung, and the one midway through the house is somewhat inaccessible—the only way to get the ladder to reach is to place it at an awfully steep angle, which they've done, and now they're standing around looking at the deep bend in it.

D announces he weighs 280 and isn't about to chance it. Stu's got to be up in the loft, working the computerized light board. So Mikey gamely climbs the thing, but it rattles so loudly Don Richardson, who's working on the set up onstage, quips, "Are those your knees?" and he descends, looking a little green about the gills. They decide to shorten the distance by rigging a plywood platform on top of the audience seats and mounting the ladder on that. It buys maybe three feet, and just enough confidence for Mikey to run up and down six or seven times, angling and rehanging the lights to illuminate the precise spots onstage that Stu has figured the show will need. D slides the whole apparatus over each time Mikey needs to reach a new bank of fixtures, and anchors the bottom of the ladder while his buddy climbs. For his part, Mikey pretends to mistake D's head for a rung a couple of times.

The scary part over—Mikey wipes his brow ostentatiously—the men take cigarette breaks in the general vicinity of the egress, and then move onstage to adjust the fresnels. Don and Doug and Dennis and Tim and George are here, painting platforms black and hanging sliding doors. One of two shoji screens has been built and lies on its side in back. Stu has carried the computerized light board down to the stage and sits at its edge, punching in cue numbers and dialing up the intensities at which the lights will be set. Smokes finished, Mikey and D clamber up and down a couple of shorter ladders here, sliding on barn doors and top hats and snoods, all apparatus to focus and shutter the light, and discarding old gels, whose square, colored leaves tack back and forth through the stale air and fall to the floor with whispering smacks.

OCTOBER 21, WEDNESDAY.

Celia, to Jimmy and Patrick during the scene where Gallimard first goes to Song's apartment: "You know, you guys are playing this thing like a goddamn melodrama, and it's making me crazy. You're playing the end of the show in every scene. And, consequently, it's boring as hell. You're not picking up beats. Put some personality into it."

To Patrick: "I don't know why he'd be attracted to you—you're boring."

OCTOBER 22, THURSDAY. TWO WEEKS AND ONE DAY TO GO.

According to the production calendar, this is the date by which all actors are expected to be off book for Acts One and Two. Patrick, who until now hasn't done a scene without script in hand, arrives tonight virtually line-perfect.

Grace sits in the back row, eating peanuts and whispering her lines, script propped on her knees. Doug has been practicing his lines at work during his lunch hour, staying at his desk with the door closed and saying them out loud; he's sure his co-workers think he's crazy. Tall Michelle runs her lines while driving Gabbie to school in the morning, Gabbie on book to cue her. Jimmy, pacing down by the front of the stage just now while he reviews his, looks up from his book and crosses himself.

Tonight they work with sound cues; even though cues are still only punched in on the boom box rather than amplified throughout the house from the sound booth, the effect is often magical, one more layer of make-believe contributing to the greater illusion.

Molly has set up shop down in the dressing rooms: a regular sewing machine, an overlock sewing machine, two dress models, an ironing board, boxes of Velcro, stencils, paints, fabrics, pins, an assortment of garments in various states hanging on a rack. She surfaces in the house from time to time to borrow a body and try something on. Celia's mother slips in to gather up material for the Mao suits from Molly. She's worked as a seamstress her whole life, and will stitch them up over the weekend. She's small, has an Italian accent, wears a purple windbreaker and a shrug. "So what kind of play is this?" she asks skeptically, while Molly loads her up. She will not come see the final production.

On the prop table: lighter fluid, a sword, a huge white megaphone, black-lacquered trays, knee pads, a tape recorder, a box of Phillies Blunts, two princess telephones, a box of incense labeled "Fragrance Cones—Night Jasmine."

On the greenroom bulletin board, a note to cast and crew to check the program for typos or changes to copy, and a reminder: "Song and

Kurogo, note your bios need to be non-gender specific, so as to maintain the necessary illusion."

On the makeup-room bulletin board, two Polaroids of Patrick bewigged and made up as a woman, one mugging, one straight.

At the end of the night, Celia asks to have everyone up onstage so she can give notes.

"Can I just say something to everyone?" says Jimmy, who has dropped and muddled a hundred lines tonight. "First of all, I'm really sorry—"

"Stop apologizing to everyone," interrupts Celia.

"But I—"

"Don't apologize," she repeats. And launches into notes. "Carolyn, project." "Michelle, you basically have to scare the bejeezus out of me in the Mao scene." "Grace, help me with what you want me to feel in the 'I want a divorce' scene. Should we feel empathy there? Right now it's distancing. It needs to be more pleading." "Orea, you've got to come right in with that chair. Pacing." "Patrick, you are an *actress*. People come from all over the world to see you. You're witty, you're . . . I'm missing personality in you. All this tender shit is not going to work, because they"—she jabs her pencil over her shoulder, indicating the audience—"are not going to believe it."

"And Jim. I need you cold on your lines. Cold, cold, cold. I don't care what we have to do to get you there. Paraphrasing is not acceptable. When you paraphrase, you add words, and that destroys the rhythm of the piece. Besides which," she sighs, "the show's long enough already." She delivers her notes like a coach in the locker room at half-time. Her voice has that muscle, that athletic lift and vigor, and at the same time an unequivocating, uncompromising taskmaster edge. "I don't think the show's going to grow until I see you work on the confidence, Jim, and I see a personality coming from my friend Song."

Tonight is the night Jimmy begins, instinctively, to turn toward Celia for nurturing. He's known all along that this role would be the most challenging he's ever done, but now his confidence is faltering. His character is onstage almost the entire play, functioning at times as narrator of his own story, then transitioning into scenes from the tale he is piecing together. In that regard, it's a memory-play, and he must be both conductor and journeyer through the labyrinths of his own dreams and distortions. And the lines are not coming to him. He knows them when he's practicing at home, when he's running through the script with John, his partner, on book to cue him, but here onstage they just slip from his mind, like tender meat from the bone, and there's so much else to remember—the blocking, which seems to change a little every night, and his props, and his onstage costume changes, and in which scenes he's meant to be arrogant and in which he's meant to be insecure—and Celia is not a cuddly director; she's tough and technical and smart and exacting, which are fine things, which are good things, but right now what Jim would really like, what he needs, is to be reassured, to be stroked and calmed and comforted a little, because he knows he can do it but it would be extremely nice to hear her say that to him.

So, after mostly everyone's cleared out, Jimmy perches on the purple stool in front of Celia and says, "Hey, Bergalongi," which cracks her up, melts her a little, and makes her dimples show warmly; it's an old nickname back from fifteen years ago, when they first met and Jim had trouble pronouncing "Bartolotti," her maiden name. Then he apologizes profusely, again, for not having his lines yet, and Celia, again, deflects his apology.

"I know you feel badly. I can see how hard you're working. But by apologizing to the cast you're taking responsibility for all of them not knowing their lines."

"I know, I just—I don't know—I know them—" His palms are pressed together between his thighs, and he wriggles his shoulders a little and swings his feet against a rung of the stool. His face is tired, sagging, and pouchy, and his rumpled hair is looking more white than battleship gray, but he sits before Celia with all the earnest appeal and sweetness of a small boy.

"Just concentrate on getting them down."

"I'm going to take a few days off next week, just to get them."

They do have a talk about confidence then, although it's not Jim's confidence they address, but Gallimard's. Celia tries to impress upon Jimmy the need to see more confidence in Gallimard, the need to see him puffed up and fat on the adoration of his orchid, his Butterfly, his Song. It's the crucial element missing from his portrayal, which is too riddled with nervous mannerisms and fumbling shtick. His Galli-mard must feel strong.

Jim listens to all this avidly, thirstily, as though he's receiving a transfusion.

"That's something we really need for this fuckin' thing to work," she finishes.

He ponders this a moment on his purple stool. "We're beyond friggin'?"

"We're at fuckin'."

OCTOBER 27, TUESDAY.

Down in the lobby Doug has spread a huge plastic drop cloth across the jazzy tiles, and on it lies a giant fan-shaped piece of muslin, with pencil marks at the future folds, and next to it a gallon jug of Elmer's, an old Maxwell House can filled with a water-glue mixture, and scraps of white tissue paper. Don comes in a little past eight from making a presentation to the Arlington Arts Council—after years of being entirely self-supported, AFD has decided to appeal for some outside funding—and Doug says, "Oh, great, I have to be onstage. Would you mind sizing this?" He hands Don a paintbrush.

Sizing the muslin with watered-down glue will stiffen it, so that the fan will stand open onstage as a piece of set dressing. Painting on torn sheets of white tissue enhances the effect, making it that much stiffer and more crinkly when it dries. Doug's original model called for one of these fans on each side of the stage, and a third, really big one behind the sliding doors at the top of the platform—this one could be lit different colors whenever the doors slid open, to create different moods. But the smaller two may have to be scrapped. Doug worked on one of them earlier, with the bone-colored muslin on a piece of plywood, and when the sizing went on, some natural color from the wood seeped through, ruining the cloth with tannish stains. That one he'll have to start over from scratch. If he can get to it. His fine features look sharp with exhaustion. This double duty of acting and set designing is taking its toll.

Don removes his jacket in his slow, amiable way and inspects the project. Of course he'll help. That's what he's here for. He just goes off to make a cup of coffee first.

"Oh, thank you," repeats Doug, harried and relieved at the same time. He sighs, blinks, scrapes a piece of hair back over his high forehead, scoots upstairs.

The house lights are off tonight, so that Stu can begin to run the light cues and see what will need reprogramming. For the moment, though, only a few milky ponds of light fall on the stage from the work lights above; the rest is duskiness and shadow, and the figures of Celia and Kelley and Mayre and the others are hard to make out at the front of the house. The sound people are positioned in their booth tonight, too; when they need to communicate with Celia and her team, one of them presses the button on what's known as the "God mike" and a disembodied voice floats down. Steven Ranieri stops in; he's the local florist who's agreed to donate three Chinese-style flower arrangements for set dressing; he needs to check on colors and size. The actors are beginning to congregate down in the greenroom when they're not onstage; the intercom has been turned on for the first time, so that they can listen for their cues from down here.

In the women's dressing room, Barbara Tyler and Betty Finnigan—director and production manager, respectively, of *Funny Girl*—have joined the little crew of assistants Molly has recruited to help sew. They sit wisecracking and sewing—Betty on the overlock machine, Barbara basting a cuff onto Doug's suit jacket by hand and pretending to be surly about it ("Can't he just grow his arms an inch?"). Both women are well aware that Celia bailed them out of backstage disaster with the last show, so, when the call went out this time around for help completing the *Butterfly* costumes, they did the only thing they could and made themselves available.

Molly, who has been putting in increasingly long hours, leaving work early to reach the theater at four and staying long after the actors have gone home to bed, dashes around as if with blinders on, focusing on the work and only the mountains of work, so that Betty and Barbara, besides contributing their hands, inject a certain welcome levity into the dressing-room area. Betty, a retired bank vice-president, trades barbs intermittently while doing some real sewing, but Barbara, the basting done, quickly ascertains that her long career coaching fashion models makes her rather more suited for other tasks; she cannot help turning her experienced eye rather critically on some of the costumes that have been assembled for the play. The truth is that Molly, working so hard to create the Chinese and Japanese garments from scratch, right down to making the tassels for the head-dresses, and designing a special obi with a pouch sewn in for the stage blood, and stitching the soft-soled shoes the kurogo wear, has not had time to focus the same level of attention on the Western garments.

Meanwhile, Tall Michelle roams the tiny corridor between dressing rooms, flourishing the prop whip she'll use in the "Mao sequence," which condenses the Chinese Cultural Revolution into a series of choreographed vignettes in which Song is interrogated by Chin, rehabilitated as a field laborer, and eventually forced to go to France and resume his role as Gallimard's lover and spy there. She thwacks it imposingly against her calf. "I'm trying to think Michelle Pfeiffer as Catwoman," she declares.

Carolyn tries on her pin-up-girl wig—a sort of exaggerated blond poodle look, spilling down her back. "I got my bikini wax today," she mentions winsomely, masking her trepidation over the fact that for her first role ever in a straight play she's going to be stripping to nothing more than a bikini bottom onstage. Barbara, tall, sardonic, and sort of scampily classy, offers an impromptu course on how to strip: stance, hair tossing, crucial pauses, and the like. Tall Michelle audits for the fun of it, and the two younger women pose and improvise in front of the long mirrors.

Just down the hall, Barbara Horrigan is fiddling with the wigs in the costume room, brushing and pinning them up in preparation for their adornment. She struggles to trim a few fake flowers off their wired plastic stems. The scissors refuse to work in her eighty-four-year-old hands. "I'm too old for this," she reflects, somewhat wheezily, but without particular chagrin. It's going on ten now. She drives herself to and from the theater in the dark.

Tension and excitement are beginning to ruffle the air. Everyone seems to be veering over the edge in terms of fatigue. Some react by goofing off, catching church giggles, and seeming detached from the glowering urgency upstairs. Some are growing fraught with intensity, curving into themselves with furrowed brow and fierce concentration; these seem detached from any sense of frolic or festivity about putting on a show. But most tread the median, dipping into the spirit of first one reaction and then the other. No one can sit still. They all play with their props, run lines, walk about in their stage shoes, and suck Altoids. Mostly, the excitement is fueled by the real, visible fact of all the people at last coming together—the sound and light people, the props and makeup people, the team of sewers, Don sizing muslin in the lobby, Barbara Horrigan pinning up wigs in Horrigan's Hideaway, the local florist stopping by to consult on blossoms—all of these people showing up as if by magic, contributing to a larger thing that's snowballing ahead now, that can't be stopped.

Late in the evening, Jimmy forgets his blocking.

"You're in the wrong place!" yells Celia.

"Me?" asks Jim, pointing at himself, confused, like a sheep in front of a honking truck.

"I thought we did all this Sunday."

"I know—I'm not a genius!"

"Jimmy? Excuse me?" That's all she says, but the entire house seems to grow cool. In the wing, the three kurogo suck in their breaths. Patrick, onstage next to Jim, grows very still.

"I'm not a genius. I can't remember." But as Jimmy says this a second time, it's more humble, more pleading, or at least Celia seems to take it this way.

"It's your job as an actor to remember," she says, but the moment of confrontation has passed.

Little breaths are released in the darkness all over the house, and the rehearsal moves on.

OCTOBER 28, WEDNESDAY. DRY TECH.

Rain is pouring loudly outside, but it's inaudible in the theater except in the shop, where you can hear drops pounding the air-conditioning unit wedged in one window. The only storms allowed into the theater are generally those created by special effect, up in the sound-and-light booth.

The stage at this moment, unpeopled and softly lit, before the rehearsal actually begins, is looking beautiful and serene. The set is nearly complete; no one but Doug and Don would be bothered at this point by all the little unfinished details. The basic pieces are in place: the brilliant red cutout on the sliding doors; the sleek curve of the ramp, now painted and faced; the shoji screens, which, with their panes of white rice paper (actually a scrim stretched behind the wooden frame), provide the one element of lightness on this simple, elegant set.

Stu, who has again lugged the light-booth computer down to the stage apron, begins punching in various cues, then hopping onstage to show Celia which areas he's lit hot, which areas warm. From time to time, she asks him to kneel or lie prone, to see whether the actor's body will be lit even in these positions. The show has light cues labeled one through eighty-nine, by far the most Stu has ever programmed for a nonmusical. The thirty-eight sound cues are labeled A through LL, to avoid confusion during the actual run, when Kelley will be calling cues on headsets worn by both the sound and light operators. Kelley moves about onstage with a roll of navy-blue spiking tape, marking the exact positions where certain set pieces must be placed during different scenes.

A dry tech, sometimes called a cue-to-cue, is a rehearsal for all of the technical aspects of a show with a minimum of acting. Actors make entrances and exits, and perhaps hit a few crucial marks during a scene so the sound people can practice running a cue on a particular line or the lighting people can make sure they've lit the right spot, but it is not really a night for the actors to emote. Of all the rehearsals in the whole production process, dry techs are the ones most expected to be grueling, laborious, stress-ridden affairs, when it's discovered for the first time that the pieces don't fit, when everything that could possibly go wrong does. It's a time when people might lose their patience, snap, accuse, and blow their tops; as if in unspoken acknowledgment of this, such rehearsals are generally begun with the highest level of civility, everyone going out of her or his way to speak politely, professionally, not a "please" or "thank you" dropped, everything strictly according to the code of theater decorum. In its own way, the theater during dry tech can resemble a NASA control room.

Perhaps inevitably, given Celia's obvious strengths with all technical aspects of production—not least pulling together a crackerjack staff—this is one of the smoothest nights of all, with the whole production team very expert and calm, and even joking with each other as they move steadily through the cues, pausing to pool their change for sodas from the machine downstairs, or to jump onstage and rearrange movable portions of set. Meanwhile, the rest of the theater feels cozily populated by an ever-multiplying staff of workers. Down in the dressing rooms, five women sit sewing and tacking and beading; another two stitch in quiet tandem on one of the greenroom sofas. In Horrigan's Hideaway, both Barbaras attend to masks and wigs. Barbara Horrigan uses nail varnish to paint the lips on the masks, and Barbara Tyler brushes out the simple black pageboy wig that Patrick will wear for most of his scenes. A few summers ago, at eighty, Horrigan had her first-ever motorcycle ride—on the back of Tyler's boyfriend's Harley. Now the Barbaras discuss having Patrick meet them at the hairdresser's, so that the wig can be trimmed properly while he's got it on. Tyler hands over the fake lashes she picked up for him. She got the lushest possible ones, "the kind the transvestites use," she says knowledgeably, and Horrigan thanks her and tucks them into her makeup box. In the tiny vestibule beyond, Molly irons and the smell of hot metal and fabric fills the air.

OCTOBER 29, THURSDAY. ONE WEEK AND ONE DAY TO GO.

Carolyn, Doug, and Teri huddle in the paint shop, running the quick smattering of lines that make up their cocktail-party scene.

Down in the makeup room, Gabbie sits on a stool and watches while Barbara Horrigan makes up her mother "to look more Asian." The liquid eyeliner curls up past the outside corners of her dark Filipino eyes.

Jimmy, upstairs by the prop table, lights a cigarette gingerly in preparation for the opening, then holds it like a live grenade.

Patrick takes his place backstage, wearing the wireless mike for the first time. His feminized voice doesn't carry as well as his regular baritone, and he's miked in order to balance his volume with Jimmy's.

He's wearing the tiny receiver strapped around his back, with a thin cord snaking up the back of his neck and taped into place by his temple. The whole thing distracts him; it itches, and he can't believe the audience won't spot it there.

Orea and Little Michelle gather in the shop with their kurogo costumes pinned and tucked onto them.

Kelley, wearing headsets and brandishing a flashlight, moves through the backstage area calling places. She's already called it over the intercom but garnered little response, which has awakened her inner schoolteacher. "Ladies and *gentle*men—when I call places, I need you *in* your places im*me*diately, or I will start with*out* you."

The run goes well. Jimmy calls "Line!" only about as much as everyone else tonight. The physical elements are all coming together—a hand prop here, a sound cue there—and suddenly it's beginning to look like a show. Of course, there are great gaffes, moments when the physical elements backfire. Jimmy, kissing Patrick at the close of Act One, gets his mouth too near the mike, and the smacking sounds are amplified hilariously through the house. Patrick, trying to slip his cigarette and lighter from the folds of his obi, cannot locate them and resorts to ever-broader fishing and groping before the props finally drop from the bottom of his obi and clatter to the floor, whereupon he sinks supplely down, scoops them up, and returns to character as such a paragon of poise that it breaks everyone up, including Celia, whose dimples have been flashing more and more lately with real pleasure: a sign of gratified relief, born of all the evident momentum and the fact that things are starting to fall into place.

She begins notes after the run with, "First of all, you all know you did quite well tonight, I hope," which, coming from Celia, is close to occasion for popping corks. Then she switches her Altoid to the other cheek and levels her gaze at Jimmy. "James. I'm really glad you were pissed at me." Beat, beat. " 'Cause it worked. You did good work. Thank you."

She is sitting on a chair on the thrust, looking down at her cast, which is for once gathered in the audience, reclined in the comfortable chairs, instead of standing or sprawling on the floor of the stage. Patrick alone stands off to the side; he was the last to arrive for notes, having been downstairs getting his wig and the transvestite eyelashes removed. Now Barbara Tyler has followed him up, to try on yet a different wig—a long fat braid—and a coolie hat, for the "The Actor is Re-Habilitated" scene.

Celia goes through her pansy-covered book, reading aloud the notes she's scrawled there. Carolyn—volume. Jim—watch the regional accent on the word "morning." Tall Michelle—play with what you're going to do on the word "deflowering." Kurogo—place the screens with the scrim facing upstage. Patrick—let's try you humming the aria straight through. (He is gazing at the floor but, as per her request, flashes her a sign, a thumbs-up, very cool and very sweet at the same time.) And then, "Okay, Patrick, first of all, when you put the wig on, there was this unbelievable *thing*. And, I don't know if you even realize it, but you put this kind of swish into your walk. I wrote, 'Keep swish in.' And the eyelashes."

"I was boggled when I saw him," says Jim.

"It is mind-boggling."

"I *feel* different in it," agrees Patrick, shyly.

"Yeah."

Patrick's creation of Song has evolved gradually, in pieces, by an apparently private and pensive process. So much of what looked like coolness in the beginning was Patrick's way of internalizing notes, cerebrally and critically. And in the beginning he offered only the voice, Song's feminized, slightly breathy cadence, and the intelligence, the sense that Patrick's mind was continually making meaning of character and motive. Then came the gliding walk, and the fluid, womanly hands. But it wasn't until he had his lines and blocking down that Patrick dived into Song, making possible new levels of contact and connection, both with Gallimard and the audience. Layered onto this has been Song's singing, which has come as an ethereal surprise to everyone, for Patrick, with his classical vocal training, has learned bits of *Madame Butterfly*, which pour from him in an effortless, haunting soprano at moments in the script. Now, with the wig and eyelashes, and the pomegranate lips, and the celebrated swish, and moments of real, seductive coquettishness, Song is coming to life as a complexly realized character in these last rehearsals.

Jim invested himself wholly and unreservedly in Gallimard from the beginning, going on undiluted instinct and unchecked physicality. From the way he established connections with his fellow actors, to the way he plunged simultaneously into his character's lines, emotions, and physicality, everything was large from day one: Gallimard's nervous tics, his self-deprecating humor, his awkwardness in pursuing an affair, his candor, his voice, his heart. Over time, Jimmy has modulated his performance, begun to contain or shift or flat-out jettison earlier ways of delivering certain lines. And now, over the past several days, he has begun to incorporate Celia's analysis of Gallimard as a more confident, at times arrogant, player in both politics and love, bringing layers to the character, grounding him in an intellectual understanding as well as a physical, emotional presence.

The method of one actor seems measured, even compartmentalized, and then carefully pieced together from the inside out, with a mountain climber's combination of deliberation and skill. The method of the other seems more a general leap of faith and then a pulling back, a subsequent mental process of recalibrating his course to the final destination, more parachutist than mountain climber. The one, in other words, is very nearly the inverse of the other—but the two actors are, in these last days, against all odds, seeming to make their respective ways toward a common ledge.

OCTOBER 30, FRIDAY AFTERNOON.

It's 1:00 P.M. Celia is alone in the house. Jimmy asked to work with her individually, so they each agreed to take the afternoon off today and meet at the theater, only Celia came early; she's been here since eleven-thirty. When Jimmy arrives, she's gazing at the stage, her pansy notebook under one arm, a pen clamped between her teeth. She's been pacing the playing area, thinking and writing, visualizing, plotting, with her mind that won't sit still. She's in her rehearsal denims. Her nails are cherry red. She's made herself a cup of green tea with one of the teabags she keeps in her purse; it's grown cold; later she'll nuke it.

Celia does not regret what she calls the altercation she had with Jim three nights ago. She thinks it was necessary to push Jim over the hump of his difficulties with the role. And she needed to stand her ground in order not to lose the respect of the cast. If it had gotten any worse, she would have asked everyone to excuse her and Jimmy, so as not to humiliate him before others. It's not that she likes playing the heavy, contrary to popular belief. But she took his remark as a challenge to her authority, and for the larger good of the production she couldn't allow that. Now, in the aftermath of that incident, she will allow herself to mete out some strokes—not anything mushy or coddling, but like this, for instance: taking an afternoon of her time to give Jim her undivided attention.

Jimmy enters via the shop, his gait and his countenance like that of a sweet-natured teenage boy who's just had a growth spurt, and removes his maroon sports jacket. He's wearing a dog-patterned necktie and a small gold tie clip. But under the surface he looks beleaguered; he's lost weight and hasn't been sleeping so well, and not just because of the late-hour rehearsals. At home his partner, John, has been hearing his anxieties and complaints every night, gently trying to give him Celia's point of view, doing what he can to help smooth things out between leading man and director. John knows Jimmy to underestimate himself habitually, and to rely on higher estimations of his worth from external sources, so he has tried to prop up Jim's spirits and confidence in a way Celia can't or won't. And Jim comes in today resolved yet again to be strong, to succeed. It's as if he's trying to strike just the right note of appeal; perhaps that would finally elicit from Celia the support he needs.

"Bergalongi," he salutes.

Celia has already taken on the murkily timeless air of the theater; she might have been here all night; it might *be* the middle of the night. "Mr. Grana." She nods. He rolls up his cuffs. "Where would you like to start?" she asks.

"I don't know. I keep thinking the transitions are my biggest bugaboo."

In the absence of anyone else, Celia reads the other parts for Jimmy, stepping in and out of scenes with him, becoming his buddy, his boss, his fantasy, his wife. She takes on the mannerisms of the other actors, who have put their marks on the roles, conveying traces of Tom's bawdy relish in the "boobs flapping" speech, Doug's unctuous paternalism in the promotion scene, Carolyn's generic come-hitherness in the pin-up-girl scene, Grace's smug amusement in the "Is she perverse?" dialogue. In each case, the transition back to Celia is breathtakingly quick, as if slack moments are not in her vocabulary, and when she begins to talk again as her director-self, it's as though she's working from a well-rehearsed lesson plan, always ready to feed Jimmy another leading question, another approach to the problem, another tool. Her speech is pointed, muscular, deft. They work the transitions from scene to scene, and they work the short, linking monologues that are so often interspersed. They talk about technical ways Jim can help the audience understand which scenes are flash-backs, and about more esoteric shades of meaning: "What's the objec-tive of that scene?" "Show us the difference between the various Gallimards." "Let's try to connect the dots."

Jimmy attends to her almost beseechingly, as though willing each next thing that will come out of her mouth to be the key that unlocks the character for him once and for all.

The phone rings in the shop. It's Hewlett-Packard. "I'm sorry, Jimmy, we're working on a hot thing at work," says Celia, but, like a seasoned teacher stepping into the hall for a minute, she gives him something to grapple with in the interim: "Is he between two worlds in this scene? If not, which world is he in?"

Jimmy loosens his tie and whispers the question back to himself as he sits on the edge of the ramp. He looks tireder in this moment, with Celia gone from the room. He likes to think of himself as a con-sumer advocate at the insurance company where he works; although that's not his official title, it's he who often communicates directly be-tween the consumers and the "docs," lobbying for approval for some extra bit of coverage, listening to and reassuring the consumers who call with their sad, worried stories. That's who he was all morning, in his maroon coat and doggy tie, a listener and nurturer, soothing the relatives of the sick in his kindly, avuncular way. Now he's someone else—an actor struggling with a role and for the approval of his direc-tor, and on top of that he's trying to be Gallimard, too, a strange bird, really, an archetypal muddle of Western arrogance and insecu-rity, seeking to love the perfect woman and be the perfect lover, and bringing himself to ruin in the act. Jimmy undoes a couple buttons at his throat and pulls at his already loosened tie as Celia conducts business in efficient tones just beyond the stage.

If asked which were more pressing at this point, nailing the role or receiving succor, his answer would just be "yes."

FRIDAY EVENING.

They're dress-rehearsing, if that term applies, Patrick's nude scene—or, as Celia delicately put it when she reminded him last night, "Are you ready to do the buck-naked thing tomorrow?" Teri has already pulled him aside and assured him that, as a mother of three boys, in addition to having been "sort of promiscuous before I got married," she's seen it all, but that, regardless, he can count on her and the other kurogo backstage not to peek when he disrobes. Orea, meanwhile, has confessed with her usual Gracie Allen candor that she'll be doing exactly that: finding a discreet crack between the traveler and teaser curtains from which to gaze. And Celia has announced that, for privacy's sake, the Academy Street entrance will be locked and unlit tonight, in order to prevent anyone from stopping in off the street. To each, Patrick has nodded or grinned or laughed; he is perhaps the least nervous person in all of Arlington regarding this particular event.

Before running the scene, Celia wants them to run just the lines, which Jim is having trouble with. He's changed out of his business clothes and is wearing sweatpants and a "Florida Sunshine" sweatshirt, and he sits at the end of the ramp, hands clasped over his cheeks, massaging his forehead as he tries to get through the dialogue with Mayre on book. Patrick comes up midway into the scene; he has been outfitted in a sort of fog-gray suit tonight, with flares at the cuffs, very dapper in a Glen Campbell way. It's the end of the play, when he's dressed as a man, and the contrast to his Butterfly-persona is striking. He picks up his lines seamlessly from Mayre, and chooses to sit smack next to Jim on the end of the ramp, a small gesture which, given his usual rather elegant remove, seems large and kind.

Celia, sitting in the back of the house, sips green tea from a paper cup and whispers the lines automatically with Mayre whenever Jimmy needs prompting. "Okay, gentlemen, let's try it," she calls when they reach the end. "Hey, Jimmy: just *relax*." He's looking unquestionably gray and fragile.

They do the scene and it works, it's lovely, it's a dance of truth and deception and malicious revelation, and it goes incredibly smoothly, Patrick removing each article of clothing on the designated line, working up to the moment when he says, "Monsieur Gallimard—the wait is over," and steps out of his briefs. His bearing is incredibly strong, even with his back to the audience; it seems to defy any embarrassment they might feel. The moment is left cleanly open then for Jim to play Gallimard's reaction, which is the point of the scene and exactly how Celia wanted it: the focus on him, the look on his face when he's confronted with Song's anatomy.

"Yes," whispers Celia, again and again. "His instincts are so good on this," she says aloud, of Patrick, and does not write in her pansy notebook but shakes her head in satisfaction: he's nailing it. After all these weeks of not being sure he was even listening to her direction, of having people rumble softly around her that maybe she should get back in touch with that other Song from auditions, Celia is seeing this young actor realize the part commandingly and excitingly.

Not to mention pulling off the nudity. For so many months, for a year practically, the chief buzz around this production has been the *nudity*, and will they or won't they, and however will they pull it off? And now, on a quiet Friday evening, quite unremarkably, Patrick simply does that, pulls it off, and stands there, plain and pure as any other fact, for perhaps a whole unabashed minute, before he gets to his line "Okay, what about this?," on which he pulls Butterfly's white robe over his body, and the great controversial event has passed. And it's clear from this moment forward that the nudity will not, after all, be the production's major problem.

Four or five times through the scene, to work out bits like how Song's shed clothes will get cleared from the set, and then Celia dismisses Patrick with a "Thank you. Thank you very much. You're all set."

Jimmy calls him "big guy" and tells him to have a great weekend, and Kelley prescribes lots of wine and rest, and Mayre tells him Happy Halloween and asks what he's doing for the holiday. Staying home and renting a double feature, he tells them—*It's the Great Pumpkin, Charlie Brown*, and *Elvira, Mistress of the Dark*—and he does one of his sweet, bright Chiclet smiles and zips up his black leather jacket and goes to wait for the bus on Mass. Ave. Tendrils of affection follow him out. He is the same person and they are the same people, but now they have weeks in common, weeks of shared work and shared sleep deprivation, shared gripes and shared jokes, and little shared victories, like tonight's rehearsal, which did go well.

FRIDAY, NEAR MIDNIGHT.

After Patrick leaves, Mayre goes to fetch David Warnock and Molly, in order to try out a dry run of the long-awaited blood effect. At the very end of the play, Gallimard transforms himself into Butterfly onstage, donning her kimono, makeup, and wig, and then commits seppuku. Dave's been readying the effect in the paint shop all evening, mixing up the fake blood, loading the apparatus, doing trial runs with plain water. It's all just a little bit 007 this final unveiling, and the others gather curiously around them onstage.

Dave and Molly, through some early research, uncovered the fact that in the Broadway production the release of fake blood was triggered by radio, via a remote-control device; further investigation proved the rental cost of such equipment to be prohibitive for community theater, so they were left to invent an alternative approach— no less ingenious, but far less expensive. This is the very sort of challenge so many amateur-theater designers relish most of all, and Dave and Molly went at it with no holds barred, coming up with the mechanism they now explain to Kelley, Mayre, Jimmy, and Celia, all clustered around them onstage.

Dave, who has the sort of gentle, methodical voice that might calm a frightened animal, describes all the parts involved. First, the stage blood—a concoction of sugar syrup, dye, and detergent (this last ingredient to aid the washing of the costume each night)—is poured into a real blood-transport pack (appropriated, like all of the other medical devices involved, from Dave's workplace), whose piece of plastic tubing he has punctured several times with a drill. The transport pack is slipped into a plastic pneumatic pressurized infusion bag, which is in turn fitted inside a firm plastic sleeve. A bulb pumps up the infusion pack, and a clasp holds the contents in place until released. This entire thing fits into a bustlelike pouch Molly has made to fit inside Jim's obi.

The idea is that, as the kurogo help dress Jim while he delivers his final speech, one of them will release the clamp on a precalculated line, and this will allow exactly the right number of seconds for the blood to travel through the tubing and begin oozing through the little holes Dave has drilled, seeping in turn through the fabric of the obi and making it look as though Gallimard is bleeding across a long gash on his abdomen. Jim will be kneeling for his final disembowelment, and his thighs, predicts Dave, will make a nice platform on which the blood can pool and spill over. "A lapful of blood," he explains, cheerfully, "which should read nicely."

An initial quantity of blood will be rigged with a Ziploc bag attached to the stage knife's retractable blade, so that a small amount can spurt out on the actual plunge of the knife. But the follow-up, the steady seepage of vast quantities of blood from the entire length of the wound, is the inspired coup de grâce, the detail that will make the effect unbearably lifelike and devastating. "We can make it come out faster or slower, depending on how much tubing we use. The more tubing, the greater volume we need, though, to get it around the horn."

"The blood," Molly interjects matter-of-factly, "is sucrose-based and can crystallize, so it'll have to be washed out every night with warm water." She has Scotchguarded the fabric of Jim's kimono already, and test-stained some swatches to make sure the blood will wash out. But it stains skin, too, so Jim will have to apply some special hand cream before that scene. Now, in a peacock-blue turtleneck draped about with measuring tape, pincushion, sewing scissors, etc., like some kind of oddly decorated war hero, Molly unties the bustle-thing from around her own waist, explaining that she attended a kimono demonstration last year and saw how the blood pack could be incorporated into some of the authentic ritual of how the kimono and obi are traditionally folded. Standing in for the kurogo, who will have to learn all this, they proceed to walk through the dressing of Jim, who stands in their midst like a bemused sacrificial virgin. Celia and Molly clothe him in his kimono, and then Molly ties an under-sash around his waist. They unfold the obi and wind that around his waist; Molly fastens it in back and then ties a rope sash over all *this*, making a square knot which she tucks in around back. Then Molly ties on the bustle-thing. Everyone's a bit staggered.

"You're talking through all this, by the way," says Celia to Jimmy, with just a trace of gallows humor.

"She says I have to keep talking," Jim deadpans to Kelley. "Can I just use all the lines I left out of the other scenes?"

"Just do the ones where the sound and light cues are," Kelley retorts dryly. "I don't care about the others."

Molly finally finishes up, tucking the tube into the front of the obi, and the clamp release around in back. A pressure gauge is supposed to pop out, like a turkey thermometer, when it's ready. They pump up the infusion bag and hear a sound like a shot—the transport pack's burst open the plastic sleeve. Someone laughs in a great squawk and then goes immediately quiet. "Hmm," says Dave in his mild-mannered way. "We'll have to duct-tape the hell out of it."

"We're gonna do this for real Sunday night?" asks Mayre.

"Yeah, Sunday night we're gonna bleed," says Celia.

But now they're all going daffy.

"Grease?" says Celia, discussing with Molly what Jim will need on his hands to protect them from bloodstains.

"What about it?" asks Jim, confused.

"Is the word."

"Is the show you wish you were directing."

Jim decides it's time to give Molly a big fat kiss on the cheek, which she takes in stride. "Don't get nervous!" he begs Dave, in mock-alarm. "It was just a kiss!"

Dave, inspecting the plastic packs, smiles. Doug comes in from the shop to see what all the commotion is about. "You're having entirely too much fun out here," he observes. He's wearing a tool belt and holding a giant piece of sized muslin. He's been having dreams about sizing muslin.

"My goal," promises Molly, "if I have to *live* here, is to have this all ready by Sunday night." No one bothers to tell her she's pretty much already moved in. Doug, for his part, is literally swaying on his feet.

"I don't think you should be using power tools," observes Mayre, her last cogent thought before she flops into a chair at the end of the ramp.

"These aren't power tools."

"I mean, whatever."

Jim is more or less reclined on the ramp, incongruously garbed in kimono, sweatpants, sneakers, bright-orange undersash. He props himself up to drink from a can of Sprite. "Is this mine?"

And this is nice, too, the privilege of all being exhausted together, smeary and ragged and giddy at the end of the night, when the theater feels soft and familiar as an old glove, and they are, for this moment anyway, as entitled to sprawl here unmasked in front of each other as any handful of unrelated citizens could be.

Ten

A Theater Primeval

One August evening at Long Lake, up in the midst of the Adirondack Mountains, right when we normally would be down at the dock brushing our teeth by twilight and maybe watching some deer splash and bound away into the woods, we pushed off, my parents and I, from the little cup-shaped beach in the canoe called the *Tintype* and paddled toward Emerson's Boat Livery. I was eleven. My brother and sister had opted to stay back and play poker by gas lamp with our grandparents at the long picnic table in the cabin. We carried extra sweaters and a big fat flashlight in anticipation of the return boat trip later that night. My parents' paddles dipped and pushed and ruddered, and I, idle in the middle, trailed a hand in the soft water, and made out the shaggy hulk of Moose Island uplake, and the lights of other camps beginning to twinkle on along the densely pine-lined shores, and the shapes of boats docked at Emerson's, where we eventually crunched up onto the sand and hopped out, being more careful than usual to keep our feet dry. We were going to the theater.

We went to the Point, my grandparents' camp on Long Lake, every summer of my childhood, drove up from the city six hours to the south in a dull-red station wagon packed with camping gear, and we might have been driving to the Northwest Territories as far as we three kids were concerned—both because of how interminable the car ride felt and how utterly remote the country up there seemed. We left our car at the boat livery and rowed or paddled to our grandparents' camp across the lake. No electricity, no phone lines, no plumbing, the only running water from a spigot outside. We burned our garbage every night in a great sparky fire, and kept our produce cold in a covered pit dug into the earth. What toys we brought looked different at the Point, not only cheaper and more garish than they had in the city, but more disposable, more inconsequential. Our chief playthings at the Point were more likely to be an antler-shaped branch we'd found, a sacred spot between the cove and the woods we'd stumbled upon and declared a fort, mazes we charted in the scrubby blueberry bushes. My grandmother had chosen, and my grandfather wood-burned into a piece of pine and nailed up in the privy, a few lines from Longfellow's *Hiawatha*; they began, "This is the forest primeval," and we never doubted their authority.

The overwhelming sense we had at the Point was of leaving behind the world as we knew it. It was a sense of shedding, of denuding our-selves for a week or two of all the trappings of what we might have called civilization; the closest we came into contact with it during our Long Lake days was when we drove into the village (in a car!) and were allowed to buy (with real money!) gobstoppers (processed sugar!) at the general store (an actual commercial establishment!). The strange thrill of these penny-candy forays, the brush with civilization they en-tailed, was dizzying. We'd head back over the lake, this time in the rowboat with the outboard motor (named *Cop-out*), weighted down with bags of groceries and the newspaper, which must have been a sort of grown-up equivalent of our gobstoppers. And soon the only rem-nants of the candies would be rings of dried colored sugar around our lips, and the paper would be quickly ochered by the sun and blown about and sandy on the little beach, and the great green essence of the Point, of what we really believed to be the forest primeval, would have re-established its eminence in our hearts and minds, and we would be far, far away again from that other, larger, but at the same time queerly smaller world we'd so recently left behind.

All of which makes it so perfectly odd that one evening, one summer, my parents and I decided to go to the theater. They'd seen a flier in the general store. A little repertory company had sprung up and was inhabiting the dilapidated buildings of a former priests' camp a few miles from the village, down a winding dirt lane called Tarbell Hill Road. Mixing a few professional actors with local citizens, it produced a revolving slate of three or four plays throughout the summer. The productions were staged in an old woodframe chapel with open rafters, which seated about seventy. The audience, comprising summer people and year-round residents, was not in short supply; we were well packed in. I was young enough both to wonder at the event of so many strangers having found their way here through the dark to congregate at this theater in the woods, and to take it for granted. That summer was around the time I was beginning to think of theater as one station near the crux of everything important in life.

We saw *Private Lives* and came back the next night to see *The Subject Was Roses*. The acting was very fine, and the sets startlingly good, considering that they got installed and replaced within the course of a day. So mesmerizingly complete were the two very different worlds conjured on successive nights on the tiny, somewhat sagging stage that there was something genuinely shocking, after the final curtain, about the return trip: first to the walls of the shabby wooden chapel, and the company of audience members, which grew about me after the applause like a sudden murmuring forest as they rose to their feet and shuffled sociably out; and then to the humongous darkness and coldness and quietness of Long Lake, where we'd shove off again in the *Tintype*, aiming across the water for the lantern left on for us at the Point.

But equally shocking to me each night, as I performed the silent, straight-backed duty of flashlight-holder while we crossed the lake, was the simple evidence, revealed, that theater could exist anywhere, even in so unlikely and remote a place as this. And in that notion—held murkily but with conviction on the occasion of those late and stately sojourns back through the vast liquid darkness to our sleeping bags— lay the clear corollary that theater itself was primeval, and therefore necessary, in some water-and-oxygen-and-sunlight way, to our species.

• • •

If I imagined, that summer, that I'd more or less stumbled upon a theater thriving in the middle of a lonely pine forest, and that this was some sort of proof—of theater's organic nature, of its inevitability—one response might be that I was certainly ripe, at eleven, to draw such a conclusion. For the theater of childhood is something everyone engages in; childhood might even be thought of *as* a kind of theater, an arena for the exploration of stories and crafting of myths. This is perhaps the most serious and ancient kind of theater: the private, daily one enacted by children, for children, often with little regard to audience and a rare absence of self-consciousness, the theater in which make-believe and reality have shifting, porous borders. It's the theater through which we all, in our early years, filter and ingest the substance of life. Theater as baleen.

All children are actors, directors, and playwrights. From the time we can talk, we are spinning dramas out of our imaginations. From the time we can bark, actually—from the time we learn to say "meow" and crawl around the house and lick people's feet—we get it, we are on to it, we are acting. And we direct our rag dolls and our Matchbox cars and even our crackers and raisins in intricate dramas which we narrate and make up as we go along. When I was really small, I named my fingers, and they were my repertory company, appearing again and again in half-whispered plays upon my knees.

As we grow, the web of our individual dramas spreads out to overlap with that of our friends. Here are requisite games of firefighter, astronaut, teacher, witch; here also the more elaborate backyard adventures, very grave, very grand: now comes Sir Ferris Wheel in his mother's old velour bathrobe, and Sir-Lady Gladiola in red cowboy boots, and there they go, riding maple-switch horses behind the garage to save the kingdom. There's never any final curtain in the theater of childhood; we slip in and out of character all day long; we reprise our roles endlessly, and bring our plots and ensembles to school with us and on the subway and to the doctor's office.

Hours and hours of our childhoods we devoted to rehearsal and performance; only a fraction of it is ever witnessed by others, and that only after we learned a certain amount of self-consciousness; it was never our motivating force. Our motivating force was something more personal and private, more simply intrinsic to the process of becoming a person. We would have done it anyway, audience or no; in the beginning it was only to satisfy our own curiosity, our own longing to experience, to narrate, to know. This is the theater primeval: the play-acting of childhood—very grave, very grand, irrepressible.

And then we learn to forget it, outgrow it, repress it, we learn to leave it behind. It gets folded up with our too-small clothes and stashed in an attic trunk, or given to Goodwill. We won't need it anymore. It'll have no currency in our daily adult lives, would only mark us as eccentric at best, creepily flawed at worst. Theater will henceforth enter our lives almost exclusively in the form of evening sitcoms and hour-long dramas, which we will accept passively, dumbly; these programs will stimulate our brains less than sleep. With some regularity, the media will unite in a frenzied but strangely robotic serving up of some real-life drama, and for days or weeks or occasionally months at a time the show will unfold everywhere: in magazines and newspapers, on radio and television, at water coolers and Web sites, and it will be like a faint, faint, pale echo of a more ancient kind of mass catharsis through theater, although it won't be acknowledged as such.

Stories will still unfold in our hearts and play themselves out across the screen of our minds. In tiny, unchecked moments, reveries will flutter down and light upon us and for an instant we'll be someone else, and far away. Then other concerns, more literal, more immediate, will press in, and the reveries will flit off again, mothlike, erasing their own memories as they vanish. We will be given no language for these lapses, no space in which to store them, no training in how to cherish or regard them. So they will not linger or accumulate but will continue to flit away, to elude, and to most of us they will not seem worthy or dear, and we will never really register their weight, much less miss them when they have receded.

But is this true?

A few months before becoming immersed in *M. Butterfly* rehearsals, I was one of several hundred adults to make my way to a small city in Michigan in order to attend an international amateur-theater festival. *International amateur-theater festival.* Mulling over these particular four words, linked together like that, made the plane ride short. I hit the tarmac filled with happy curiosity and a lurking skepticism. What sort of people came to week-long international amateur-theater festivals anyway? The expected attendance, I'd been told, was around fifteen hundred, and groups from eighteen different countries were scheduled to perform—these selected from an applicant pool that had included *fifty-seven* different countries. Whatever sort of people they proved to be, there was no apparent shortage of them.

Who would have thought such appetites could prevail, worldwide, among so many? Not only did all these people engage in amateur theater on their home turfs; they had decided to raise the money and take the time to make the journey—thousands and thousands of miles, for many of them—to the small, solidly Midwestern Twin Cities of St. Joseph and Benton Harbor, Michigan, in order to perform for one another. For five days, they would all meet at Lake Michigan College, and share meals of overcooked spaghetti and salads swimming with mini-marshmallows, and attend workshops and performances, and celebrate the spirit of amateur theater with a bunch of strangers from all over the world. What passion! What folly!

As I quickly learned, there was nothing anomalous or even very novel about this event. It was the third in a series of such festivals, given every four years since 1990 under the auspices of the American Association of Community Theatres; the other two had been held in Des Moines, Iowa, and Racine, Wisconsin. (It is perhaps not pure chance that all three had been held in the Midwest, where community theater is traditionally well supported on a much greater scale than in other parts of the country. As one board member of the Iowa branch of AACT told me with a sort of backhanded pride, "There's not a heck of a lot else to do out here.")

All week long, the festival was abuzz with talk of upcoming events. The twenty-fourth World Congress and Theatre Festival, sponsored every two years by the International Amateur Theatre Association (IATA), would be taking place the following summer in El Jadida, Morocco. Plans for something being billed as the World's Greatest Amateur Theatre Festival were under way for the millennium; this would involve hundreds of simultaneous "mini-festivals" to be held in countries all over the world. Aruba's eleventh international festival would be coming up in couple of months; then there was one in Caracas the month after that, and a conference in Canada the month following; the fifth World Festival of Children's Theatre had just finished up in Lingen, Germany, and the sixth of these was already being planned in Toyama, Japan; and furthermore, IATA—which comprised eighty countries and five continents and over a hundred thousand amateur groups, and had just relocated its headquarters to Tallinn, Estonia—had recently accepted two more national centers (Bangladesh and Zimbabwe) into the organization, as well as twenty-five more associate members, from Bulgaria to Pakistan to Papua New Guinea to Tunisia to Turkey to St. Lucia. And all of *that* represented only even the barest tip of the iceberg. Some of the conference attendees, an important-looking little clutch of them who kept cropping up at all the major meetings all week long, had schedules that kept them on the road with amateur-theater commitments twelve months a year.

Meanwhile, for the rest of us milling about the chilly passageways and cavernous atria of the enormous, state-of-the-art Mendel Center at Lake Michigan College—this plunked bunkerlike amid a rather banal, flat landscape of fruit farms and strip malls baking tarrily in the stark, unseasonable heat—a sense took hold of theater's centrality to life. How could it not? Here we all were, scores and scores of us, having come from so many walks of life; how could what had summoned us not be something central?

One woman had flown to the festival from Hanes, Alaska, a former military base, population two thousand. She had a small business there making gourmet cat-food out of local salmon. Her mother, with whom she was traveling, had helped found the community theater in Hanes forty-five years ago. Her father, a military man now deceased, had designed sets and managed props, and used to joke that he knew the precise inventory of every basement and attic in town.

There was a gregarious, preternaturally confident woman from Washington, D.C., who had conceived of, written, directed, and was appearing in the official United States entry at the festival, *Sistas in Heat*—essentially a distillation of ten years' worth of her journal entries.

Her small company, Nomads Theatre Workshop, which billed itself as "a leading African American theatre group in the USA," had raised the money to get to St. Joseph/Benton Harbor by holding barbecues and selling hand-dipped chocolates and books of original poetry.

There was Sir Mort Clark, a venerated, cultivated kook of a man who'd been knighted by Princess Caroline (or, anyway, awarded the Chevalier Medal of Culture) in Monaco for his work in amateur theater. A handful of other festival participants had been awarded the same medal, but Sir Mort milked the distinction theatrically, and worked aggressively to spread seeds of insouciance and playfulness throughout the festival. A roly-poly, white-haired figure, sporting towering, flamboyantly patterned top hats and a masks-of-tragedy-and-comedy button the size of a dessert plate on his Hawaiian shirts, he conducted improvisation workshops and dispensed great rattling handfuls of Mardi Gras beads to everyone in his path.

There was a great pack of strapping, amused Finnish teenagers with fabulous physiques and poise; and several dozen extremely well-chaperoned Japanese children in matching jackets; and a couple of U.S. servicemen in civilian dress and brush cuts, representing AACT's Region X, the Military Overseas; and a group of Russians with hopeless teeth and excellent laughter; and various national and international theater-organization officials, almost preposterously decorous in dark suits and starred name badges, weighed down by their attaché cases and solemn bearing.

The international ambience clashed happily with the Middle American setting. The foreign guests gamely sampled the paper-thin slices of roast beef and canned green beans and creamed corn produced by the cafeteria workers, and spent no small amount of time fiddling intently with the vending machines. All the banks of pay phones scattered around the building were well exercised by a polyphony of voices in different languages. The balcony of the main theater (which the locals pronounced "thee-*ay*-ter") was hung with eighteen different flags, one for each of the countries that had been scheduled to appear. After every performance, the circular, cement-roofed driveway in front of the building flash-flooded with smokers from around the world; for the first few minutes after any given production had ended, the only sounds out there would be the click of

lighters and the dry *shhk* of matches, and, wordlessly, hands of all different color and ancestry and provenance would reach out and offer
flame to one another. Beyond them, security guards would chat and
stroll in the wide parking lots, and the uninterrupted sky would put
on its eternal pantomime, going peach and pink and Madonna blue,
basting the clouds in gold till they looked like dough dripping butter.
Everything began to seem like theater, every interaction, every silence
heightened and observed.

My greatest surprise, and it kept surprising me, every day of the
festival, until by the end it had achieved a patina of almost beatific absurdity, was the lack of translators or interpreters. Each of the performances—many of them ran easily two hours, and a number
featured talk much more prominently than song, music, dance, or
movement, and one was essentially a monologue—were delivered in
the native language of the production company. And in each instance, except for the English-language productions from England,
Ireland, Canada, and the States, the great bulk of the audience sat relatively uncomprehending. Some of the plays were adapted from
works by well-known playwrights, from Ionesco (Romania's entry) to
Aristophanes (France's) to Shakespeare (Russia's), but many others
were original or more obscure. Those groups that had submitted a
synopsis for the program had tended to keep their descriptions rather
brief and general. The result was that even the three adjudicators
(Canadian, American, and Filipino), there to offer comments at the
end of each performance as well as judge the festival winners at the
end of the week, repeatedly opened their remarks with a kind of dis-
claimer ("Since I don't speak ———, I will confine my comments to
the beautiful staging, which certainly transcended any language barrier"). At first, I thought such attempts at adjudication were a sham,
smacking of obsequious insincerity, but after the performance by the
South Koreans—most of whose large company, denied visas at the
eleventh hour by our State Department, never made it to the festival,
and who instead of their planned production therefore presented a
one-man piece about a beggar—the Filipino judge broke down crying during her adjudication, explaining chokily that she'd been over-
come by memories the performance had evoked of beggars in her
own country, and I had to reconsider.

After three or four days of this, witnessing about four performances a day, people appeared to be finding themselves strangely affected by the experience. We saw a row of German youth with tin cans on their heads, eating blue Jell-O. French women in trenchcoats, wielding flashlights in the dark. Japanese children dancing with umbrellas and bales of hay. A lovesick Croatian baker eating a huge loaf of bread shaped like a woman. A Romanian king dancing a tango.

As the house lights came on one afternoon after yet another lengthy performance in a foreign language, a woman sitting behind me with a Kelly-green cardigan and a Texan accent as thick and languorous as honey leaned forward and confided, "I keep thinking if I listen hard enough I'll spontaneously begin to understand," and I had the thought that she spoke for many of us; there was that level of concentration in the audience, among all those amateurs, those lovers of theater: that quality of keen and hopeful craning forward, of willing oneself to fall into communion with the story unfolding.

Leaving Michigan at the end of the festival on a sticky-bright June morning, traveling through the air in a vibrating metal tube, I was reminded of another return trip many, many summers earlier, paddling back across the dark cold of Long Lake in the *Tintype*, returning to the regular world from a theater world. And although I was already in the sky, I felt a strange, quick sense of flying in my limbs and heart. It wasn't just the knowledge of theater existing in the distant pine forest, and existing in Croatia and Finland and Korea, and existing in the land of gelatin salads with mini-marshmallows, and in countries at war and countries at peace, and in the time of the Greeks and the time of the Bard and the time of dotcom. It was the sudden, momentary notion of it—as if of an actual image spied through a fleeting, magic lens—exisiting everywhere.

Eleven

Tech Week

The multiplying cadre of mostly middle-aged and elderly women stitching in the dressing room and greenroom has grown quieter and more assiduous; they take up sofas and chairs and move their hands with the silent grace of undersea plants. Fifteen of them will be listed in the official program; the Sunday before opening, seven are at work for the better part of the afternoon and evening. Molly has taken it upon herself to move beyond Altoids, bringing in muffins and fresh fruit, and during the course of the day the greenroom's kitchen countertop becomes hilly with other people's offerings and discards: deli-sandwich halves, plastic packs of cookies, leftover Halloween candy, and Fishermen's Friend throat lozenges, which are tiny innocuous-looking gray pellets that taste alarmingly but sort of intriguingly like charcoal briquettes.

Most members of the cast and crew have been here working specific bits since two this afternoon, if not earlier, and by the time the evening's tech rehearsal is set to begin—the first full run-through with sound and lights—they are milling about the theater in somewhat floppy states of mind, the result of too many hours cut off from natural light and too many cups of caffeine. Floppiness notwithstanding, there is a sense of purpose, a sense of business tonight, that is different from before. Tech week has commenced; it's the final countdown. All the loose ends, figurative as well as literal, must be sewn up now to be ready by opening. Friday night is it.

The sign-up sheet appears for the first time today, tacked to the greenroom bulletin board; from here on in, all cast and crew listed will be responsible for checking off their names upon arrival.

A sign-up also has been posted for the closing-night cast party, to be held at Don and Nancie Richardson's, with each attendee asked to submit eight dollars to the production manager before then.

David Giagrando, the production manager, has not been visible for much of the rehearsal process, but he is here tonight, summoned as much as anything by his own name appended to the sign-up sheet. For lack of willing recruits, he's enlisted himself as light-board operator, meaning that he will be the person on headsets up in the booth punching in, at Kelley's bidding, each light cue Stu has programmed into the computer. It's a job, as David is quick to point out, that Baron could be trained to do, and in fact the ash-gray schnauzer is here, too, trip-trapping closely at David's heels, as if in anxious-apprentice mode.

More Polaroids of the actors in sample makeup and wigs have been taped to the wall in the makeup room, along with scrawled reminders like these:

Song

1—base tan #2
rouge—eyelashes—eye liner—lipstick—eyebrows
5—over #1—white base—rouge
geisha—heavy eye w/brow and lips
put on wig last
onstage—prop tray: baby wipes—tan #2—men's rouge—water
    w/sponge
remember to zip fly!!

Tom, as per director's orders, has cut his hitherto longish graying brown hair, and looks at once vulnerably shorn and imposingly smart, with the back of his neck all tender and new, the trim tidiness about his ears all strict and masculine. In its own way, the haircut is more transformative even than Patrick's lashes and lipstick and wig: Tom's change is less immediately revocable, and it signals the real, tangible fact of something important and looming at the end of the week. In spite of all the accumulating evidence otherwise, it's difficult to believe that the play is going to come together and go on, in front of an actual audience, before the week is through.

It's difficult to believe in part simply because this is the way it always is, it's practically a theater tradition; during the week before opening, what's called "tech week" or "production week" or "hell week," everything seems hopelessly plodding or in shambles. No matter what you do, you can't get the show to run any shorter than three hours and forty-seven minutes, and the lights keep going to black right in the middle of the last scene of Act One, and the leads keep laughing when they go to kiss, and the door keeps coming off its hinges, and the mustache keeps falling off the villain, and someone in the sound booth keeps mistaking an old John Denver tape for the fireworks sound-effects tape, and that sort of thing ad nauseam, until the night before opening, when somebody finally repeats the old theater saying, "A bad dress rehearsal means a good first performance," and everyone nods sagely and with relief, and then comes opening night, and everything is success. So some of this is par for the course and in keeping with a time-honored theater tradition, a sort of superstitiously mandated Murphy's Law insurance policy.

But in the case of AFD's *M. Butterfly*, some of this trepidation is actually warranted. Jimmy's difficulty with his lines has become remarkable, for the late date at which he's still forgetting them, for the extent to which he's forgetting them, and for the randomness with which he's forgetting them—scenes he glides through perfectly one night seem to have vanished from his memory the next; there's no predictability to the lapses. The cause of the difficulty is a great mystery. It's obviously not lack of experience, since he's been performing in community theater for the better part of four decades, and brought home EMACT's best-actor award five times. It isn't for lack of effort or enthusiasm, either; as everyone saw, he's been pushing himself toward getting off book since the first week of rehearsals, and as everyone knows, he's had his heart set on this role for a good year. Could it be age-related memory loss? a few people have quietly wondered. But, after all, Jim's not *old*, and only a few months ago he carried the Noel Coward comedy *Present Laughter*, playing a lead with very nearly as many lines and as many scenes onstage as Gallimard has in *Butterfly*, and did so triumphantly—with ample paraphrasing, it must be said, but also with ample confidence and pleasure and audience-winning gusto. Then is it stress? others have suggested, Jimmy among them, stress unmitigated, if not actually triggered, by the very different styles of this particular actor and this particular director, the one thriving on and engaging so openly in warm strokes and encouragement, the other adhering to such uncompromising standards and so rigorous a work ethic? The question will never be definitively answered, although Jim—and who can speak to the question with more authority than he?—will maintain in the end that the difficulty was due partly to this stress and partly to the elliptical, flashing-backward-and-forward nature of the script. If only he had another week or two. But he doesn't, and what is painfully clear to everyone is that the mounting anxiety around not having his lines down as opening night draws close is making the situation worse and worse.

Tonight being the initial tech rehearsal, Kelley is busy juggling for the first time the multiple responsibilities of calling light and sound cues as well as making sure the actors are in their places, and every little thing is accounted for, not to mention conferring over the headsets with Celia as they make note of and attempt to solve glitches, and all of this means she's not following the book as closely as usual, so a number of times in the opening scenes Jim calls "Line!" and receives no prompt. He waits, and gropes visibly within his brain for the memory of the next line himself, and nothing comes, and he calls "Line!" again and is met by silence, and he looks around and sees Kelley not bent over her script at the edge of the thrust, but in whispered conference with somebody, or just some dislocated voice over her headset, and still he waits, not snapping in frustration as some actors might, ever-mindful of the important work that others are doing, but across his face passes the most terrible look of desperation and disbelief, as though his own brain, his own years of experience and skill are betraying him. A few times Patrick prompts him, gently, from memory, in an un-Song-like baritone, and they are able to continue for a bit.

Once, Little Michelle lets a shoji screen fall and it crashes to the floor and startles Jimmy. Another time, the lights are cut and the actors carry on, tentatively, in darkness. Doug's wig slips over his face. Tom trips on the track of the sliding doors and knocks a piece of the molding loose. Sometimes, Jimmy is bathed in shadow when he forgets his blocking and neglects to move into the light that has come up for him across the stage, and then Celia talks him into his place. She does not bark at him tonight, shows no impatience with his slips. Without prior indication, at this late hour, she has metamorphosed into a gentle rock. The worse the rehearsal goes, the more calmly and patiently she steps in to steer everybody through it. Her voice is even, almost kind; she might be talking a scared cat out of a tree. She goes onstage at one point to strike a piece of furniture the kurogo mistakenly left, and then whispers an instruction to Teri, in the wing, her hand laid softly on the other woman's back.

Some things go gorgeously. Carolyn does her stripping scene for the first time for real, standing behind a shoji screen whose scrim panels, backlit, reveal her only marginally obscured body. She strips to black underpants before her light goes out, turning upstage as she removes the black bra, so that her final exposure is not as great as Patrick's in the later act, but still it takes an odd sort of courage and detachment, as well as the comforting disguise of the great poodley wig, and a lot of not entirely candid reassurance about the degree to which the screen mutes her nudity. Then, during the break between acts, Carolyn is very funny about scrutinizing the tickets she has ordered for her friends ("Oh, that's way too close—I have to exchange them"). Celia compliments her down in the greenroom—"That's not easy, babe!"—and Barbara Tyler helps bolster her nerve by demonstrating, with great seriousness and a native sultry finesse, a few more stripper tips—"Dangle the hose before you let it drop. . . . Look down over your shoulder as you slide off the bra strap." For his part, David Giagrando makes her laugh by assailing her during the break with a loud and chipper, "Great breasts!"

Meanwhile, the trick costume Molly designed for Patrick, for the Mao sequence, works beautifully, like magic, the kurogo tearing the specially slashed-up-the-back and Velcroed Mao suit away, so that in an instant the green pants and jacket have vanished and Patrick crouches before them in the entirely different blue peasant costume he has had on underneath. One of the kurogo claps the wide-brimmed coolie hat, with long pigtail attached, on his head, and he's transformed; four years have passed and Song has gone from Chinese-opera star to rehabilitated fieldworker on a commune in Hunan Province. It's a tiny, breathtaking moment, beautifully executed.

The kurogo in general have begun to do wonderful things. Celia worked with them just this afternoon to strengthen their overall role in the play. The changes make up a sort of last-minute artistic addition, taking them beyond the glorified furniture-movers they have felt themselves to be and turning them into "silent actors" who slip into poses amplifying the feelings of Song in many scenes. Three "specials" will be added to the light plot to illuminate each of the three women as they ring the action, creating a subtle, living periphery which in turn helps illuminate what is transpiring for the key actors in the scene. To the extent that they evoke a Greek chorus, or, more aptly, the intricately inked border around an illustration in a medieval text, they help cast a stylized, mythic quality onto the action. It's a lovely, effective conceit, kept subtle by the very pale washes of light and the loose black-and-gray garments of the kurogo, who seem to dwell between shadow and psyche. Very few of the cast members will even notice the addition, since it has been made so late, and the actors reside mostly in the greenroom now when they are not wanted on-stage, so that within the ensemble the role of the kurogo is again hardly counted or remarked upon; still, Teri and Orea and Little Michelle move into these new moments with care and ingenuity, and the effect is very strong.

Also strong is the visual element of the round, red, mandalalike sliding doors at the top of the ramp, and the blue cyc (short for "cyclorama"—a great expanse of pale-blue cloth stretched along the back wall of the stage) behind it; tonight, for the first time, lights turn the cyc white or golden or scarlet or cobalt at various moments in the play, and shine through the jigsawed pieces of luan stunningly. And all sorts of individual moments play well: Grace's cuttingly heartfelt exit line, "I hope everyone is mean to you for the rest of your life," which never fails to get a laugh, even from the same old crew of people who have heard it night after night; and Tom's infusions of cocky, bold levity in virtually every Marc scene, and Tall Michelle's scene with the whip, in which she has become quite impressively terrifying, and Patrick's cradling-crooning scene, in which he sings so hauntingly to the Cabbage Patch doll, which he has even begun to hold like an actual baby. So many moments are crystallizing beautifully.

And yet. In between these moments comes mishap after mishap, the whole evening straight through—more shoji screens crashing down, more actors plunged into sudden, arbitrary darkness, and, most troubling of all, more and more and more lines mangled and muddled and missed altogether. Celia remains outwardly calm; inside, the doubts are fast clicking together. During the second act, she slips on a pair of headsets. "Kelley, is he doing the right lines? Is he even in the right place?"

"No, want me to stop him?"

"Yes."

Kelley does.

Jim cups his whole face. "Oh shit, oh shit, oh shit."

"Okay," whispers Celia on headsets, "I have no idea what we do if that happens."

"It's only Sunday," David says. That becomes the evening's refrain.

David, meanwhile, gets sassy on the headsets, which breed their own kind of disembodied intimacy. Every breath, every swallow, every rustle of paper and sniff can be heard over them, and yet the wearer may be in pure geographical privacy, ensconced in the sound and light booth, tucked away behind the curtain stage left, or simply roaming in the darkness about the house. David is up at the light board, with Peter Ambler running sound beside him and Baron yawning at his feet, and every now and then he sends his voice, like the color commentary in a sports cast, randomly out over the air waves. "The lights look good. When the actors manage to stand in them. It's like, hello, Acting 101: look for your light."

And later: "Baron, are you having fun? Do you need a dog in this show?"

"That depends, can he learn lines?" retorts Kelley, her voice low and clear in David's ear, her body somewhere out in the darkness.

"He can speak on cue."

"That's true."

And later: "I really think Song looks like a woman."

"I know, it's amazing."

"Once he's all gussied up. I only wish his voice were a little higher."

"Warn light cue fifty-nine and sound cue Z."

"Warned," says David.

"Warned," says Peter Ambler.

And later, succinctly but meaningfully, as Patrick does the nude scene for the first time in front of the entire cast and crew: "In Arlington, Massachusetts, folks."

At the end of the run, with the cast gathered in various states of makeup and dress on the edge of the stage, Celia begins her notes by broadcasting out loud, as those on headsets have been echoing quietly all night, "It's only Sunday. Everyone relax. Obviously, the first tech is always like this, lights are wrong, props are wrong, that's typical of tech night, so don't anybody get upset about that."

But after the cast is dismissed, all but Jim and Teri, who stick around to try the blood effect, that final thing goes awry, too, the red syrup leaking all over the floor before they even have a chance to strap the apparatus in place.

"It's only Sunday," mumbles David, and Celia shoots him a glance rich with feeling. In the course of a few hours, it's changed from a useful reminder to a mantra.

On bunny notepaper:

To Whom It Concerns,

Why is M. Butterfly being done with nudity/adult content. It can be done fully clothed, even the movies don't need all nudity. Please stop and leave your clothes on you'll do better and elders would enjoy play more.

There is enough in movies etc. that are not called for. We need
decency in Arlington please refrain from any more nudity.
Thanks.

—*Arlington residents*

This arrives at the theater Tuesday in a manila business envelope, written in an apparently elderly female hand. In the same batch of mail arrives a tan greeting-card envelope containing a highly similar text typed all in caps on plain white paper. The second letter adds, "WE NEED TO STOP THIS THAT IS WHY SO MANY PEOPLE, KIDS ARE ON THE WRONG TRACK." A perfunctory glance at the handwriting on both envelopes makes pretty clear that the missives have been sent by the same person, and Celia, though hardly warmed by the correspondence, is not particularly unnerved by it. Although she did also receive a phone call this weekend from a member of long standing who expressed dismay over the upcoming nudity planned for the Arlington stage. Still, they always expected to ruffle a few feathers, and ought hardly to take this as a shocking blow.

The decision had been made early on to include in all materials advertising *M. Butterfly* the information that it contains "nudity and adult content," and it is likely in response to such notices that have been appearing in the papers recently that the letters have been sent. Few actual AFD members have ever gone on record as objecting to these items personally; they have tended more often to frame their opposition to doing this show as being motivated by concern over the prospect of offending *others*, primarily those in the upper age brackets. But B. J. Williams, the most senior member of last year's play-reading committee, which had selected *M. Butterfly*, snorted over these objections. She knows many of the senior citizens who ordinarily come to AFD shows; she takes an aerobics class with some of them at Arlington's Senior Center. "Frankly, I think they'd be thrilled," she predicted, speaking of the nudity, and pointed out with a certain slyness, "It's certainly nothing they haven't seen before."

Obviously, senior citizens are as diverse a population as any, and hold no single unifying perspective on the matter. If the Friends have shown special concern not to alienate the elderly, it is with sound fi-

nancial motivation, since the membership is composed disproportionately of that particular group. On the other hand, B. J. Williams
is right to snort, if only because presumptions about their collectively
delicate sensibilities are patronizing; they perhaps carry with them the
ageist assumption that the elderly won't be able to *handle* having their
sensibilities challenged or affronted, that they need to be shielded
from that possibility. Barbara Horrigan is the perfect walking refuta-
tion of such ideas. She has never tried to hide the fact that she doesn't
like the play; she finds the nudity unnecessary, the plot ludicrous and
unappealing, and Carolyn's second-act penis speech flat-out distaste-
ful. Yet she's an experienced, intelligent woman who hardly needs
protection from ideas, and has decided of her own volition to lend
her expertise, wholeheartedly, to the production's makeup-and-wig
designing. She's just a lovely example of the complicatedness of
things, of all the ambiguities and apparent contradictions that exist
within every individual as well as within every community made up
of human beings, community theater not least among them.

At AFD, the Thursday night before opening is traditionally an "invited dress," a dress rehearsal that a select audience is invited to attend
for free—good public relations for the theater, good practice for the
actors—and for years the select audience has been members of Arlington's Senior Center, housed across the street. This audience is famously unreserved and unpredictable. According to legend, they
bring hard candies, and sandwiches in plastic wrap, which they then
proceed to unsheathe fumblingly during hushed moments onstage.
They walk out when they've had enough, regardless of whether a
scene is in mid-progress. They have few qualms about stating their
opinions of a show, *during* the show, at decibels ordinarily associated
with subway stations and construction sites. They're also unabashed
in their enthusiasm when it strikes, and can give the warmest, most
glowing ovations. In the case of *M. Butterfly*, no one is sure what to
expect of the seniors, or whether to expect their attendance at all.

Celia, not a shielder, decides to share the news of the poison-pen
letters and the disgruntled phone call with the cast and crew, but does
so in a way that communicates her own confidence in the good taste
of the production, and no one seems terribly rattled by it. Anyone
who comes to *see* the production can then judge for herself or himself

whether or not it's offensive, reasons Celia; she won't be bothered by
self-appointed critics who decline ever to view the piece. The only
niggling worry they cause is the prospect of half-empty houses: will
large numbers of people stay away altogether? Box office sales have
been on the sluggish side.

They are not, however, her immediate concern.

Tuesday night's run begins with Jimmy at a horrifying loss for
words in his opening monologue. He begins improvising, then buries
his head in his hands. "I'm sorry. I'm sorry. I know how important
this is."

"Describe the cell," Celia calls out from the audience, and it's a
grim thing for her to choose to do, not prompt Jimmy with an actual
line, but instead offer him an alternative technique for how to get
himself through the moment should it happen in performance.
"Where's the door and window?" she prods. He's silent. "Start it over
from the beginning, that's all."

Slowly, after long gray seconds, with a line from Kelley, he recom-
mences.

Here is a story, probably apocryphal, about another actor who ran
into a strange bit of trouble onstage. It takes place about seventeen
hundred years earlier, in Rome. Genesius the Comedian was performing before the Emperor Diocletian one day during the third century, in a play satirizing the Christian sacraments. In the midst of
depicting a burlesque baptism, he was suddenly converted to Chris-
tianity. When he confessed the faith, then and there, the emporer had
him immediately tortured and beheaded.

This is not a story Jim knows, although he wears the medal of St.
Genesius, patron of actors, around his neck every day. It was a gift
from Sister Christopher, an Episcopal nun who worked backstage at
AFD for many years. Jim used to call her Sister Honey. She had the
medal blessed, Jim believes, by her bishop. He has not taken it off in
some thirty years. For decades now the gold medal has been the same
temperature as his chest. For decades he has not removed it even for a
performance, although actors routinely shuck any jewelry incongru-
ous with their parts during a performance, no matter how cherished,
from heirloom keepsakes to wedding rings, and for a performance
Jimmy does remove the ring he otherwise wears at all times on his left

ring finger. But St. Genesius rides. Jimmy will permit Molly to bandage it with a piece of Scotch tape, and so prevent it from catching the lights and spitting back a flash of gold in an audience member's eye. But it rides. And if the talisman has protected him all these years, perhaps its power has derived partly from Jimmy's ability to declare its importance to him. In cherishing the medal, Jim allows himself to cherish freely that part of him which is an actor, to cherish that part of him which believes the theater is sacred. The medal links Jim's greatest personal passion with something higher. It is a slice of warm gold against his skin, a charm that tells him who he is, a sign of faith that the answer to that question is part of something greater.

But tonight, for the first time ever, the answer to that question is coming up blank. Everything's distracting him, confusing him. They've got him in a suit with bell-bottoms and a fly that doesn't open . . . and the script has him bouncing from a Paris prison cell in 1988, to a satirical re-enactment of a scene from *Madame Butterfly*, to a school in Aix-en-Provence in 1947, to a fantasy/memory in his uncle's house when his character was twelve, to the German ambassador's house in Beijing in 1960 . . . and Celia's been telling him that the whole cast is nervous about him . . . and she keeps making little changes in his blocking, and in the lighting and the onstage costume changes, so that he can hardly remember whether he's knotting his tie during that speech or this one . . . and he's lost weight, and he can't sleep, he isn't sleeping, he hasn't slept.

Just before Act One, Scene 12, whose lead-in is the line "I had the strange feeling that the ax would fall this very evening," Jimmy begins to cry. "I can't do it," he chokes.

Celia asks for a hold. "He's okay," she says, with the brusque command of a police officer dispersing a curious crowd. "He just needs to relax." She approaches him and speaks more softly. "You were fine last night. Eighty-five, ninety percent of the play you had fine." She plays not to the emotion of the scene, not to Jim, but to the task the scene necessitates, which is one of invention, one of creative problem-solving. "What if you had your book onstage? We can make it like he's reading from his diary." Her tone is almost casual, as if she were suggesting something on the order of "Why don't you hand your champagne glass to Marc at the end of the scene," and she appears to be waiting for a response in kind.

"I can't believe I'm doing this," is all that Jim can bring himself to say, after a moment, in a broken voice.

And then she really does disperse the crowd, giving everyone ten minutes, and the rest of the actors drift in respectful, awkward silence down to the greenroom, where they are left to answer the questions of those already downstairs—"Did we get to Act Two? Is this a break? Oh shit, am I supposed to be up there?"—as gracefully and carefully as they see fit.

Celia, meanwhile, is less sure of her options at this point than her outward demeanor suggests. She uses the break to consult quietly with a few people, and concludes that it's too risky not to have Jim on book for performance. They'll have to figure out a way to incorporate the script as a plausible prop, an artistic choice. It seems a dreadful feat, though, not least because it'll give Jimmy one more thing to worry about: lugging it around, riffling through the pages, trying to find his place. With all of the potential disasters that have hovered over this production since it was submitted as part of the annual slate, no one dreamed that this one would come to pass.

Jim comes back after the break, shaken but composed. He gets through Acts Two and Three off book, with occasional prompting. The rest of the cast begins giving him a wide berth now, out of respect and concern and a sense of preserving his dignity, but to Jim it only adds to his feelings of humiliation. Grace alone, who is an old friend, remains close by him, literally so, coming in closer as his anguish becomes more evident, sitting beside him on breaks and reassuring him and always just appearing physically beside him now, silent usually, but by her presence and proximity transmitting love.

TWO DAYS BEFORE OPENING.

The next morning is clean and brisk, full of cold, pale sunlight and russet leaves, more on the street than on the trees. Last night the full moon had a kind of mother-of-pearl circle around it, which some say means trouble and some say means rain, but which was so beautiful it might just have meant luck. By ten-thirty in the morning, the AFD driveway contains two cars, Celia's and Jim's, whose ACTOR-1 plate declaims itself baldly unto the street. Inside they are working. Jim has taken this whole week off; Celia is missing her fifth day of work for the production.

No matter the fine weather; inside is constant as ever: dim, with sawdust and muslin and blacks. Jimmy's in a T-shirt, sweatpants, sneakers. Celia's in her jeans and denim workshirt, untucked. They're both looking rather the worse for wear, Jimmy with great pouches under his eyes, and the crags of his face etched more deeply. He looks tired and humbled, and nevertheless resolutely eager. Celia is looking strained in a more guarded way—partly the manifestation of her abdominal pain, which she is still keeping to herself, and partly a reflection of *M. Butterfly* strife. It's as though all of the most tiny and obscure muscles in her body are united in a steely effort to hold herself, and her production, together.

"I've thought of one other possibility," she tells Jim now as they sit in the front row together. A cue mike. Apparently, it would cost twenty-five dollars a week and look just like Song's body mike, or like those tiny, flesh-toned earpieces Secret Service agents wear; the audience probably wouldn't even be able to see it. Or a breast-pocket journal, says Celia. That's the other possibility. She presents these options not especially winningly; though she does not seem to be trying to provoke guilt or remorse, neither is she making an effort to cajole or bolster Jim into believing she is artistically enchanted with either proposal.

Of course, he knows. Neither is he. The breast-pocket journal seems the worse choice; he can't fathom the awkwardness of flipping through the pages. He says he'll pay for the cue mike. Even though several people have purchased items for which they'll never submit receipts, the production is already over budget. Costumes alone have come in at $1,327, $827 more than the estimate, and *that* had been higher than for most straight shows, whose costume budget typically falls between $150 and $400.

Working with a cue mike will be hard, too, they both realize. Who will be speaking on the other end? Not Kelley, who'll be too busy calling the show. Not Celia, who'll have other responsibilities as director. Whoever it is will essentially have to miss viewing the show. The person will have to follow the script, line by line, with a ruler perhaps, and anticipate the very moment Jimmy needs a line fed to him, but not distract him by leaping in too quickly with a prompt, should he only be taking a pause. What sort of signal will Jim give to differentiate between the two types of silence? Both Jim and Celia agree that the person has got to be Mayre. She's got the experience, with this production and with theater in general; they both trust her personally and professionally, and she'll be a solid presence, reliable and calm. Celia goes to the shop phone and calls David Giagrando at work, to set him to the task of renting a cue mike, and then calls Kelley and asks her to coordinate with Mayre.

"I can't believe this," says Jim again when she returns, and it's both a true statement and a way of apologizing, of expressing how sorry and genuinely stunned he is to be putting them all in this predicament two days before the opening. "You know, I, I, I got distracted by the cap slipping in the Sharpless scene, and then I think it was . . . then the fact that my bathrobe was tied by a necktie in the first scene, and I was thrown, it threw me that I had to bring on the glass for the scene with Marc. . . ." He's not prevaricating; he's groping, really, for an explanation, for clarity, for a reason upon which to hang the burden of his defeat, as if to do so would enable him to step away from it at least momentarily and have a look, gain an understanding of what has happened and why. It's a helpless kind of litany, an unrewarding struggle.

Celia won't indulge. "I've seen you bring on a glass before. You've been doing it for forty years." She doesn't mean to rub it in. If anything, her constant reminders that he's an actor, that he's been doing this for most of his life, are meant to instill enough confidence, or at least enough conviction, to enable Jimmy to buck up, buckle down, snap out of it. She approaches theater with a certain coolness of intellect and demeanor, and her method with actors consists partly of setting the bar very high and then matter-of-factly clearing it, over and over again, herself.

Jimmy, on the other hand, is virtually all instinct and heart, great unabashed heaps of it, and when these fail him, as they have now for the first time in his long career, he is left bankrupt and bereft. Celia is not here to coax and stoke his gifts back to life. She is here to help instill something methodical and concrete, a rational grid of escape hatches which can be employed when Jim gets into trouble.

So they start. The task is to identify spots where escape hatches are most likely to be needed. The first time he stops and needs a line, Celia says, "Okay, that's an example. If you need that line, how are we going to let her know?"

"I could say, 'Well . . . ,'" suggests Jimmy.

Celia squints and gnaws a wine-colored nail.

Later she supplies another line when he goes blank. "Okay, are you going to need that one?" she asks.

"I don't think so," he answers, seriously, after consideration.

She writes "cue possibility" in her script, the beginning of a running tally of places where Mayre ought to be particularly alert.

Now and then Celia alters a bit of stage business, trying to pare down and simplify any of the blocking that may be distracting Jim. Once, she realizes an excised bit is instrumental, and she reinstates it, muttering, "Jim, I'm sorry to keep doing this to you," and he is quick to say, "That's all right," as though it's a terrific relief just to be on the receiving end of an apology.

They begin to hide clues on the set. He misses his next transition, which comes in conjunction with a prop: it's the scene where he pulls out a stack of porn magazines and lies on his stomach to peruse them, narrating to the audience as he does so. Celia tries to link the action with the line in his head. "You lay down the magazine and say, 'Act Two begins with Butterfly.' Do it. Lay down the magazine and say, 'Act Two begins with Butterfly.'"

He lays down the magazine and says, "Act Two begins with Butterfly."

"Now let me ask you something—if we write that on the front of the magazine, will that get you into it?"

"Yes."

"Okay, give me the fuckin' magazine." The epithet isn't used angrily, nor could it be called jovial; it's somewhere in the middle, uttered in a spirit of joint determination, more along the lines of "Okay, let's get this fuckin' thing on the road." She goes to the shop, comes back with a marker, and scrawls his line on the cover of a *Pent-house*.

"Celia."

She doesn't look up.

"Thank you for this. I really need it."

"I know."

"I know *you* know. But thank you, I—"

She cuts him off as though she does not hear. "Okay, let's go from 'I returned to the opera that next week.'"

Here are Celia and Jim, separated by age and gender and role, by myriad different interactions experienced over the course of their life-times, as well as by the immediate fact of each of their very disparate needs, disparate desires, in this moment. And yet this moment finds them voluntarily here, alone together, far from colleagues and family and friends, far even from the sunshine and the season and the hour on the clock, and it isn't enjoyable, what they are doing, it's grueling and it's painful. They're angry with each other. Those feelings are currently tamped down, but Jimmy blames Celia in large part for the difficulties he's having; if only she were warmer and more supportive, if only she didn't keep changing the blocking, if only, especially, she hadn't been undermining him all these weeks, wringing bitter guilt from him with her comments about the whole cast being nervous he'll mess up. For her part, Celia is frustrated with Jimmy because of his unpredictable failure, his having landed them all in this most basic, most amateur of predicaments.

Although neither of them would believe it, they are in a way very lovely in this difficult moment. The fact of their uniting here on a Wednesday morning in spite of real physical and emotional hurts, in spite of their frustrations and humiliations and profound inability ul-timately to connect with each other in a way that feels good to either of them—the fact that they have united here anyway for the sake of saving this play that they both passionately want to present to the community—this is an astonishingly lovely thing, in its own way something greater than the decency one anonymous Arlington resi-dent implored them to consider. It's the sort of "anecdote" that would make Nancie Richardson cry, quietly, without being able to put into words exactly why.

TWO NIGHTS BEFORE OPENING.

The troops are out. It's Wednesday evening and the actors have been given the night off, but Barbara Tyler and Ellen Kazin and Betty Finnigan have taken up residence, with a kind of merry prankster boisterousness, in the greenroom area. It was Tyler who sounded the call to duty, moved to intercede in the area of Jim's wardrobe, which, she decided after viewing last night's supposed full-dress rehearsal, is pitiful. A fly that won't open! Never mind that the clothes don't flatter him, don't do anything useful for either the character or the actor. Grace's costumes, too, are not working. That argyle suit is simply not something a French diplomat's wife would wear. Late last night she pulled Celia aside and gave her a nice salty piece of her mind, upon which Celia gave her leave to help out, provided she works things out with Molly first. So here they are now to ransack the costume room and whatever else may need ransacking, this indomitable trio of brassy fairy godmothers: Tyler, Kazin, and Finnigan.

Molly, just down the tiny flight of steps in one of the dressing rooms, is puffy-eyed, ferociously industrious, silent. She feels humiliated, exposed, not unlike Jim; each has been unable to deliver wholly on the promised job; each has been deemed in need of outside assistance. In Molly's case, the Asian costumes, built from scratch, have proved such a time-consuming challenge, and she is such a perfectionist, unwilling to compromise on their quality or authenticity, that, truth be told, some of the Western costumes have been scraped together somewhat more hastily and haphazardly than would have been ideal. On some level she knows this. In fact, ordinarily Molly would be the first to impress upon people that just because a costume is contemporary and Western doesn't mean it requires any less thought and attention.

But her passion to produce excellence in the elaborate Asian constructions for this show has necessarily made her a little myopic. And her instinct when swamped is not to call for help, but to work herself that much harder; she's been staying up until three and four, sewing

furiously in the lonely theater or her own basement workshop, then reporting to her day job, only to hurry back to the theater at quitting time. Further taxing her energies this last week has been the blood effect, which she and Dave have had to rethink. In *Agnes of God*, dressers mounted the complicated apparatus on the actor in the wings. In *Butterfly*, the costume must be donned onstage, in the presence of the audience, and all the components—kimono, obi, blood bag, tubing, clamp, timing, etc.—are proving too complicated for the kurogo to learn to master now, at this late date. So she's further saddled with designing a new pocket in the obi for a preplanted blood bag, which will be ruptured and slit side to side by a needle taped to the fake knife. She simply hasn't an extra moment, as anyone can see. But still it stings, to have a portion of her work publicly decreed unsatisfactory and more or less wrested from her.

Coming up the triplet of stairs into the greenroom now, she trips, heavily; her palms smack the floor; everyone looks around, drawing breaths of concern, but she rights herself immediately, makes no eye contact with anyone; her eyes are reddish; she goes on about her business. Weeks later she will look back philosophically and feel compassion for herself and gratitude toward the self-appointed three musketeers, but tonight she is a woman with far too little sleep.

As for Tyler-Kazin-Finnigan, they are pretty damn funny, bringing an air of therapeutically insouciant levity to the theater that seems clearly good for Jim, at least. They bustle about him, clucking and plucking at his sleeves and pant legs, pawing through racks of suits and dressing gowns in the costume-storage room, making the hangers sing on the metal rods, finishing one another's sentences and topping one another's put-downs continually and effortlessly, almost as if the patter were scripted, and just generally surrounding Jim with their reassuring bodies and noise. Jim and John Kawadler, and Barbara and her boyfriend, have for years spent New Year's Eve at the Kazins' little lake house in the middle part of the state; their bonds are more familial than collegial, and Jim feels taken care of in their presence.

The greenroom phone rings. It's Stu for Ellen, with a question about his supper. "There's that turkey in the fridge. Do you care if we rip up your red bathrobe?" she tacks on with no preamble, all pert and pointed with her freckles and cap of red hair, like a busy bantam hen. She hangs up and grabs her car keys and coat. "I've got to go raid Stu's closet. Be right back."

Even without most of the cast, the theater is highly populated. Upstairs, the other Stu is tinkering with what has become a hundred-odd light cues—by far the most he's ever programmed for any show. The result, however, is the opposite of showy; the object is not to have the audience eventually sitting there thinking, "Gee, another great lighting effect . . . And another!" If he does his job well, most laypeople in the end will never even be conscious of the lighting or the number of cues. They will simply have *felt* that the same nearly naked spot onstage changed from jail cell to diplomat's office to opera star's apartment; they will simply have *felt* that this moment was sad, and that one devious, and that one sexy.

Up in the light-and-sound booth, David Giagrando tests Jimmy's cue mike. It turned out to cost a hefty bit more than the original estimate; the company wanted $450, but after some haggling he managed to rent it for $300. There's certainly nothing left in the budget to cover this expense, but a private donor has offered to pick up the tab. Now that they've rented it, the temptation to play Secret Service agent proves irresistible. "Okay," David tells Kelley, listening on the other end, in a husky, discretion-conscious voice, "the president's limo is pulling up. We need to get Monica out of the building with as little attention as possible."

Jean Hogman, mother of Michael Hogman, who choreographed *Funny Girl*, and a mainstay of Molly's sewing force, arrives with cases of soda, juice, bottled water, and candy, which will be sold during intermission. For now it gets locked in the secretariat, the storage space off the lobby, under the stairs, where stationery and the odd prop— an antique wicker wheelchair, a couple of battered valises, and some Art Deco wet-bar accouterments—are stored.

Lorraine Stevens, who has been working at home as Molly's chief stenciler, painting the intricate patterns Molly designed and cut stencils for onto the many-layered pieces of the Peking Opera costumes, sits tonight on a greenroom sofa, stitching humble hems.

Dot Lansil was here earlier in the day, doing her usual Wednesday toilet cleaning; she's home in bed now, but tomorrow night will come early to mop the floors before the senior-citizen dress rehearsal.

Barbara Horrigan, who will not attend every performance—not for lack of stamina, but because the whole first weekend she'll be out of town with Lorraine, staffing the annual festival of the New England Theater Conference in Hartford, Connecticut—is here to oversee the two men who will actually apply the makeup she has designed. In the shop, one brushes more rouge onto the Peking Opera masks with a rabbit's-foot brush. Downstairs, the other perfects the technique of transforming Patrick into a woman; Patrick has been asked in tonight solely to lend his face to this purpose.

Doug Desilets, tool-belted, with a green gel in hand, roves blearily, with an adrenaline edge, through the house. Don Richardson, with his perpetually unruffled air, paints a bit of gold trim on the edges of Doug's set.

John Kawadler, box-office manager, tallies orders and assigns seats quietly in the box office. Attendance is still hovering in the vicinity of 50 percent for five out of the six performance dates, the exception being the second Saturday night, which is pretty well booked, thanks largely to Jimmy's having sold a block of fifty-seven special benefit tickets, at a jacked-up price, to his colleagues at work; five dollars on each of those tickets will go to breast-cancer research. Meanwhile, orders are still trickling in, and more tickets may sell at the door.

Mayre and Celia, their respective mugs of instant coffee and green tea gone cold beside them, sit in the dark front row of the house and discuss the finer points of cuing Jim. Mayre will be stationed in her own private corner of the loft, outside of the light-and-sound booth, where the follow spot would normally be located for a musical production. She'll have a music stand and a tiny clamp-on light to help her follow the script, and she'll be on headset for communicating with Kelley, as well as on the cue mike for feeding Jim any lines he might need, so she'll have to get used to operating both at once and make sure she's speaking into the right mike at the right time.

Ellen returns from her home, two towns away, with great piles of her husband's clothing, which she and her comrades begin trying on Jimmy. They isolate a few contenders and usher their model upstairs to show Celia, who approves a suit jacket and a dressing gown. Tomorrow, Ellen will drive some of her own cocktail suits over to

Grace's house and they'll do dress-ups and try to come up with something properly stylish and French-feeling. She'll also hit Marshalls and Filene's Basement, if need be, to purchase some black trousers for Jim that actually fit.

A little after ten, Betty Finnigan looks up from her sewing. "It's a good job there's *some* nudity in this show, because we're having enough trouble getting sewn what we do have."

Jean Hogman, her stocking feet up on the ugly coffee table, is working on a pink opera-costume. Lorraine Stevens is on the brown couch, stitching an orange hem, which she now holds up and scrutinizes. "Are they going to be able to see I'm using white thread?" she asks no one in particular.

Ellen pauses the perfect beat. "Can I have some of what you're on?"

"I'm a perfectionist," Lorraine informs them, mock-haughtily.

Celia comes down to use the Coke machine. "Is everything okay? Is everybody happy and talking?" she asks, with a meaningful glance toward the dressing room where Molly has been working in such seclusion all night.

"I am!" declares Ellen.

"*She'll* talk even if no one's listening," puts in Jean Hogman heartily.

Then David comes downstairs to pester Ellen about casting him in *Blood Brothers*. Auditions are months away, but he's begun a playful lobbying campaign early. He makes various dramatic and vague threats about the dire fates that may befall her should he not get the part he craves, until she feels moved to regale everyone (again) with the story of how she once didn't cast her own *son* in a play she was directing ("Can you say therapy?"), and then everyone else launches into accounts of shows in which someone or other was famously not cast, and then they segue (somehow) to Chinese food and hot dogs and then to actual *dog* dogs, and David says, "Baron, speak," and the schnauzer yaps, and David asks Ellen if she might consider casting *him*, at any rate, and then another (apparent) segue gets them on the subject of making the balloon costumes for *Seesaw*, back in 1976, with Kazin and Tyler and Finnigan working late one night in a supposedly otherwise empty theater, when an unexplained crash put them all into a panic about the theater ghost (all theaters have a requisite ghost); the other two women fled into the street, leaving Kazin, clad at that point in balloons, too wide to fit through the doorway and thus all alone in the theater with the amorphous presence—and here private laughter takes over and the story dissolves as the trio is unable to speak coherently for a little while.

The whole thing is like broth to Jim, who sits on the couch, buoyed slightly by the loony warmth, though still looking a little hollowed, a little pale.

DRESS REHEARSAL.

By eight, the house is a quarter full, and alive with murmuring and the prophesied rattling candy wrappers. Many of the seniors remain in their coats, and a few in their hats as well. Signs taped up abundantly around the house forecast adult content and nudity.

Celia comes into the greenroom and tells everybody, "We have a small but mighty group of seniors up there." She seems excited and nervous and happy to have made it to tonight; she's all compact energy and dimples. "Have fun, everyone. Let's go!"

Jimmy, sporting a new Gallimard ensemble tonight—part Stu Kazin, part Marshalls—with the wire from the cue mike taped behind his ear and snaking down his back, asks if everybody could hold hands for a moment and "say a prayer or whatever." Hands shoot out willingly. They form a large, brief, lopsided circle, hang on for a moment, then let go.

Tall Michelle kisses Gabbie's head; Gabbie is cross-legged on the silvery-jade sofa, copying out her homework in orange pencil: ". . . a patch of beautiful daisies so I picked some daisies here and there." Patrick, costumed and made up but wigless, with a stocking cap flattening his hair, experiments with the newly added, draping white cuffs on his kimono. They reach past his knees as he bends and makes flowy movements with his arms. "I like how they emphasize the hands." Mayre stows a ladder in the broom closet, then goes up to assume her station in the loft, ready to supply prompts. Tom pops an Altoid from the economy-size tin someone finally brought in. Carolyn, all sparkly in her beaded black cocktail dress, admires Grace's new threads. "Where did that come from?" she asks innocently, and Grace crosses the greenroom tactfully to explain. Molly sits in the wing-back chair, still sewing. The kurogo traipse upstairs to don their opera masks and take their places.

Upstairs, the lights dim and Jim's voice gives the prerecorded welcoming announcement. It's just a coincidence that he happens to star in this show; the same tape is played before every AFD performance. His voice on it is resonant, confident, tinged with his endearing Boston regionalism; it's his cordial-host voice. Backstage, the real Jim touches the earpiece of his cue mike, says a last prayer. *Please God, let me get through this. Make this work for me.* The lights go to black and someone in the audience says, "I can't see. I can't see anything," and then the lights come up and Tall Michelle bangs the gong and the music cue starts and kurogo come floating out from behind the sliding doors and it's begun.

Celia starts out sitting in the back row, but her energy won't allow it, and soon she's on her feet, pacing, bouncing on her toes, gnawing bits of fingernail in the back of the house. When they hit a joke she roars appreciatively; when something goes amiss she whispers "Shit!" and makes sounds of exasperation. She switches on her flashlight and writes on a yellow legal pad; she whips on the headsets by the entrance and issues low directives to Kelley, up in the booth. Then something goes right again and she's bobbing her head, dimpling with unbridled pleasure, snapping her fist in the air.

It's sort of a typical dress rehearsal, not a fiasco, but with just enough going wrong to make everyone really nervous about opening night. One half of the sliding doors breaks and sits still on its track for most of the show. Patrick's body mike seems to be picking up signals from a CB radio; a steady shoosh of static and indiscernible trucker patter comes over the speakers whenever his mike is turned up. During the courtroom scene, a bathrobe that ought to have been preset comes suddenly flying out of the wings and lands in a puddle of white. The blood effect fails again.

As for the audience, they are rather vocal, particularly related to the sex bits. Carolyn's strip scene ends just before she gets to her underpants, and as the lights go to black, one man in the audience lets out a loud, disappointed, very heartfelt, "Awww . . ." which is followed by a good dusting of chuckles. "Is that a girl or a boy?" someone else asks repeatedly during Patrick's early scenes. There are lots of titters during Carolyn's penis speech later, and solid guffaws during Jimmy's speech about his first, awkward sexual experience. When Patrick finally strips, in the play's penultimate scene, an audible chorus of "Jesus!" rises from the group. Two women rise and sail briskly out several lines later. Celia politely switches on her flashlight to illuminate their exodus. Funny how they waited until *after* he was dressed again, she cannot help noting. The fifty-odd audience members applaud vigorously at the end, especially for Patrick when he emerges—one woman rises to her feet for the occasion—and then for Jim, who takes his bow last.

It's a swift, stark, almost edgy curtain call Celia has directed. The final tableau has them arrayed on various levels of ramp and platform and stage floor, no one touching, and as the lights dim for the last time, with a swell of the strange, haunting music that has become familiar to the audience over the course of the past two hours, Jimmy folds his arms across his chest and Patrick slips a hand into the pocket of his suit pants; they all gaze directly at the audience and strike their final stances and disappear in the dark. It's very cool and full of attitude; it might be an album cover.

What finally becomes all but certain around eleven o'clock on Thursday night is that they are going to pull it off, in some fashion at least; enough of the elements are going to occur smoothly enough that the show will move along coherently from opening to curtain; it will hold together. What is also clear, to anyone who knows Celia, is that if this is the extent of the production's success she will be bitterly, gravely dissatisfied. If the mounting of this show has been in some senses like waging a battle—against stereotypes, against provincialism, against prudishness, against unwillingness to change, against assumptions about the audience's impoverished intellectual appetite or aesthetic curiosity— its execution must result in nothing less than a resounding victory, in both artistic and commercial senses, a victory to be capped by laudatory reviews, an awed buzz among the most respected and competitive bigwigs in the community-theater circuit, and a first-place win at the EMACT festival this spring. Whether or not the fierce and lofty pursuit of such a goal will turn out to be hubris remains to be seen. But the cool, enigmatic confidence of the play's ultimate image belies the fact that this past week has been riddled with worry, humiliation, and doubt.

CAKE.

The next morning, in Lorraine Stevens' blue kitchen, a chocolate sheet cake rests on a glass cake-plate, waiting to be iced. The kitchen is warm and very quiet. A blue wall-clock ticks, and a blue bottle with a dusty-pink rose and a spray of baby's breath sits on the table beside the cake. Outside the window, cold golden November sunshine casts long shadows. Lorraine's breathing makes an ample, comfortable sound as she gets out her mother's old rectangular tin of cake-decorating tools.

This is something like the ninetieth opening-night cake she has made for the Friends. The first one she made was for *Can-Can* in 1975, and she made them off and on, for shows she and her husband, Ernie, were involved in, until 1984, when she began producing them for every show. The theater used to pay her twenty-five dollars a cake, but ever since the renovation began, she's done it for free.

It's funny how far she's come in the eyes of the group since she was a little girl. Lorraine is one of the few members of the Friends with an active, personal, memory of the group's haughtier days. She grew up in Arlington, where she was close friends with a child named Lois until they were eight or nine years old, at which point Lois acquired a new stepmother who forbade her to play with Lorraine anymore. The stepmother, active in the Friends, considered Lorraine's family— headed by her carpenter father—socially unacceptable. She encouraged Lois to play with the children of other AFDers instead. Lorraine was so hurt by being deemed unworthy that she vowed never to have anything to do with that snobbish, elitist group.

Without measuring spoons or cups, Lorraine mixes a concoction of milk, butter, and confectioner's sugar, begins to smooth a plain white background onto the cake. She used to bake them from scratch, following an old recipe for Wacky Cake, or War Cake, so named because it used no eggs. Sometimes she'd make something called Fireman's Wife Cake. But nowadays she relies on Betty Crocker; it tastes just as good and takes a third of the time.

With the background completed, she adjusts her eyeglasses, picks a shish-kabob skewer out of the tin, and peers at the *Playbill* propped beside her. The cover shows a large red letter *M.* followed by a red butterfly. The program is a souvenir from the 1990 production at Boston's Colonial Theater. Luckily, Ernie saves all his theater programs, along with his collection of scripts, on a special bookshelf in their bedroom, so she was able to pull it out this morning to use as her model.

With the skewer she traces the outline of the butterfly in the white, then mixes up two smaller bowls of icing with red and black food coloring, respectively; she chooses a tip from among the dozens in the tin, fits it on the end of a cloth funnel, slathers icing into the funnel, and squeezes. After a few changes of tip and a few changes of funnel cloth, the *Playbill* cover has been reproduced in slightly wobbly but serviceable form on the sheet cake. Something's missing, though. Lorraine switches tips, writes "Congratulations" in black script across the top. Ernie comes in from the hardware store, smelling of autumn and cigarettes, and peers critically over her shoulder.

"It's lopsided," complains Lorraine, genuinely peeved. She may not like the show, but that's no reason to stint on the cake.

"You could add a flourish next to the word, and put something over here." Ernie points.

She adds the year and a couple of flourishes. A fine red border all around and she calls it quits. The wall clock ticks; the shadows outside are not so long. Lorraine tells Ernie how many metal tips she used, so when he's doing the dishes later none will escape down the disposal. She retires to the den with a cup of coffee, settles comfortably into a chair, opens a package of cigarettes. Her fingers are stained reddish from food coloring, as are her teeth a little bit from licking the knife.

All around her, on four walls, hang photos and program covers from shows spanning decades, collectively as laden with stories and relationships as any family album. She misses the days of some of those plays. They worked with smaller budgets then; more stuff was homemade, piecemeal, and so what if it wasn't exactly historically accurate? It used to be more fun. People understood it was an avocation, not a vocation. Directors would schedule more breaks, more time for coffee and chitchat, for the cast and crew to get to know each other. Used to be more house parties, more going out after rehearsals, to a big Chinese restaurant called Forbidden City. Not there anymore. Used to be on Route 2. Used to have twenty, thirty people gathering after rehearsal there on Friday nights. In the old days. It was happier. Well. She just hopes it goes on forever. That's the wish.

Twelve

Places

The difference tonight is not overt. Oh, there are the bouquets Tall Michelle has arranged next to the silver elephant in the greenroom: a bunch of sunflowers with a card addressed to Crew and a bunch of red roses with a card addressed to Cast. And a glass bowl of chocolate lollipops, with a card from Ellen Kazin, has been set on top of the piano. And Lorraine's sheet cake has been deposited on the table by the captain's box. And a fresh economy-size tin of Altoids waits on the coffee table, unopened. And Celia is out of her blue denims, sporting instead a sleek black turtleneck, slacks, and gray blazer. And in the lobby a scarlet kimono has been thumbtacked to the bulletin board, and beneath it the brightly tiled floor gleams: evidence of Dot's having mopped that afternoon.

But mostly what is different is impalpable. It's clichéd: it's the buzz of opening night, which really exists, as sappy or hackneyed as that may sound. It's the knowledge of imminent exposure, of extraordinary nakedness, and not just in Patrick and Carolyn's sense of the word, or even in the sense Jim means it when he says he feels more naked in his public humiliation than either of the actors who show their skin. Every one of the cast tonight will be bare before strangers, willingly, willfully baring herself and himself in an effort to communicate, touch, arouse response. No matter how close they come or fail to come to succeeding, the effort alone will be a thing of beauty, rare. Each of the players will carry with him or her a little protection from absolute nudity, a sort of thin paper sheath called *craft*. And in the hours and minutes before curtain, each in her or his own way goes about tending to that craft, as an outfielder might oil her glove before a game, or a soldier might clean his gun before battle.

Now Carolyn, in the ladies' dressing room, sponges pancake base all over her body, including throat, stomach, and underarms. Tom, on the crimson sofa, polishes his tan boots with a small round tin of shoe polish. Grace, made up but not yet in her first costume, wanders about with a grave sort of aimlessness in the red-and-white kimono-style dressing gown she brought from home, in keeping with the spirit of the production. Little Michelle, wearing her wide gray kurogo pants and a bra, stitches a hook more securely onto the side closure of the pants. Tall Michelle, eating chicken on a bagel in front of the soda machine, chews in rhythm with the lines she is reciting in her head. Orea and Teri, in their muslin sacklike undergarments, identical black ponytails (Teri's having been sprayed that color), and Asiatic makeup, glide about with little practiced kurogo-steps, their hands clasped nunlike in a mixture of solemnity and insouciance; they recite in a singsong the order of events in the blunt shorthand they have developed: rape scene, penis scene, *sake* scene, the opera. Doug's wife has given him an opening-night present of two silver worry balls in a Chinese silk box, and he shows them around and worries them melodically in his hand. Patrick, wearing a stocking cap and a yellow cape around his neck so as not to stain his costume while his makeup is being applied, alternates between moments of such remote concentration he might be in a trance and sudden bursts of his sweet, goofball laughter at a quip from one of the makeup crew. Jimmy, wired for sound as it were, finds himself a spot on the brown sofa, the one most tucked away, between the piano and the photocopy machine, and there he focuses and tries to steel his nerves. Grace comes and plants herself beside him: comrade and silent anchor.

"Tonight's secret word is 'duck,'" floats Kelley's voice mysteriously over the intercom. "I repeat: the secret word is 'duck.'" Later she makes her way to the greenroom and quizzes cast and crew to make sure they got it; it's her way of testing the intercom and getting people used to paying attention to any announcements that may come over it, such as "Five minutes to curtain," or "Places, please."

Meanwhile, Mayre must check that Jim's cue mike is functioning. She comes down at one point, concerned that her test messages haven't been getting through. "Jim, did you hear me?" He didn't. "Are you turned on?"

He innocently unzips his fly to check (the receiver is strapped inside his waistband), and everyone bursts out laughing.

There are plenty of moments like these. Barbara Tyler, still sewing snaps onto a kimono at seven-thirty-five, growls, very gangsteresque, "Now, James, remember, I've got fifty bucks riding on that tie." (She and Celia have a joking bet on whether or not he'll manage to get his necktie on during a certain scene.) Celia calls the cast together shortly before curtain and tells them, over the growing patter of feet overhead as the house slowly fills, about a tradition she'd like to follow: each night, a different unsung hero of the production will be presented with a symbolic token of appreciation, a white glove, which she or he must wear somewhere on her or his person for the remainder of the night. "That'd be difficult for Patrick," someone remarks, which sets the others to begin creatively addressing that dilemma, until eventually they wear that subject out, and Celia presents the glove to Teri, and everyone applauds, and Teri, who came so close to quitting, declares, "I know where it can go," and saucily hoists up her opera costume to stick it inside her tights. More laughter and applause. Then everybody is kissing everybody else, and slapping one another on the back, and Jimmy says, "Have fun, bubbee," to Patrick and kisses him grandly on the cheeks, and Kelley's voice comes over the intercom, and they are being very seriously shooed away from all this cozy silliness in the greenroom and upstairs, into the dark wings, where they will wait, singly or in twos or threes, listening to their own breath and hearts, unnaturally huge and alert.

From down in the box office comes the signal, over headsets, to go. Kelley, up in the booth, responds into her mouthpiece, "Cue one-one and announcement." The house lights dim. Jim's recorded voice floats forth confidently, handsomely, from the speakers; before every performance, the same program manager's recording about no flash-bulbs, and emergency exits, and how to become a member is played. In real life, in the wings, a less assured Jimmy says a prayer. Hidden at the top of the platform, the kurogo whisper eerily behind their im-mobile, expressionless opera masks. The announcement ends and the house lights go to black and for a moment the stage is a quiet, ethe-real sea of varicolored glow-tape, and then the cut-out spaces within the circular red element are backlit an intense yellow, and Tall Michelle, down right, bangs a hand-held gong and sweeps back into the wings, and then the recorded music begins, each of these cues being called softly by Kelley over the headsets and punched through by fingers up in the booth. The round element parts in two as the doors slide open to emit the three kurogo dancers, and the lights fade up on them as they swirl down the ramp, wielding fans and silk swath and sword, and then Song appears, mesmerizing, fluid-armed, in a slow dance between the parted halves of the door, and the Chinese-opera music dissolves into the "Love Duet" from *Madame Butterfly*, and one by one the dancers leave, Song last, and a stark light reveals Gallimard down left, looking feeble and anguished in a dressing gown, and he speaks the first words of the play beseechingly—"But-terfly, Butterfly . . ."—as she withdraws, and then he is all alone on-stage with his first monologue to deliver and forty-four minutes left in Act One. At the back of the house, Celia is doing her caged-tiger routine for all the ushers to see: very coiled, very tensed, dimples and furrows etched deep.

Tiny slips. Mayre, perched in the loft outside the booth, follows the script intently, whispering cue lines to Jimmy every so often. Once, he misses his blocking and heads into the dark; "Go right," she corrects gently, and he alters his course and steps into the lit area. "Thanks, Mayre," sighs Kelley, and you can almost hear the heart at-tack retreating. In a number of scenes, the preset sound levels are too high, and there are hissed admonitions and scrambling adjustments to bring the music or sound effect down so that the actors can be heard. Kelley and David fall into a little happily bitchy banter on headsets: "These guys must have a contest going to see who can jump each other's line the fastest." Or when the opposite problem occurs: "There's that tractor-trailer driving through the hole in that paragraph." "Did it crash into the one that drove through right before it?" But their very indulgence in such sarcasm seems a sign of how basically well it's going, and a few times they are reduced to sincerity. "Can you believe he's only twenty-two?" says David after Patrick has pulled off a particularly affecting moment, and "That works," says Kelley simply, when the gobo casts a jade foliage cutout onto the shoji screen, and the music lilts just so, and Jim's narration winds over it like a sad, inevitable thread.

Most of the audience have no knowledge of the trial this production has often been. There is no history; there is only the moment, and the spectators float in the timeless, placeless darkness of the house, filling their sights and minds with the time-warp sequencing of the play, its lights and colors and sounds and textures wrapping them all in a transformative embrace.

The act ends; the audience applauds. Mayre says, "That was good, sweet pea. I'll check in with you later," and detaches herself from headset and cue mike. Baron, in the loft, yawns loudly, with a great pink curl of tongue, and shakes himself out. Down in the lobby, volunteers are opening up the cash box behind the refreshment stand. The line for the women's room begins forming. Smokers head for the cold, huddling companionably on the bricked patio. Around them, through the trees, burn the lights of neighboring houses.

Celia sails into the greenroom with tears trembling in her eyes and the first person she sees is Jim, on his way into the bathroom, and she shakes her head and says, "Jesus Christ," her dimples dark and alive in her beaming face. "I'm crying."

"You're crying," says Jimmy. "I've been crying for the past four weeks." He looks so relieved, so mightily lightened, it's as though all his ballast has been suddenly removed, as if he might drift at any moment, unsteadily, in glad disbelief, a few inches toward the ceiling. Not that his humiliation has been lifted—he will suffer under that hot weight for months to come—but at least perhaps he's reversed course now; at least it may not get any worse. And for this moment

Celia, never a mush, gives him the thing he has wanted most from her all these weeks. She wipes her eyes and shakes her head again at him, beaming. He has touched her and she has let him see it.

It goes this way, for the rest of the night and the rest of the weekend and the rest of the run. The production is solid; more goes right than wrong—although the blood effect continues to fall flat (the hypodermic taped to the stage knife fails to pierce the bag; the kurogo put the obi on upside down, so the bag gets pierced at the very top and emits only a paltry trickle; and so on, a different malfunction every night), and the sound levels continue to seem just a little off, and Mayre continues to prove soberingly necessary up at her cuing station, and all manner of minute line and prop and cue error occurs, in ways that are hardly noticeable to the audience but keep the cast and crew on their toes, alternately cursing, striving, giggling, tinkering; this is, after all, live theater.

The audiences, for their part, fill out respectably, with an average attendance rate by the end of six shows of 73 percent, down from *Funny Girl*'s 91 percent, but, then, no one expects a drama to bring in the same kind of numbers as a musical, and compared with attendance rates for other dramas over the past seven years, it's actually a little better than average. And except for the pair of anonymous letters received during production week, and the two women who walked out of the senior dress immediately following the nude scene, and a young man at the second Saturday performance who, after Song's real gender was revealed, said disgustedly and clearly from his seat, "Shoot the faggot," the reactions of the audiences have been mostly positive. Even the longtime member who'd called Celia at home to register her concerns decided in the end to see the play for herself, which, she confessed afterward, by way of complimenting the director, altered her view 180 degrees. Another longtime member, a woman of eighty-one years, sent a donation to the board for the purpose of helping support the renovation and in her accompanying note wrote, "P.S. *Loved M. Butterfly!*"

As for official reviews, community-theater productions rarely receive any. In the Friends' early days, the *Arlington Advocate* used to run not exactly reviews, but evaluations-cum-synopses, which tended to be somewhat stilted in their style and uniform in their enthusiasm.

"*Lady Windermere's Fan* Capably Presented by Local Talent to the Delight of Large Audience. Handsome Gowns Worn by the Ladies. Production Well Coached," read one headline of 1925. "Friends of Drama Play Was Sparkling Success. 'Best Amateur Production Ever Saw,' Say Critical Critics," read another headline, in 1929. And in 1935, "Friends Delight Children With 'The Wizard of Oz.' Youngsters Forget to Lap Lollipops During Enthralling Performance. Actors Stimulated to Great Heights." A sort of spun-sugar feedback: momentarily thrilling, but lacking in any real substance.

The *Advocate* no longer reviews plays, but a few venues exist that occasionally provide an outsider's opinion. A local theater aficionado maintains a Web site called *Larry Stark's Theater Mirror*, where he posted a review of *M. Butterfly* that read, in part, "This was a Major Theatrical Achievement on any level. Considering the prominent signs about nudity and language, I think it took guts for a Community Theatre to attempt this play. . . . This is certainly one of the best PLAYS I have seen all year—and I feel I did indeed see it, not a 'commendable attempt' at realizing all its levels and intricacies. . . . I don't think that the 'INC.' in AFD's name makes the group 'professional'—but this production does!"

Later, posting his nominations for that year's IRNE (Independent Reviewers of New England) Awards—which consider professional as well as amateur productions under one umbrella—the same critic nominated *M. Butterfly* in the categories of best actor (both Jimmy and Patrick), best set design, best ensemble, best director, and best production, writing about this last nomination, "I will vote for *M. Butterfly* not just because it was a magnificent production of a brilliant play, but because it represents a courageous break with the general conservatism of community theater companies. . . . [A] surprising exception to the Neil Simon comedies and old musicals that are the usual community theater fare. Brave—Bravo!"

An official EMACT representative attended the show at AFD's request and provided a three-page written report that included these impressions: "From my first moment in the theater, I was enthralled by Doug Desilets' set design. . . . Stu Perlmutter's design defined the term 'theater magic.' . . . The costume design by Molly Trainor was breathtaking. . . . The production values of this piece were brilliant.

Congratulations to Celia Couture for creating a theatrical experience that is visually exciting, breathtaking to behold and meticulously crafted."

But perhaps no review touches Celia as deeply as her husband's. Gerry Couture, that most cheerfully but commitedly self-professed disparager—not only of this particular play's subject matter, but of the whole ridiculous idea of adult amateur theater—did eventually subject himself to sitting in the audience one night, whereupon he found himself able to amend his original assessment. He liked it. Or, as he beneficently declared in his own inimitable phrasing, "It's *not* a pig show." And he loosed his quirky, half-bashful grin, and acted generally amused at himself and the event of his earlier misapprehension. And not just because he is her husband, but, to the extent that he is Everyman, or at least one highly skeptical and hard-to-please version thereof, his opinion is some kind of profound measure of whether the show succeeded, which is to say whether it effectively made its way to the thresholds of people's hearts, and once there was admitted entry.

CLOSING PARTY.

The cast-and-crew party, as AFDers try hard to remember to call it, is held at the house of Don and Nancie Richardson, and is themed, in the tradition of AFD shows, after the production. In this case, no one felt quite up to preparing the Chinese cuisine that might seem most obvious, so, taking advantage of Gallimard's character, the party is being termed an "Ambassador's Reception," which Nancie figured meant both elegant and easy: she could throw a roast in the oven and call it Tenderloin Medallions du Boeuf au Jus.

"Easy," of course, is how Nancie would put it, downplaying the work involved in hosting a party for some forty people. They began getting ready at seven-thirty this morning. The Richardsons' home is a spotless, cozy ranch on a hilly dead-end in Arlington, and when people arrive after Sunday's closing matinee, the sky is dark and starry and a great pungent fire burns in the hearth and wine is flowing from the numerous bottles guests have brought, having heeded the BYOB notice assiduously. The long dining-and-living room is the place to

congregate, especially around the fire or around the table, laid eclecti-
cally with crackers and roasted garlic dip and herring in wine sauce
and pâté and little Italian meatballs and mixed nuts. The $13.48 left
over from everybody's eight-dollar cover charge will be scrupulously
stuffed into the silver elephant later on. Don and Nancie host one
cast party a year, another of the countless unsung services they provide the theater, their child, their club.

The cast and crew have turned out not quite in full, but nearly so.
A few have brought significant others along, but most have shown up
alone, or, rather, in the company of other members of the production; the event is thick with family feeling. In spite of the dark
patches of the production process, and the ways the production itself
may have fallen short—not in terms of aesthetics but in terms of creating a community—what is striking at the closing-night party is how
much the feeling of family prevails. Simply by dint of having gone
through these past seven weeks together, shoulder to shoulder, Altoid
to Altoid, silence to silence, quip to quip, something has been created. And is now being dismantled. Even on the happiest, lovingest
production, the family comes apart when the show ends, both dis-
solving irretrievably in the magical act of the final curtain, when the
lights go up and the illusion seeps away, vacating everything but
memory. So there is a trace of melancholy tonight, too, and that is
nice, a goodbye without any melancholy being hollow.

Orea is easily the saddest to see the production end. Her bio in the
program read, "O. Nicolls is ecstatic to be here and while debuting at
the Friends with this production is no stranger to theater having performed for four years at St. Louis Academy and winning a scholarship
for theater arts." The fact that some twenty-five years had elapsed between those performances at her parochial high school and her secular
debut with the Friends, though surely lost on audience members pe-
rusing the program, heightened for Orea the sense of finally realizing
a weathered old wish. She bought a white three-ring binder in which
to begin her first theater scrapbook, and purchased an extra ticket,
paying the full thirteen dollars for it, just to paste inside. The pages
after *M. Butterfly* are already filling up with audition notices she's
clipped from the paper or downloaded from the Web; she's hungry
for the next play.

There have been difficult spots, of course—getting yelled at by Celia has made her cry backstage; and the one-hour drive home every night, on the heels of ten-hour days at Hewlett-Packard and then rehearsal, was grueling; and the whole endeavor has bred a little tension between her and her husband, a manager at Raytheon who gets up for work at three-thirty in the morning and would therefore always be asleep by the time she got home at night, so that they've hardly seen each other in weeks. He came to a performance, but declined to greet her in the greenroom afterward, and wouldn't be introduced to her new friends, instead waiting for her outside in the street. They drove the hour home without discussing it, and then, in the late-night kitchen, she finally went ahead and asked him what he'd thought, and he said, "A play's a play. I thought it was stupid."

"But what did you think of *me*?" she'd pressed.

"Orea," he chastised. "You had one line."

The next night, he bought her flowers. She knows he just missed her, that's all, was even maybe a little scared to see her so rosily excited by an interest outside their home, their shared realm. But that moment in the kitchen was crushing just the same.

Still, she's been thrilled by the whole experience. Being made up each night in Horrigan's Hideaway with all the lightbulb-framed mirrors, just like in Hollywood, she felt treated like a queen. Being measured and fitted for costumes, and seeing her name on the nightly sign-in sheet, and sitting on one of the shabby sofas going over her scenes in her head, and waiting, masked, backstage for the music cue, and floating down the ramp with her pink scarf and the dust motes all swimming in columns of hot stage lights, and the sense of the audience like a single shadowy creature behind those lights, all focused, all intent, delivering their attention to the action onstage—well, it *has* been a dream. A dream come true.

"I'm so heartbroken it's over," says Orea passionately now, perched on a chair in Don and Nancie's living room, her eyelids still swoopy with black liner applied to make her look Asian, and Teri pats her knee. "I'm so hungry," she says a moment later, in the identical tone, and Teri laughs. "Orea, you kill me." "I *am*, though," protests Orea, and they rise to fill plates with the main course, which has replaced the appetizers on the buffet.

Teri has come the furthest in her feelings about the play, from her initial enthusiasm way back when she accepted the part, to the very depths of kicking-herself regret over having committed to the role of glorified furniture-mover, to a newly dawning appreciation for how much the kurogo ultimately added to the emotional richness and style of the piece. She took the part largely for the opportunity to work with Celia and the rest of the high-caliber production team, and began to regret it almost right away, not least because she doesn't have the luxury of auditioning for anything else this year: that's the unspoken agreement she has with her husband and three boys. Once a year she gets to indulge her love for theater, maybe twice if one of the roles is very small, which Teri sort of thought the role of kurogo would be, ha ha.

Midway through rehearsals, Teri approached Celia and told her flat-out how much she was hating the experience. She'd been under the impression she'd be called to rehearse two nights a week; instead it was four. She and the other kurogo had thought they'd been engaged mainly as dancers; instead they felt more like slave laborers, toting chairs and props, constantly having their duties revamped, getting yelled at when they missed something. Rehearsals were bringing her almost to tears, and she couldn't even really go home and vent to her husband, who was struggling to put the kids to bed by himself every night while she theoretically was out fulfilling her creative needs. It wasn't even satisfying on a social level. The cast never really bonded; they hadn't gone out for drinks after rehearsal once, and didn't seem any of them to be having a particularly good time. "I have to share something with you," Teri told Celia that night, after another intense rehearsal. "I made such a mistake saying I'd do this. I feel so subservient, like a slave, like we're glorified props people."

"That's not how I think of you," Celia had assured her, and enlisted Teri then to help her work with the other kurogo in shaping their function more significantly. This was around the time when she began blocking them into more scenes, until finally they were onstage for almost the entire show, not only as porters and set changers but as nonverbal communicators. Their purpose got grounded deeper and deeper into the vision of the play, culminating the week before opening in Celia's request that Stu add the three "specials"—overhead lights rigged solely to illuminate the kurogo in their silent acting. And she asked Teri, that night of Teri's venting, to lead the group by example as the most experienced of the three, so that she had a personal mission and artistic challenge now, and by closing night Teri, who had not invited a single person to attend the show (why bother?), had heard from many sources how much the kurogo added to the show, how beautifully they danced, but, more important, how like the soul of every scene they were. And now Teri can say she is glad, it was worth it; she swallowed her pride for the greater good and wound up stretching herself as a performer, learning from Celia as she had originally expected and wished, and doing the most experimental bit of theater she's ever done. Not that she isn't looking forward to beginning to catch up with her family tomorrow, not to mention her sleep.

Jim is least ambivalent about being glad it's all over. Jim, from the beginning the happy heart of the cast, the buoyant welcome-wagon, gathering them together and nurturing each individual with his indiscriminate sweetness, has suffered something he's never suffered before, and it's been worse than any pain he can recall, worse than the ruptured appendix he once had. The hardest part has been letting other people see him lose it. Him of all people, James Grana, ACTOR-1, five-time winner of the EMACT best-actor award, AFD program manager, and longtime leading man. After last Saturday evening's performance, one of the kurogo had mentioned that they were all trying to stay out of his way and give him space; she'd meant it caringly, he supposed, sympathetically, but it was a great blow to his heart. Did they all see him as so fragile, so unstable, a great quavering, doddering figure with only that thing in his ear to keep him from wrecking their show, God forbid anyone should distract him for a moment?

The bitterness will take a long time to abate. He feels his confidence has been crucified. He's never had anyone see him like that before, turned inside out, helpless, hopeless, unclothed. He's lost nine pounds in the last two weeks, and had nightmares that will continue weeks beyond closing. That's part of the anguish; he doesn't really get to leave it behind. For one thing, of course, he's got to reprise the role for EMACT this spring, and he anxiously expects that Celia will be dissatisfied with anything less than first place. But that's not even the worst of it.

Jim's not a gypsy. He's not Patrick, who may or may not ever set foot on Academy Street again. AFD is a second family, a second home. He's afraid this experience may have damaged his reputation with the Friends; afraid it'll lose him future roles, and the directing job he's had his sights on for one of the plays on next year's slate. But it's not even the feared loss of specific roles and jobs so much as the thought of showing his face at board meetings, at play-reading committee meetings, in the greenroom, in the audience—the places that have long been as comfortable and welcoming as his own favorite couch at home. It's the thought of coming back and seeing all the old familiar faces and knowing they've heard the story about how he faltered, how he almost didn't manage, how he had to be rescued with a cue mike. When Doug asked him to be the one to present Celia with her gift at the party tonight, Jimmy demurred and suggested Patrick instead, as the new kid on the block, unconsciously harking back to days when the honor of pouring the coffee after membership meetings went to the most promising new recruits.

It's customary at the end of a production's run for the cast to present gifts to all the techies. For *Butterfly*, Grace and Doug have undertaken to organize the collection of funds and the selection and purchase of gifts, and after everyone has eaten, they gather the group together down near the fireplace, and the ceremonies begin. All of the cast except Jim take turns making little speeches and presenting, variously, Japanese soup bowls and teapots and teacups to the many members of the crew and production team, all smartly packaged in magenta-and-navy Chinese-food takeout boxes. Celia's gift is saved for last. Patrick, who is looking dashingly impressive tonight in a tuxedo and black leather zipper-boots, does the honors. It's impossible not to register a kind of reversal from the days of early rehearsal, when Patrick was the quiet one in gray corduroys, seeming shy, a bit defended, keeping to himself, and Jimmy was in his own broad way the suave and solid master of ceremonies. Although it is Celia's gift about to be presented, it is so clearly Patrick's moment. Framed by the large double doorway to the living room, he stands gracefully erect and delivers, as if off the cuff, in his beautiful baritone, a speech of such pointed and resonant wit that the group, including Celia, is laughing out loud from the very first line, a kind of gut-wrenching, truth-validating, tension-releasing laughter that leaves everyone doing those ridiculous little gaspy-sigh sounds at the end, and gazing admiringly at the youngest person in the room.

"I've been accused by our director of not letting her know what I think," he begins. "So, Celia, here it is. Rarely have I worked with a director who's cursed as much, told me I had no personality, and assured me I'm not my own worst critic." He eventually ends with a tribute to Celia's vision, her dedication to that vision, her attention to detail, and on in that vein, painting a portrait they can all recognize of a talented and impassioned director. Then he helps hand over her gift, a huge flat rectangle wrapped in brown butcher-paper, elegantly inscribed with Chinese characters (which, it is quickly confessed, Grace's husband copied out of a Chinese takeout menu; the actual meaning of the calligraphy is something like "General Chow's chicken and broccoli in oyster sauce"). Inside is a framed poster with art for Puccini's *Madame Butterfly*.

Celia drinks in the image silently and thanks everyone in a voice pitched low with emotion. But the short speech she makes confirms only her drive, her fierce expectations, her stark, muscular competitiveness: "We're gonna kick butt at Brandeis."

Within a few weeks of closing, the abdominal pains that plagued Celia all during the rehearsal-and-performance period get much more severe, and she is hastily admitted to the hospital to have her gallbladder removed. Immediately upon recovery, she immerses herself in the task of preparing a forty-five-minute cutting from the *M. Butterfly* script, to be staged at Brandeis in May.

The night after closing, Patrick goes into rehearsal for another play. Within a month, he has auditioned for five or six more, made two industrial films, and begun rehearsing a new play at the Chinese Culture Institute. By the time the group reunites for Brandeis, he has received a glowing review in the *Boston Globe* for his performance in a professional production at the Boston Center for the Arts, and Pet Brick has begun preproduction work on the evening of Beckett plays.

As for Jim, he goes home and tries to eat and sleep and restore what has been scraped away these weeks. In the new year he auditions for the role of Narrator in AFD's production of *Blood Brothers*. The part is described in the audition notice thus: "On stage throughout, he must have presence, passion, and a strong singing voice—a true triple-threat performer." He is cast. The show goes up just a few weeks before Brandeis, and Jimmy emerges from it nourished, a success; he's won his sea legs back—or his stage legs, as it were. The stage has felt like home again: *haimish*, happy, fun. "Of course!" says Ellen Kazin, who, not incidentally, directed. She gives a fabulously expressive *why-should-it-be-any-different?* shrug. This is her whole point. This is what she's been saying. "If it's not fun, stay home."

SIX MONTHS LATER. THE EMACT FESTIVAL FINALS.

Backstage at Brandeis University's huge Spingold Arts Center, the cast and crew convene in a cramped cinderblock dressing room. It's the day before Memorial Day, and they've all been summoned away from various holiday-weekend activities. A couple of people canceled trips to the beach in order to be near a phone this afternoon. Little Michelle got the call on her cell phone while going through the car wash. Teri was at a friend's pool party, and had to scarf her paper-plateful of chicken and chips before dashing off to Waltham. Stu Perlmutter was called away from a friend's wedding, for which he was an usher; he showed up at Brandeis still wearing his tux. And although several members of the company have grumbled and sighed over having to drag themselves back to *Butterfly* for EMACT in general, none of them complains about being called here tonight in particular.

Of the twelve community theaters participating in the festival this year, four have been invited back to perform in the finals; that AFD is one of them is, if nothing else, some vindication of the extra time they've had to spend on this show. The cast and crew have been meeting up at Hewlett-Packard several times a week for the past month to rehearse. The cutting Celia winnowed—about a third of the play—includes all of the original cast members, and as much of the entirety's complexity as she could retain while keeping the script cogent, as well as feasible in terms of costume and makeup changes.

The condensed version seems to serve the piece well, as one of the festival adjudicators sort of damningly observed yesterday afternoon in the postperformance open adjudication, which is intended as an educational opportunity for all festival participants. Overall, the adjudicators had reacted positively to *M. Butterfly*, but until the actual announcement went out this afternoon, no one was certain they'd make it to the finals.

And here they are. One last time crowding around makeup mirrors, dabbing colors on their skin communally, warming up their voices and limbs. Molly is still stitching, like a joke, but it's for real: patching one last time the gashed obi. The crew members mill quietly, efficiently, testing headsets, timing costume changes, checking props. Someone produces a tin of Altoids and it goes around the room for old times' sake. Mayre bustles around like an embodiment of the Boy Scout motto, with a first-aid box in one hand and a necklace from which depend four rolls of tape: duct, glow-in-the-dark, neon, masking. Kelley comes in to announce a line run and Jimmy begins, "Butterfly, Butterfly . . ." and thereupon goes blank. Everyone pretty much cracks up. Celia of all people giggles and says, "I think I'll wait out here," and removes herself to the hall.

As it would turn out, that night *Butterfly* sweeps. At the awards ceremony, which gets underway around midnight, the Friends receive best make-up, best costumes, best lights, best set design, best direction, and a special adjudicators award for the kurogo dancers, as well as the plum: best production—all of which mitigates any disappointment over losing the acting awards to other nominees. That this production has been marked by trial and minor defeat makes tonight's glory sweeter and more surprising. As a group they are on their feet, clapping and cheering, seven times—more, actually, because they cheer, too, for friends, here with other community theaters, who pick up the awards that they don't, so by the end of the ceremony, in the tiny hours of Monday morning, they have sore throats and glassy, sleep-deprived grins, but when they traipse out to the parking lot it is not to drive away immediately to their separate beds, but to drink toasts, a last tailgate party before they do finally quit each other's company as—for the last time—a kind of family.

But not so many hours earlier, all of this was still unknown, and

Celia had waited anxiously outside the dressing room, chewing a nail while purposefully not listening in on the line run taking place on the other side of the door. There was never any question of using the cue mike for Jim at Brandeis. He'd done well in rehearsal all month, and at yesterday's performance carried off the role without a hitch; still, the idea of his blanking on lines hit a little too close to home. She willed herself not to contemplate the possibility, and turned her thoughts forcefully to what she'd seen at twilight on Friday, when they'd been transferring sets from the big rented yellow moving truck into the theater's freight elevator.

A monarch butterfly, brilliant orange and black, had appeared; it fluttered and dipped and wound past her as she stood there on the loading dock. As intellectual and rational a director as she is, she took it for a sign. So she dwelt on this instead, on this sign, in the dingy, narrow hallway as she waited, which was all she could do anymore, after all: wait and release her work—nearly eighteen months of work on this play—to the ensemble. For that is the ultimate mandate of theater: to be released. She could no more control now how the ensemble would carry out her vision than she could control how the audience would receive it. Like every conversation we have every day, that part is entirely an act of faith.